Hot Rodder's Bible

Gerry Burger and Steve Hendrickson

MOTORBOOKS

About the Authors

Gerry Burger began his automotive journalism career in the 1970s doing freelance work for *Hot Rod, Rod & Custom, Street Rodder, Muscle Car Review*, and other automotive magazines. In 1981, he started a quarterly publication, *Rodder's Digest* magazine, on his kitchen table. He owned and operated *RD* until he sold it in 1995, and continued as editor until the magazine's demise in 1999.

A life-long hot rodder, Burger has built and owned numerous hot rods, including a '31 Model A coupe, a '40 Ford pick-up, a '39 Ford pickup, a '33 Pontiac sedan, a '32 Ford hiboy roadster, and the infamous *Rodder's Digest* '47 Chevy sedan delivery. He's currently working on a '55 Pontiac two-door sedan and a '57 Ford two-door wagon, and is the executive editor of *Street Rod Builder* magazine and senior editor of *Super Rod* magazine. This is his first book.

Steve Hendrickson is a second-generation hot rodder whose career started as an editor for *Street Rodder* magazine in the mid-1980s. After returning to his home state of Minnesota, he joined the fledgling *Midwest Rod & Machine* magazine, which was purchased by *Rodder's Digest* in 1989. He stayed on as senior editor of that magazine until 1999.

Hendrickson's current hot rod projects include a '47 Oldsmobile convertible (known to *Rodder's Digest* readers as "Project Big Olds"), a '32 Ford three-window coupe, and a pile of Model A parts that will one day be a back-to-basics hot rod.

First published in 2001 by Motorbooks, an imprint of MBI Publishing Company, Galtier Plaza, Suite 200, 380 Jackson Street, St. Paul, MN 55101-3885 USA

For details write to Special Sales Manager at Motorbooks International Wholesalers & Distributors, Galtier Plaza, Suite 200, 380 Jackson Street, St. Paul, MN 55101-3885 USA.

Library of Congress Cataloging-in-Publication Data

Hendrickson, Steve.
  Hot rodder's bible : the ultimate guide to building your dream machine / Gerry Burger & Steve Hendrickson.
    p. cm.
  Includes index.
  ISBN 0-7603-0767-9 (pbk. : alk. paper)
    1. Hot rods—Design and construction. I. Burger, Gerry. II. Title.

TL236.3+.H45 2000
629.228'6—DC21   00-068711

On the front cover: A 1932 Dodge Roadster powered by a 1957 Chrysler 392-inch Hemi engine with a 350 turbo transmission. One of only three existing models, it is owned by Hal and Susan Burrows. Peter Vincent

Edited by John Adams-Graf
Designed by Jim Snyder

Printed in the United States

Contents

Gerry's Preface 6
Steve's Preface 8
Acknowledgments 9

Chapter 1
A BRIEF HISTORY OF THE HOT ROD . . 10

Chapter 2
FINDING YOUR HOT ROD PROJECT . . . 28

Chapter 3
BUILDING A BETTER BODY 36
   IN THE SHOP:
      Removing Rust 55
      Fixing Dents 62
      Hammer-Welding a Patch 68
      Replacing Rotten Body Wood 75
      Installing "Bear Claw"
         Door Latches 82
      Chopping an F-150 Ford Pickup . .85
      Top Chop Techniques 93

Chapter 4
THE HOT ROD FRAME 108
   IN THE SHOP:
      Custom Tubular X-Members 125
      Custom Motor Mounts 133
      Installing a Subframe
         Front Suspension 137

A ROUGE'S GALLERY OF HOT RODS . .145

Chapter 5
HOT ROD SUSPENSION BASICS 162
   IN THE SHOP:
      Installing an Aftermarket Independent
         Front Suspension 182
      Swapping Power Steering 186
      New Rear Springs for Fat Fords .190
      Choosing the Right Wheels 194

Chapter 6
HOT ROD BRAKES 198
   IN THE SHOP:
      Installing Big Brakes
         on a Mustang II Front End 209
      Plumbing a Hot Rod Chassis . . .212

Chapter 7
HOT ROD ENGINES
AND DRIVETRAINS 222
   IN THE SHOP:
      Designing an Automatic
         Shifter Linkage 240
      Making a Retro-Tech Air Cleaner . .243

Chapter 8
HOT ROD INTERIORS 246
   IN THE SHOP:
      Hanging a Steering Column 258
      Anchoring Seatbelts 262
      Installing a Four-Point Harness . .264
      Installing New Gauges
         in Old Dashes 267
      Restoring Heaters 271

Chapter 9
15 THINGS TO DO
WITH YOUR HOT ROD 274

Appendix A
THE TEN COMMANDMENTS
OF HOT RODDING 281

Appendix B
SOURCE GUIDE 282

Appendix C
CLUB LIST 287

Index 288

Gerry's Preface

*H*ot Rod. Has your heart accelerated just a bit? Do those two words conjure up memories of solid lifter cams, fenderless coupes, roadsters, and high-performance engines? Do rolled and pleated interiors and blown big-blocks quicken your pulse? This is all part of the great world of traditional hot rods. This is a book about building great hot rods. Perhaps it is most important that you understand what a hot rod is, and from whence it came.

If a hot rod is any one thing, it's personal. That's a good thing in today's impersonal world. It is no doubt one of the things that draws thousands of avid enthusiasts to spend nights and weekends toiling on ancient hunks of iron to make the transformation to a real hot rod.

What exactly is a hot rod? Now there's a debate that is continued over workbenches around the world today. It is safe to say a hot rod is a car that has been modified to enhance performance and styling. Now we're painting with a pretty broad brush on that description! Under that great umbrella of hot rodding come many subgroups. Street rods, customs, street machines, trucks, and muscle cars to name a few. All are hot rods, but we will be dealing with the traditional hot, the 1948 and older modified cars.

There are those out there who would lead you to believe that real hot rodding has no rules, but that, my friend, is just not true. Certainly there is no written rule book on how to build a hot rod. A hot rod should be a reflection of the owner's personal tastes and desires; that's true. To build a good hot rod that you like and that represents the breed well, you should have some basic guidelines. After 30 years of photographing and writing about hot rods, I've seen my fair share of great cars, near misses, and outright failures. I will for the first time write down some of the unwritten rules of hot rodding.

UNWRITTEN RULE NO. 1

The rule is this simple and complex: Your modifications must not simply change the vehicle, they must improve the vehicle.

Accepting that axiom, there is still ample room for interpretation. Let's take a quick example: lowering a car with suspension changes. Lowering a car is typically considered an improvement in hot rodding circles. It is not an improvement if the wheels are no longer centered in the wheel openings, the suspension has no travel, and you can't turn the car around in a 40-acre field. So, to the rule book we must add the word *well* and apply it to all modifications.

This is a book about doing things well. In the following pages, we will explore many of the options and techniques available to the modern-day hot rodder. Engine choices of every make, era, size, and description are legal game in hot rodding. Suspension from straight axles front and rear to exotic aluminum independents with inboard brakes—all choices for the hot rodder. There is ample room for both vintage modifications or high-technology rods or any blend of these building styles in the world of hot rodding. Regardless of style, the hot rod must be done well.

UNWRITTEN RULE NO. 2

Much like designing a new car, a house, or a highway, a good hot rod needs a theme, a constant design direction for the whole car. It can be dictated by year, technology, or graphic style, but the whole car must flow together mechanically and esthetically. Just as you wouldn't design an interstate highway with speed bumps, you wouldn't use a billet steering wheel on a period-perfect, full dress flat-head-powered Model A. This is an illusive process, tougher than it may appear and is almost always the difference between a hot rod, and a great hot rod.

I am a real advocate of the home-built hot rod. In this book, numerous professional hot rod builders will comment on and add insight into the makings of a great hot rod. We hope this information will help home builders "raise the bar" on their next project and build a car that represents their best-ever effort. This is a book about designing and building hot rods at home. But for those of you who are without the required skills or energy to build your own car (and it takes a considerable amount of both), there are shops all across the country that can perform the work for you. Check these shops out like you would a doctor. Most shops are staffed by reputable, hard-working hot rodders who will construct a car that is well built. Others are not.

I think that a hot rod should be fast. OK, we're talking street performance here, but it should still be able to have a reasonable level of performance. It should have the potential to excite the driver. Building a car that is very streetable and capable of 1/4-mile times in the low 14-second range is really quite simple. I prefer my hot rods to run in the lower 13s if possible. Once again, it's about choices, but at least make an attempt to put some power under the hood.

UNWRITTEN RULE NO. 3

A hot rod should have a high-performance powerplant. Bear in mind that a "built" nailhead is slow by today's standards but a great example of power available in the early 1960s. Likewise a brand-new LS-4 pumps out gobs of hi-tech power. Both engines satisfy rule #3.

In this book we will not address the actual building of hot rod engines. There is an abundance of material on that subject, and we suggest you research engine building as a separate issue.

UNWRITTEN RULE NO. 4

Try it yourself. You will be pleasantly surprised at just how capable you are at building hot rods. Many parts of the construction process are well within the reach of the average guy. New kits have taken much of the hard work out of the process. With a good wiring kit, almost anyone can wire a hot rod successfully. Likewise, bolt-in kits for suspension for many cars make home building easy. Try whatever you like, but be certain things like structural welding are done well. That means professional quality.

UNWRITTEN RULE NO. 5

Hot rods are fun. It is my fervent belief that the only real purpose of a hot rod is to have fun driving and constructing the car. A good hot rod is not a shrine, a carport queen, or a trailered car. It is a car that takes to the open road and the drag strip, and cruises town. A rolling piece of self-expression that performs well, and has an attitude that commands attention.

UNWRITTEN RULE NO. 6

There are no rules. Well, no rules that can't be stretched, bent, pushed, and pulled. The trick to breaking any rule (known as finding an "edge" in racing) is that is must be well broken. Pushing of the existing standards has made some of the greatest hot rods of all times (and some pretty marginal ones too I might add). Stretch the rules gently—a little movement in a new direction goes a long way. Do remember you're building the car for you; it is most important that YOU like the car (if others appreciate your efforts that's a good sign too)!

Now that you have all the rules you need, I hope you purchase this book (so I can finish my latest hot rod) and enjoy the information within. Be you a novice or experienced hot rodder, this book should inspire you to get out in the garage and begin the long, rewarding process of building your ultimate hot rod.

—Gerry Burger

Steve's Preface

*H*ot Rod. See, two can play this game, and Burger's right, that's a word that should quicken your pulse if you're any kind of American at all. Why? Because hot rods are a uniquely American phenomenon, born of a country that has an innate need to go places, get things done, and get there faster.

Hot rods also satisfy that built-in American need to do things better and to stand out from the crowd. The first hot rod was built because some anonymous tune-up artist figured he could make his buggy go faster than the factory could. The second one was built when another guy figured he could make his car go faster than that guy's car. The first time those two cars met on the street, drag racing was born.

So, what exactly is a hot rod? Fifty years ago, Bob Petersen's first editorial in *Hot Rod* magazine defined a hot rod as a car that had been modified for improved performance and appearance. With the addition of improved safety, that definition stands today, whether you're talking about a 1929 roadster on Deuce rails or a Honda Prelude with nitrous injection.

Are hot rods art? Hell no. Art hangs on a wall in a stuffy museum, or gets splattered on the wall in a warehouse-district loft. Hot rods do things. They go places. They're functional. In that sense, they may qualify as a craft or maybe even folk art, analogous to quilts, pottery, and other useful, beautiful objects.

Some hot rods do, however, merit some museum floor space because, like it or not, they have historic value. Cars like the Pierson Brothers' 1934 coupe and Doane Spenser's Deuce roadster set the trends and broke the records that the rest of us have been chasing after ever since. They're timeless reminders of what we were and how far we've come.

So why a *Hot Rod Bible*? Well, in the last couple of years there's been a lot of hue and cry about the lack of young hot rodders. Some magazine and industry types think this is because hot rodding as they know it has become too expensive for young folks. They argue that with a base price of $40,000 and up for an "acceptable" hot rod, kids can't afford one.

That's bunk.

The magazines are in an odd position, because to satisfy their advertisers, they have to show how to install the advertisers' products. And those products seem expensive to a 20-year-old kid with a hot rod jones. The plain fact is, a hot rod does not have to be expensive, or pro-built, or finished, or a steel 1932 Ford roadster, or fuel-injected, to be enjoyable. All it has to do is move safely for a kid to have fun. That means that a primered 1950 Chevy pickup with a split manifold and a set of mags will do the trick, and we *know* such a vehicle can be gotten on the road safely for a couple of grand. And the beauty of that plan is that the truck (or car) can be worked on as it's driven. The bottom line is this: Fun hot rodding *is* affordable.

In this book, we'll help you figure out what you want in a hot rod, show you how one goes together, and then show you what can be done with it. Most of the chapters are in two distinct sections, kind of like many college courses. You can think of the first half as the lecture, which provides the basic info you need to understand the concepts (Just try not to fall asleep in class, OK?). The second half is like the lab, where we go into detailed how-to sequences that'll show you how to apply your newfound knowledge.

So get comfy, grab a cold soda, and start studyin'. There won't be a test on Friday, but if we do our job, the final exam will be the construction of your own hot rod. As we used to say in the magazine business, "Read It, Build It, Drive It."

Have fun, and let us know how your project turns out.

—Steve Hendrickson

Acknowledgments

GERRY'S ACKNOWLEDGMENTS

A book such as this comes together from many sources. For the most part we have tapped into archives accumulated over the past 25 years. Good hot rod engineering, design, and building tends to be timeless, so many of these chapters would have been as correct 15 years ago as they are today. On the other hand, a lot of this book could not have been written 15 years ago because the level of engineering, parts and kits availability, and affordability of tools has changed dramatically in that time.

I'd like to thank some of the people who made this book possible. Thanks to Tom Medley for the encouragement and coaching some 28 years ago to a fledgling freelancer. Garry McWhirter was always there helping out (when he wasn't at a NASCAR race) and provided some of the photos used within this book. Of course this book would never have come together without my coauthor, Steve Hendrickson, who did a lot more of the organizational work on this project than I. John Dianna was kind enough to allow reprints of four color features from *Street Rod Builder* and *Super Rod* magazines, two of the great titles from Buckaroo Communications. Thanks, John, for that and for allowing me to be a part of your brand-new company.

Of course I'd be remiss were I not to thank those at home who tolerate late nights, weekends gone, and mumblings about deadlines. Vera gets to tolerate the bulk of this these days, but to my two children, Ty and Amy, thanks for always helping get the job done, whether it was on a car or on a magazine, over the past 25 years.

And thank you all the hot rod builders out there who continue to amaze me with your creative talents, amazing energy, and great attitudes. I have made my livelihood by being a part of this great hobby, and were it not for all the home builders out there, I surely would have had to find a much more mundane job than I have enjoyed. I hope that this book is a help to you all, and that you enjoy our joint efforts.

—Gerry Burger

STEVE'S ACKNOWLEDGMENTS

We have a lot of people to thank when it comes to this book—people who have helped us in the past and who've believed in us.

Thanks to my family—Roger, Julie, and brother Eric—for helping out when help was needed; my wife, Becky, for knowing from the get-go that her daily driver might never see the inside of a garage; and my boys for enjoying time spent in the garage.

I also need to put in a word for some of the folks who got me into this business. Starting way back, thanks to Bill Moeller who taught the most advanced class in English I've ever taken—10th grade composition at Fairmont High School. That brings me to 1985, when I applied for a job at *StreetScene* that was already taken. Joe Mayall gave my name to Geoff Carter, the editor at *Street Rodder*, and two weeks later I was living in sunny Southern California, embarking on a career in hot rod journalism that hasn't ended yet. Thanks to Joe for getting it started, and to Geoff for teaching me most of what I needed to do the job right. Others who helped along the way include Tim Remus and Mike Urseth, my partners at *Midwest Rod & Machine*; Garry McWhirter, the third stooge at *Rodder's Digest*; and of course Gerry Burger, who either liked what I was doing or was quite a masochist—we had a very good nine years with *Rodder's Digest*. Finally, thanks to Zack Miller and John Adams-Graf (our editor) at MBI Publishing Company, who convinced us to embark on this project. I'll get even with them yet.

—Steve Hendrickson

Finally, we both need to thank the thousands of loyal readers who followed our every triumph and our every gaffe in *Rodder's Digest*. Remember when those troublemakers were cuttin' up in school and your teacher said, "Don't laugh, you'll only encourage them"? Thanks for laughing.

—Gerry & Steve

A Brief History of the Hot Rod

The very term *hot rod* has an energy about it. It has transpired from mysterious origins to become universally recognized around the world today. Where did the term come from? Endless speculation with no real proof is all we have in the search for the origin of the term. On a logical level, the term could have come from the connecting rod, the extra heat, and associated cooling problems of a high-compression bored engine. Could the term be slang shortened from "hot ride"? You can choose to believe an existing explanation or manufacture your own; the interesting thing is that the term has such lasting power. The earliest use of *hot rod* is traced to around 1946.

While the sport/hobby has evolved over the years, it is still about people hammering away at building real hot rods. Hot rodding is a hobby that is completely acceptable in most circles, and crosses all economic and social levels. In the formative years early hot rodders didn't have social acceptance, and for the most part were regarded as a fringe element that was more trouble than anything else.

Typical of early hot rods, this Model A coupe is powered by a 348 Chevrolet engine. The chopped top and channeled body create a classic hot rod profile. Black primer is the exterior finish and spun-aluminum Moon discs complete the late 1950s look.

A very traditional hot rod, this 1929 Ford Roadster pickup rides on widened 1935 Ford wire wheels. Other traditional touches include a dropped, drilled, and chrome-plated front axle, dropped headlight bar, and a chrome roll bar behind the seat. Dick Lewis of Litiz, Pennsylvania, built the period-perfect roadster in the early 1980s and still owns the car today.

Reminiscent of early track roadsters this modern rendition captures the very essence of hot rodding—the small, light body, ample horsepower, and lack of frills. In the 1930s and 1940s these cars could be seen racing on local ovals, the dry lakes, or the Bonneville Salt Flats. The "Track-T" is an icon of early hot rodding.

Lest you think all hot rods were Fords, we offer this Chevrolet roadster as graphic proof to the contrary. This 1930 Chevy could have been a street/strip car in the early 1950s. Remove the headlights, windshield, and exhaust system, and it was a racecar. Bolt these pieces back on for the trip home. This car is actually Dick Bertolucci's race-only roadster. The car runs a straight six and performs very well at the local drags. The car is flawless.

This car sure was the talk of the 1981 Street Rod Nationals. Why? This seemingly normal 1934 Ford roadster was actually the first 1934 roadster manufactured by Gibbon Fiberglass. Commonly referred to as "glass cars" for their fiberglass construction, these bodies made hard-to-find body styles instantly available. George Packard, who was instrumental with the design and production of the car proudly displays the finished product in 1981. The "glass decade" had begun.

While the Model T has fallen from favor in recent years, it was a major part of the hot rod revival that happened in the late 1960s and early 1970s. This Colorado-based "T"-touring was built in the 1970s by John Horendeck and remains unchanged today.

In the 1990s the return of traditional rods began. Having worked through the billet aluminum time of the 1980s, the pure and simple hot rod look was gaining momentum once again. Frank Leonetti built this purple flamed five-window coupe. The coupe has since been reworked and is now owned by rock-and-roll singer Brian Setzer.

Social respect would be earned slowly over the years, as hot rodders accepted more social responsibility and society came to understand, and even admire, the talents of hot rodders.

Most historical accounts will credit Southern California for being the birthplace of hot rodding. This is both true and false, if that's possible. After World War II, servicemen returned home with some money in their pocket, new skills, and a huge thirst for automobiles. Modified cars from the prewar era were the basis for going fast, and hot rodding literally exploded onto the scene. Southern California was no doubt the hot bed of hot rodding in that era. There were plenty of rust-free cars to be had, the dry lakes and later the salt flats were within driving range, and *Hot Rod* magazine started there in 1948. No doubt about it, there were more hot rods per square

mile in most Southern California towns than there were in towns in other parts of the country. That does not mean there were no hot rods in other parts of the country.

Let's turn the clock back a bit. I believe that hot rods are a direct product of the search for speed. If that is the case, then one cannot overlook the earliest racecars as the true roots of hot rodding. The question, "When was the first automobile race?" can usually be answered, "As soon as there were two cars in the same town." As early as the turn of the century, the Vanderbilt Cup was being pursued on Long Island, New York. Indianapolis Speedway opened in 1909. Two years later, the first Indianapolis 500 was run. The cars that were raced in those early outings were basically manufacturers' cars that were stripped or rebodied for lighter weight. All unnecessary

Traditional hot rods also include "fat-fendered" cars, manufactured from 1935 through 1948. Harvey Triplett built a very traditional 1940 Ford tudor sedan flathead-powered under the hood. Wide whites, steel rims, and a proper hot rod stance complete the 1950s look.

Pickup trucks have always been a part of hot rodding. This 1939 Ford truck was built by Gerry Burger in the early 1970s. Not nearly as desirable as the 1940–41 trucks, the 1939 was one of Ford's ugly ducklings.

items were removed and the engines were reworked for more horsepower. Gee, that sounds a lot like a hot rod.

All across the country racetracks were cropping up, everything from banked wood-plank ovals to dirt tracks and the simplest race of all, the hill climb. Speed equipment and engine modifications were around "back East" and in the Midwest. I believe that to say that hot rodding was born in one state is a huge disservice to the many pioneers of modified cars that were located not just in the United States, but all around the world. The European Grand Prix cars were also in existence in the early 1900s. All racers learned speed secrets from each other. I like to think they were all hot rodders.

The first Pikes Peak Hill Climb was held in 1916, and when the dust had cleared from the four-day event, a man by the name of Rea Lentz took home the huge purse of $2,000. Lentz had outperformed all the big-buck factory-sponsored teams with big-name drivers. Lentz's car was a homebrewed Roman Demon, powered by a 402-ci Curtiss airplane engine. It was the smallest car with the largest engine. Now I ask you, was Rea Lentz not a hot rodder? Sure, the term had yet to be coined, but his efforts of 1916 embody the very soul of what hot rodding represents. Home-built ingenuity and the belief that he could build a better car than the next guy are what propelled Lentz up that huge hill.

By as early as the 1930s, dry lakes racing was going strong on the West Coast. Often secret weekend races were arranged through word of mouth, and hot rods and spectators would meet for "organized" racing as opposed to the impromptu street races. The turnouts for these races were getting larger, and more dangerous. There clearly was a need for some standards in the dry lakes racing sport.

In 1938, the Southern California Timing Association was founded and brought timing equipment, tech safety inspections, and a degree of legitimacy to the racing hot rodders. Classes were formed so hot rodders could compete with similar cars. Participation was high since this was the only straight-line, top-speed contest available at the time. Circle track racing and the associated track roadsters were still popular, but it was the top-speed contest that seemed to fit hot rodders best. Many of the track roadsters would also compete at the dry lakes, and later on the famed salt flats of Bonneville.

By the early 1950s a new hot rod style of racing, the drag race (another term that has no conclusive documentation of origin) had been founded. All across the country, airfields and other suitable strips of pavement were set up for timed speed trials. Often, in the elimination rounds of these drag races as many as four and five cars would be run abreast down the wide landing strips. Racetracks took on many different lengths as drag racing was seen as a way of getting "the kids off the street" and onto the strip to race. I was told stories of a drag strip in North Carolina that had a concrete starting line for about 100 feet and then it was hard packed red clay for the rest of the quarter mile. It is the only

Until 1949 when Oldsmobile and Cadillac introduced overhead-valve engines, the flathead reigned supreme. This "full race" flattie now resides in a powder blue 1932 Ford roadster built by Royce Fewell.

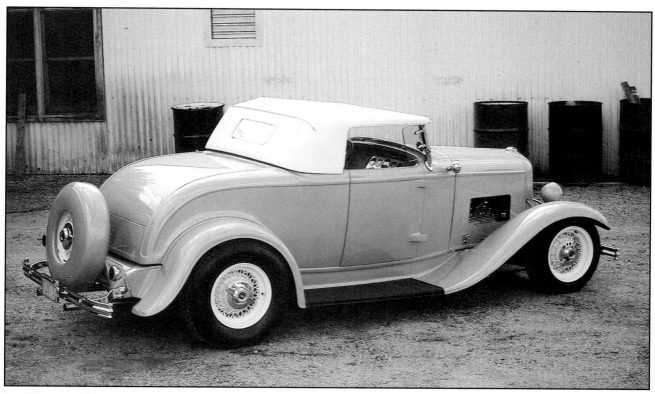

ABOVE AND BELOW

The Fewell roadster incorporates everything you could hope to find on a 1955 street rod—frenched door hinges, Buick Skylark wire wheels, chrome bumper brackets, and flawless bodywork. This is a timeless hot rod profile. A blue-and-white rolled and pleated interior is found inside. On the exterior, stock cowl lights remain intact, while King Bee aftermarket headlights are employed.

Once again we demonstrate the non-Ford hot rod. This time it's a 1939 Oldsmobile with a radical top chop and a great set of flames over black paint.

story of "dirt track drag racing" I have ever heard, and to date I've not been able to find anyone who has photos from this small-town strip. Just imagine leaving that strip of concrete to catch second and third gear on dirt. I'll bet there were some great races held on that "mixed medium" surface.

Once again the need for an organization was apparent. Robert Petersen, Wally Parks, and others formed the National Hot Rod Association (NHRA). This organization brought about the standard quarter-mile drag strip and class and safety rules, and went across country on Safety Safaris to promote safe, organized drag racing as a way of stopping the problem of local street racing. The effort paid off with drag racing evolving on a professional and amateur level.

During the early years of racing, hot rodders would drive their coupe or roadster to the track, possibly make a few tuning adjustments, "uncork" the exhaust system for open exhaust, and the car was race ready. The following Monday, barring any unforeseen mechanical problems from the race, that same car was daily transportation. It was that way well into the 1950s—the dual-purpose car, street and strip—was all the hot rodder could afford.

As drag racing became more competitive, the hi-performance aftermarket industry was born. What were once small one-man shops were growing into genuine manufacturing companies. Their products were advertised in the pages of *Hot Rod* magazine, spreading the word all across the country. Still, the best way to advertise speed equipment was to win races. Thousands of local spectators would come to watch the races, and they turned into the speed shops' next customers. From this competition to win, the "race only" hot rod was born. The true racecar made none of the compromises that a street/strip car had to. Cam grinds could be wilder, compression higher, interiors lighter, and gear ratios lower. Soon it was difficult, approaching impossible, to compete with a dual-purpose car.

In later years classes would be formed to allow hot rodders to race their "daily drivers" in stock, modified production, and lower gasser classes. To this day, many a weekend warrior makes his way to a drag strip for a day of racing in any number of classes. Today drag racing is a big part of the large family known as hot rodding.

With the advent of the full racecar, many of the hot rods were relegated to strictly street cars. That doesn't mean all racing stopped— many a street car would line up next to another local hot rod and race on deserted local roads strictly for bragging rights. The street hot rod, or street rod as they would be known, evolved into

Almost anything can be converted into a fine hot rod with a little imagination. This 1948 Jeepster represents a rare rod. Note that all the body panel seams are filled, the top is chopped, and it's all covered in deep salmon-color paint.

Under the hood, the Willys Jeepster has a 409 Chevrolet. The addition of three two-barrel carburetors and chrome dress-up items complete the high-performance look.

Pontiacs make great street rods too. This 1934 Pontiac touring sedan was built by author Burger in "resto-rod" style. The large sedan carries all the original sheet metal and lighting for a very restored look. Under the hood was a very healthy 400-ci Pontiac motor. The combination of the powerful engine and the restored body brought about the term "resto-rod." In the 1960s this car might also have been referred to as a "sleeper."

a car that had the look of a racecar and more power than most other cars, but was civilized enough (now there's a relative term) to be used on the street.

In 1955, Chevrolet introduced an engine that would forever change the face of hot rodding: the first Chevrolet V-8. Until this time Oldsmobile, Buick, Cadillac, and Chrysler V-8s were the choice of hot rodders, along with the venerable flathead Ford V-8. This parade of overhead-valve V-8 engines was fast making the flathead motor obsolete. Let's face it, a full-race flathead was having a tough time producing the same power as a stock Buick, Caddy, or Olds. The problem with V-8s up

until 1955 was that they were wide, heavy, and expensive. With the birth of the Chevrolet V-8, hot rodders suddenly had an ample supply of a relatively small, lightweight, and affordable V-8 engine. The Ford Y-block V-8 from 1954 to 1957 was no competition for the new Chevrolet. The 265/283/327 small-block Chevrolet became the motor of choice for hot rodders.

Also in 1955 the Corvette was available with V-8 power, and even a Chevrolet sedan with the hot, new 265-inch motor held great hot rod potential. By 1957, Chevrolet had improved and expanded the engine to 283 inches and in fuel-injected form, the little motor cranked out 1 horsepower per cubic inch. The day of the factory hot rod was fast approaching.

By the early 1960s a full-on horsepower race was gaining momentum from the big three automakers. Cubic inches, compression, and carburetion were all on the rise. In 1964, Pontiac stuffed their big 389-ci engine under the hood of their smallest car (Rea Lentz, 1916 hill climb champion, would have supported this theory) and called it the GTO. The factory hot rod had arrived.

This 1936 Plymouth is clean and simple. The basically stock body rides on a new lowered suspension. Power comes in the form of a slant six-cylinder motor. No, it doesn't have to have a V-8 to be a hot rod.

That same year the Mustang would arrive, albeit some six months later as a midyear 1964-1/2 offering, a small car with a V-8 under the hood. Soon every auto manufacturer had a hi-performance offering that would not stop until cubic inches had surpassed the 460 mark, and horsepower ratings were intentionally *under*-rated at 435 horsepower—from the factory!

For the first time hot rodders could drive to a local dealership, go over an extensive options list, and order up a hot rod fresh from the factory with the color, power, and look they desired. These new "muscle cars" brought with them all the prestige and image that seemed to attract young women, making the package complete. These factory super cars mounted a real challenge to the traditional hot rod. Soon even *Hot Rod* magazine was full to overflowing with these cars, and the performance aftermarket scrambled to supply parts to squeeze even more power out of these potent packages. The traditional hot rod was definitely taking a back seat to the muscle car by 1968.

I built my first ground-up hot rod in 1969. It was a Model A coupe that I purchased from a restorer for the grand sum of $50. Just the body and frame, no fenders, hood, or grille. It rolled on stock suspension. That coupe would eventually have a boxed frame, Pontiac motor, Chevy rear and transmission, and be channeled and painted, all in my home garage. It

Ford and Chevrolet both built "three-window" coupes from 1932 to 1936. Here a pair of three-window coupes is found side by side for comparison. The Ford is in the foreground. These cars are referred to as three-windows since they have two side windows and one rear window. Coupes come in both three- and five-window configurations.

Fiberglass bodies have become so popular with hot rodders that you can now buy any number of different make and model bodies. This Plymouth fiberglass body is an excellent-quality reproduction body.

The woodie wagon has enjoyed an almost cult following from its inception. Made famous by surfers in the 1960s, these cars make great street rods. This 1940 Ford woodie is a fine example of a hot rod woodie.

Another all-time favorite of hot rodders is the 1940 Ford coupe. The timeless design of this car means that very little is required in the way of body modifications to build a great-looking hot rod. Joe Milazzo built this coupe in Jupiter, Florida.

You just can't talk about hot rods without including the ever-popular T-bucket. Based on the 1918–1923 Model T roadster pickup, the shortened-bed version that hot rodders love makes the body appear to be a bucket, hence the term *T-bucket.* Billy Coleman put a hemi between the rails of his T-bucket.

It's rare and it's a resto-rod. Finding parts for something as rare as this 1933 De Soto coupe is tough. It is best to buy one of these as complete as possible since there are no reproduction parts available for the car. Curt Land did an outstanding job building this coupe.

From the rear, it is apparent that all the genuine De Soto parts were on this car. The beautiful lines of the car make it a real attention getter.

One of the most popular commercial body styles with hot rodders is the sedan delivery. Based on a car chassis, these small panel trucks are great road cars with plenty of cargo area. Add to that the basic good looks, and you can see why they are popular. These vehicles were manufactured from the mid-1920s up through the mid-1960s. Shown here is a pair of very nice 1947 Chevrolet sedan deliveries.

was licensed and driving (less a finished interior) for only $900. When it rolled out of the garage, it caused quite a stir in my hometown. Most of the traditional rods had disappeared in favor of muscle cars. The traditional hot rodder only had one real source of information, and that was *Rod & Custom* magazine. The magazine, with Tom Medley at the helm, kept the faith for a few lean years, believing when others didn't that traditional hot rodding would make a comeback.

Government, insurance, and oil company intervention peaked during the make-believe oil shortage of the 1970s. Insurance on muscle cars was escalating, gasoline was expensive and limited, and the new round of smog controls spelled sudden death for the muscle car. Slowly, in small private garages across the country, traditional hot rods were being dusted off, new ones constructed, and old ones improved. Much the way it had all begun after World War II, individuals collectively created a groundswell of support. In an effort to define just what the traditional hot rod was, the term *street rod* was adopted. Seen in print as far back as the early 1950s, this term came to define the modified 1948 and earlier traditional American hot rod.

From this groundswell came the formation of local clubs. In the 1970s and 1980s hot rod/street rod clubs blossomed all across the country. Club members helped each other build better, more reliable, and safer street rods. Many of these individuals would make brackets and components to assist others in upgrading steering, brakes, and wiring. History was repeating itself, only on a larger scale. A whole cottage industry arose from these beginnings, with companies producing street rod parts and advertising in the several street rod publications now in print.

In 1969 the National Street Rod Association (NSRA) was formed and the questions were posed on the pages of *Rod & Custom*. What if there was a national rod run? Would anyone come? Would everyone come? Once again, Tom Medley was instrumental in the concept of a national rod run. That first national rod run was called the Street Rod Nationals and the hot rodders arrived, in unheard-of numbers for that era. More than 600 street rods rolled in to the fields outside of Peoria, Illinois. The rest is,

as they say, history. Some 25 years later the number of street rods attending the Street Rod Nationals is approaching 15,000, and the street rod industry has grown into a large group of successful companies.

Today there are kits available for almost every aspect of street rodding. We have come full circle to calling the cars *hot rods* again, a term that over time has become downright acceptable. There are hundreds of rod runs across the country, sponsored by local clubs and major promoters like the National Street

Rod Association and Goodguys Rod & Custom Association. Both of these organizations have memberships in excess of 50,000 and show no signs of slowing down. It seems in this busy hi-tech world, hot rods provide some personal flavor that many people find missing from their daily lives. Add a little hot rod camaraderie and the outright fun of driving a car that is hand built, and it is no small wonder the sport is thriving.

So street rodding is here to stay. It's bigger and better than ever, and while many may point to the 1950s as the golden era of hot rodding, I fear they are wrong. Right now is the greatest era of hot rodding to date. Never have the numbers of cars been so high, the quality so improved, or the variety as diverse. Welcome to the wonderful world of modern hot rodding. Enjoy the hobby and wear the moniker "hot rodder" proudly, knowing where its heritage comes from. Armed with this brief walk through the history of hot rodding, let's have a look at what it takes to build a great hot rod today.

Finding Your Hot Rod Project

Before you can start on any kind of hot rod project, you have to have the raw material. After figuring out what you want, finding just the right pile of tin to work on is often more than half the battle.

WHAT TO LOOK FOR

Before you go shopping for a hot rod or a project car, you have to do a little homework. The three things to keep in mind are your wants, your needs, and your abilities—together they'll determine what kind of car you should buy. For instance, if you want speed above all else, that pretty much rules out anything with a four-cylinder. If you need room to carry the wife and kids, a two-seat roadster is out of the question—you're in sedan territory, pal.

Next, assess your mechanical and fabrication skills. If you're just starting out, you may want to find a project car that's already running, and you might want to find a car that has lots of aftermarket parts and kits already available for it. It's a lot easier to buy and install a rear suspension kit on a 1948 Ford than it is to scratch-build a complete suspension system for that 1938 Nash you have your

This is the sight that everyone hopes to one day see—the Holy Grail of hot rodding, a 1932 Ford three-window coupe in an honest-to-God chicken coop. It's not as common as it used to be, but deals like this are still out there, and it's getting more common to find 1970s hot rods that have been stashed away.

The same 1932, after extricating it from the chicken coop and cleaning it up. How was it found? The new owner (one of the authors) was wearing a jacket that identified him as a hot rodder. That got a conversation started that eventually ended in this purchase. The lesson: Always let people know you're interested in old cars!

heart set on. Then again, if you have a lot of experience with cars and are a competent welder, just about anything goes. If you have the skills, you can start with a car that's as odd or as rough as you like. We know one guy who built a beautiful 1932 Buick Victoria phaeton with twin-turbo big-block Chevy power. He started with a grille, a hood, a cowl, and a set of fenders, and built the rest himself, including the body and chassis. Unfortunately, most of us aren't that talented.

Financial ability is another consideration. Seems like everybody wants a steel Deuce roadster, but they're scarce and expensive. Most guys start their hot rodding careers with a more common, less desirable car, and eventually, through a process of hard work and trading up, get into the car that they really want. If you have the bucks, go ahead and buy whatever you want, whether it's a finished car or a project. The good news for the rest of us is, you can still go hot rodding on a budget, as long as your expectations are realistic.

Another friend of ours is a good example. After several years of horse-trading parts and entire projects, he ended up with the pieces to build a Model A chassis powered by a Chevy small block and a Turbo 350. The suspension was simple, with traditional buggy-spring suspensions on both the front I-beam axle and the GM 10-bolt rear. The body is a shortened, chopped 1929 Model A Tudor with a Model A grille shell. The original intent was to build it as a stubby little sedan, but one day he got to thinking about the cost of glass, a top insert, weather stripping, and all that other closed car stuff. Then, in a slightly irrational but nonetheless inspired moment, he got out the Sawzall and cut the top off. So far it has no windshield, one bucket seat, and no paint to speak of, but he can drive it around the yard, and it'll probably be legal and safe enough to drive on the street soon.

The key to his hot rodding happiness is that he knows he can't afford a pro-built car, and he doesn't feel a need to "compete" against those kinds of cars. He's out to have fun, and he knew how to build a car with the right look on a tight budget.

WHERE TO LOOK

Where you find your project car depends on what you're looking for, and it's not always so much where you look, but whom you know. *Networking* isn't just a term for modern corporate-speak, it's also one of the best ways to find a hot rod project. Find and join the local club

A small ad in a local auto shopper publication resulted in this purchase: two very complete, reasonably solid 1929 Ford Tudor bodies for the princely sum of $195. The best parts of both are going toward a 1929 Tudor tub project, and the extra parts have been bartered or sold.

Swap meets are still a good source of hot rod fodder, especially those held in conjunction with large hot rod events. This 1929 Tudor project had most of the important stuff available for a decent price at the NSRA Nats North in Kalamazoo a couple of years ago.

and the state association in your area. Join one or more of the national associations. Almost all of these organizations have newsletters or magazines that have classified ads, and they're a good source of cars and parts. But more importantly, joining a club gets you access to the local car guys. They have the same interests you do, and they're almost always willing to share information and skills with a newcomer.

In addition, there's often a sort of "insider" network in the clubs. There are guys out there who have project cars and parts that they won't sell to just anybody. You might know a guy for months or years, then one day you'll mention that you'd really like to build a track roadster. It'll turn out that this fellow has a nice 1927 T body tucked away in the rafters, and he'll maybe sell it to you for a decent price, 'cause he knows you and figures you'll build the right kind of car out of it. Now, having said that, if you are the recipient of such generosity, you damn well better build something out of that car! There's no quicker way to ruin your car guy reputation than to take advantage of another hot rodder's goodwill.

Beyond clubs, where else can you find a hot rod project? Keep an eye on the local paper's classifieds, and on the local auto trader–type publications. Granted, most of what you find there nowadays are rusty Mustang IIs and the occasional four-door Falcon, but once in a while a good hot rod project will turn up. Belonging to a club will come in handy here, too. Chances are good that someone you know will know the car, or at least they can go look at it with you and offer their opinion.

Don't forget about swap meets and car shows, either. Look through the events column in either *Street Rodder* or *StreetScene* magazine, and you'll see hundreds of events every year, from one end of the country to the other. On any given summer weekend, I guarantee there will be at least one car show, swap meet, or major rod run within a day's drive, no matter where you live in the continental United States. I can further guarantee that every one of those events will have at least one car or project for sale in your price range. Granted, it might not be a car you want (lots of affordable 1948 Chevy four-doors out there, know what I mean?), but I can think of worse ways to spend a summer. Keep at it, and eventually you'll find something you want and can afford. Patience is the key here.

If you go the swap-meet route, be prepared. Many of the project cars you'll find at a swap meet are either unreliable or undriveable. If it's going to be a big event with lots of cars for sale, you have a pretty good chance of finding something good. Get there early, and if you can, beg, borrow, rent, or buy a car trailer to take with you. It's a lot easier to strike a deal on a car if the seller knows he can go home with an empty trailer, instead of going out of his way to deliver that project to your garage. Keep in mind,

Some of the older, larger salvage yards still have some good stuff as well. This T coupe is being "tried on" by a prospective owner at French Lake Auto Parts in Annandale, Minnesota. Note the good 1940s and 1950s cars in the background, too.

though, that there's a reason that most swap-meet specials are unfinished, and you need to figure out if it's the car's fault or the owner's. If it's the car's fault, be careful. If the owner simply wasn't able to finish it, dive right in!

Finally, there's just plain dumb luck. Here's a big hint: Wear something that identifies you as a car guy. All the time. If it's a weekend, wear that "Deuce Coupe" shirt, or a car club jacket. At the office, wear a tie with Ford ovals on it, or a tie tack that looks like a Deuce grille shell. If the situation allows, always have something visible that identifies you as an "old car guy." Somebody will notice. Maybe it'll be an old-timer who used to be into that stuff, and still has a Fronty-powered T speedster parked in the back of the garage. Maybe it'll be a kid on a skateboard who used to play in that 1940 Ford pickup in his grandpa's barn.

Ready for a story to illustrate this point? One that has all the makings of a hot rodding urban legend? Cross my carb and hope to drop a valve, what follows is true: Several years ago, I stopped for gas in a convenience store near my office, about 5 miles from my home in suburban St. Paul, Minnesota. I was wearing my *Rodder's Digest* jacket, and the kid behind the counter asked me if I was into hot rods. We got to talking about the cars I had and what I did, and he says he's into Mopar muscle cars—Road Runners and stuff. We talk a bit more, and he lobs a question, one that every hot rodder hopes to hear in a situation like this: "So, what's a 1932 three-window worth?"

Puzzled, and a bit stunned, I asked why he's asking. He replies that there's one in his back yard, that it belongs to his uncle, and that it's been there for a number of years. OK, I think to myself . . . deep breath . . . calm down, don't let the voice squeak . . . and I ask, "Is he interested in selling it?"

Well, the answer is obviously no . . . turned out a couple of guys had tried to buy it, but the uncle was never interested. Oh well, it was probably a Model A in the best-case scenario anyway, right? Just to be sure, I gave him my card and made a mental note—right next to the one that reminds me to breathe.

A couple of months later, I ran into this kid again, and asked him about the Deuce. This time, he allowed that the uncle might be interested in selling, as he was going through a divorce and probably needed a little cash. Of course I asked for the uncle's number, but the kid said no, he'd rather pass the info along himself. But he also offered to show it to me. Hmmm, progress.

After a couple of missed meetings, I was pretty certain that the kid was just blowing smoke, and I was just about ready to write off this alleged Deuce. In my mind, the picture of the car had slid from a 1932 three-window, to a Model A coupe, to a 1929 Dodge four-door sedan. But, as luck would have it, one day I saw him at the convenience store as he was leaving, and he offered to

show me the car right then. Off we went to a little old farm house that had been swallowed by the suburbs . . . and behind the house, in a small vale, was a former chicken coop. We went in a door on one end, and there in the shadows, under a thick layer of dust, was not a Dodge four-door, not a Model A, but an honest-to-Stroker 1932 Ford Deluxe coupe, outfitted with juice brakes, a dropped axle, and glory of glories, a 1956 Buick Nailhead for power!

I won't bore you with further details, but after a year of tracking down and pestering the uncle, I towed that Deuce coupe home, and it's currently in my garage, waiting its turn under the wrench. The morals of this story are threefold:
• Let people know you're a car guy.
• Follow up on those leads.
• Above all, be persistent—as persistent as you can be without having to see a judge about one of those pesky restraining orders. It will pay off—at least it did for me.

WHAT TO AVOID

Of course, the outcome isn't always that good. For every cherry Deuce you find, you'll probably have to look at a couple hundred rusted, bent, worthless, and otherwise nasty automobiles.

Be wary of aborted projects. Someone tried to chop the top on this 1954 Chevy sedan delivery, but ran out of steam when he discovered that he couldn't get the quartered top back together without warping. A very good metalworker could probably save it, but chances are this one's no more than a parts car.

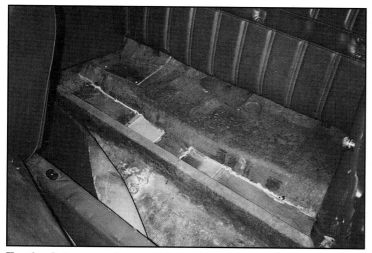

Here's what you want to avoid in a project: somebody else's bad work. This convertible had some horrendous patches that simply covered up old rust. Under the backseat, pieces of fenders and old road signs are glued, screwed, and brazed in place. The passenger floor where it meets the toeboards is equally crude, with brazing and pop rivets holding chunks of car hood in place. Yechh.

I recall one other trip in search of a Deuce roadster body that turned out to be a hacked-up, battered, rusted hulk of a decapitated five-window, with not a single savable panel on it. We went home empty-handed that day, even though the owner dropped the price in half and practically begged us to take the thing off his hands. Evidently, he knew how bad it was too.

As you wander those swap-meet aisles or crawl under a forgotten project in a cold, dark garage, here are a few important things to watch out for.

Rust

Demon oxidation is a major problem in hot rod fodder, especially in parts of the country that experience winter and salted roads. Now, some rust is not a problem. Small holes in the floor are easily patched, and holes in the bottom of a quarter panel are no big deal either (patch panels are available for more common cars, and fabricating patch panels for most others is a doable job). What you need to look out for is structural rust, rust so pervasive that the strength of the car's body is compromised. For instance, check out the strength of the body mounts, floor supports, and rocker panels. These are usually hollow and fill up with road dirt, which traps water and leads to rust. Of course, sometimes a car that's very rusty underneath might be just what you're looking for. Channeled cars or cars with Pro/Street or custom tube frames usually need all-new floorboards anyway. In this case, you might get a better deal on a car that has rust in stuff you don't need anyway.

Look also for rust in weird places. Some of these old cars have sat outside for years, where they gather leaves, dirt, and other water-trapping debris. It's not uncommon to find rusted drip rails, perforated cowl-vent lips, and hole-filled windshield openings. None of these are easy fixes.

Rotten Wood

Many old cars, GM products in particular, had bodies that were framed mostly in wood, with the sheet metal panels literally nailed on. Even Fords had some wood in them, though mostly nonstructural, and rotten wood can be a serious problem in any of these cars. In the case of structural wood, you can buy wood kits for some of the more common cars, like Fords and Chevrolets, but for others, you're on your own.

If your dream project needs wood, you have two options: you can buy or make the replacement wood pieces, or you can replace the wood with steel. This usually involves bolting the body to the frame, then assembling the pieces and tack-welding them together. A steel tubing and sheet metal framework can then be constructed that replaces the wood and holds the body together. You'd better have good welding and fabrication skills, and plenty of patience for this job.

Plastic Filler

Many of the old cars available today have been "messed with" in the past. Sometimes that means they've had bodywork, and I'll be the first to tell you that plastic filler can hide a multitude of sins. Seams that are pop riveted or screwed together, missing metal, pinholes, and bad repairs can all be covered and made to look good with a bodyman's paddle and a little filler. Sometimes a lot of filler.

To spot filler, look for filled seams that shouldn't be filled, wavy panels, and evidence of problems on the inside of the body. Small magnetic gauges are available that can tell you how thick plastic filler is in a given area. If you suspect a car is a "Bondo bucket," buy one of these gauges. It could save you from having to fix somebody else's poor work.

Odd Cars with Missing Parts

Buying a bare 1948 Ford coupe body generally isn't a problem. There are currently enough four-door parts cars in the world that finding sheet metal, trim, and other goodies for a car like this is relatively easy, and lots of reproduction parts are available for Fords and Chevys as well. But beware the rare car that's not all there. You don't have to stray very far from the norm before parts get hard to find, and expensive to buy. Yes, that incomplete 1938 Packard coupe would make a neat street rod, but have you priced a grille for such an animal lately? Good luck.

Basket Cases

The problem with a basket case is that too often a couple of baskets of stuff are missing— and it's usually the good stuff. A basket case is also the sign of an aborted project, and you have to ask yourself, "Why did this guy give up on it?" It may indicate that something is seriously wrong with the car, or that the necessary parts to complete it couldn't be found.

However, there are two sides to every coin, and sometimes a basket case is a good thing, especially if it's in pieces because it was on the way to being restored. Oftentimes, some of the expensive, easy stuff is done, like chrome plating. And if some mechanical bits are missing, well so what? You're probably going to put a small-block Chevy in it anyway. Just make sure that any hard-to-find pieces that you'll need are there.

Bad Workmanship

Sometimes a project is abandoned because the owner/builder was in over his head and screwed it up. If some of the work is done on the car, make sure it was done right. For instance, an all-too-common error in chassis work is getting the axle centerlines in the wrong place, either through error or carelessness. Make sure that any chassis work is done correctly, that the welds are good, and try to make sure that the pieces will fit back together correctly when you get it back home in your garage. This is where hot rodder friends can be a huge asset. They might know the builder's skills, or they might be able to help you evaluate the car based on their experience.

Aborted Chop Jobs

We've seen a couple of these in junkyards— some guy with a torch and a hacksaw figures a top chop can't be all that difficult and goes to town, hacking and cutting away. Then the roof ends up in four quarters, he discovers that the top needs to be lengthened to fit properly, and that the doors and window moldings need extensive reworking. The project eventually finds its way to the junkyard with its roof still in pieces.

If you're considering a car with an incomplete chop, look carefully. Make sure the openings are done such that the glass will still fit when it's cut down. Often, the windshield openings end up with a "twist," and glass doesn't take well to being bent into shape. Measure the window openings from side to side. Check the quality of the cuts, and try to see if the chop was well planned—a planned chop will have a minimum of cutting and welding. If you're not careful, you might end up with a car that needs to be turned into a convertible. Which, come to think of it, may not be a bad deal in some cases.

Missing Paperwork

Does the car have a clear title in the current owner's name? If it doesn't, be prepared to spend what seems like several lifetimes wrangling with your state's department of motor vehicles (DMV) to get the car titled and licensed. This is easier in some states than others, and it actually should be somewhat difficult if you think about it. After all, a car without a title could easily be stolen.

If you're considering a car with no title, first make sure that it isn't "hot." Next, talk to your local DMV office to see what the procedure for titling the car would be. Chances are, you'll have to post a performance bond, and the car will have what's called a bonded title for several years. A performance bond is basically insurance, in case someone else comes along with a title and lays claim to the car. If that happens, you could end up with no car, but the performance bond will cover the loss, or you may get to keep the car with the performance bond paying off the person with the title. Your auto insurance agent can probably help you obtain a performance bond.

It gets even more difficult if you're buying an incomplete car, or just a body. Many states will not issue a new title unless it's for a whole car, and they will probably require receipts for all the components if it's something you have assembled. The bottom line is, know what the rules are before you buy something without a title.

Here's some personal experiences with titles: Several years ago, I bought a basket-case 1929 Model A pickup project in California. The car came with a title that was still in the original

This 1929 Model A roadster was somebody's ditch-runner back in the 1950s; the author's father got it in trade for some work on a local dirt-track car. The chassis was crude beyond belief, but the body was saved and will soon be on the street again.

owner's name, a farmer from Paradise, California. Since the truck left the farm, though, it'd been through about six owners and a messy divorce before it got to me. I had the title, I had the truck, I had a receipt from the guy I bought it from, but the DMV just laughed. Lucky for me, AAA in California handles DMV transactions, and I found a genuinely helpful counter person who knew just what to do. I ended up signing a stack of affidavits and vouchers about an inch thick, testifying to the fact that I'd tried to get ahold of all those former owners but couldn't. She added some more forms for good measure and sent the whole mess off to the DMV. A clean title arrived in the mail about two weeks later. My guess is that an overworked, underpaid DMV clerk took one look at that stack of paper, groaned out loud, and stamped it "approved."

Vermin

There are other dangers to searching for a project car; for instance, remember that a car that's been sitting for a while could be home to anything from a family of raccoons to a nest of black widow spiders, and you have to watch for snakes in some parts of the country as well. Look carefully, and be ready to run from anything from wasps to wolverines when you investigate a backwoods relic.

Keep in mind also that most of these warnings apply to buying a finished car, as well. Ask why the owner is selling it, inspect it carefully, and give the car a careful test drive. Get second opinions, and avoid buying with your heart instead of your head. In other words, use common sense, and know what you're getting into when you hand over the cash for a car.

Building A Better Body

SPRING CLEANING 37

ASSESSMENT AND PREPARATION 38

AFTER ASSESSMENT, REPAIRS 41

FIBERGLASS BODIES 51

BODY MODIFICATIONS: Performance, Style,and Attitude 51

IN THE SHOP:

    REMOVING RUST 55

    FIXING DENTS 62

    HAMMER-WELDING A PATCH PANEL 68

    REPLACING ROTTEN BODY WOOD 75

    INSTALLING "BEAR CLAW" DOOR LATCHES 82

    CHOPPING AN F-100 FORD PICKUP 85

    TOP CHOP TECHNIQUES 93

OK. You've successfully dodged the vermin (both four- and two-legged), you've paid the bill, run the paper chase, convinced the significant other, cleared the garage, survived the borrowed trailer ordeal, and dropped your newfound treasure on the floor where it'll begin its resurrection. What next?

Well, when hot rodders started cutting into 1932 Fords in the 1950s, remember that those cars were only 20–25 years old at the time; that'd be like working on a late 1970s car today. Now our chosen hot rod fodder is anywhere from 50 to 70 years old, and we can expect to spend a lot more time fixing rust, dents, and the sins of past hot rodders. Before we can do that, though, we have to clean it up and see just how much work is needed.

SPRING CLEANING

Chances are, your future hot rod has been sitting for a number of years, and has accumulated a heavy layer of everything from dust to pigeon guano. The engine and underside are probably hermetically sealed under a layer of grease and road grime, and the interior has that unmistakable odor of old mohair upholstery

and rodent droppings. You might even find some departed former residents under the seats, and it's entirely possible that some of the braver mice stayed put during the trailer ride, with an eye toward establishing new digs in your garage. In other words, a good, thorough cleaning is in order. Now, the following steps are assuming that what you have is a nonrunning car—something that will get a full hot rod redo, including wiring and upholstery. If your car is a runner, you'll probably still want to do some of this simply so you can assess the body's condition. However, if the car has wiring and such that you plan on using, be careful with the washing and scrubbing, and disconnect the battery. That is to say, use common sense.

Start with the interior. Put on a pair of cheap, throwaway cotton gloves, a long-sleeved shirt, a hat, and a dust mask (remember that rodent droppings can transmit respiratory disease, and you don't want to inhale any of the dust you're going to generate). First, remove anything that's loose. Floor mats, carpet, assorted junk, parts, cardboard boxes—anything that can be removed without tools. Next, unbolt the seats and set them aside. If you plan on reusing the

Looking for a new body? Just about any Ford, a bunch of Chevys, and some Mopars, Willys, and other bodies are available in fiberglass from a number of manufacturers. One of the best is this 1932 Ford three-window body from Wescott's Auto Restyling. It features steel framing and crash beams in the doors; and the doors, deck lid, and windshield are all hinged and latched.

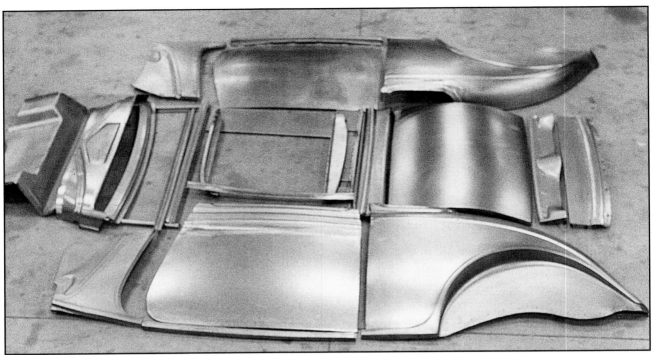

Of course if 'glass isn't your thing, some of the most popular bodies are also available in steel. This shot shows the stamped steel panels that go into a new steel 1934 Ford cabriolet from Steve's Auto Restorations. They also build roadsters. Steel roadster bodies for 1928 through 1932 Fords and 1932 Chevy roadsters are available from other manufacturers.

seats, what you do with them depends on condition. If they're in good shape and reusable as is, vacuum the fabric thoroughly, cover them in plastic, and put them in dry storage. If the upholstery is rough enough to be unsavable, tear it off and store just the seat frames. No sense providing the local mice with bedding.

Next, carefully remove the door panels, kick panels, and other interior pieces. If they're good enough to use as patterns, store them with the seats. Save the door handles, screws, and other door hardware in zip-seal bags, and label them. Likewise, remove any carpeting or floor mats, padding, and insulation on the floor. Lastly, remove the headliner. To do this, you'll probably need to remove the windshield frames and some other trim pieces. If the headliner is in any kind of condition, roll it carefully and save it as a pattern—your upholsterer will thank you later. You might also want to remove the gauge panel and any other dash hardware, or pull the whole dash assembly if it's possible. Remember to bag and tag all the parts while you do this, and take pictures of things during disassembly to assist you in reassembly.

By now you should have a pretty bare-looking body. The next step is to clean it up. If you have a shop vacuum, go and borrow your neighbor's shop vacuum. Trust me, you don't want to use *your* vac to suck up this junk. Vacuum the floor, inside the kick panels, inside the doors, the glove box, ashtrays, behind the dash, above the windshield header, and any other nook and cranny where there might be a mouse nest. Make sure you get rid of anything that can trap and hold water, to help prevent future rust.

When you're left with nothing but metal, roll the old girl out in the driveway and give it a thorough scrubbing with soap and water, inside and out. What you want to do here is flush out any loose particles, dust, or other contaminants that will interfere with your work or hold water. When you're done, rinse everything thoroughly, and leave it in the sun to dry with the doors and deck lid wide open. Might even want to put a fan in there to speed up the process.

ASSESSMENT AND PREPARATION

It's clean, it's dry, it's empty. Now is your chance to really see just what you bought. You need to look for four things: rust, wood rot, collision damage and dents, and abuse.

Rust

Rust can be roughly divided into three categories: structural, floor, and cosmetic rust. We'll discuss structural rust first, as it's most serious and affects the integrity of the body. Rocker panels, body mounts, floor supports, and door panels are all places to look for it. For starters, check out the rocker panels, inside and out, top and bottom. Rockers are usually a long box section that can hold water, so it's normal to find some rust here. If just one face of the rocker is rusted, you can probably patch it. If two or more faces are rusted, or if sections of the rocker are missing or have been cheaply repaired, replacement is the best option. While you're looking at the rockers, inspect the bottoms of the door posts where they join the floor and the rocker panels. They should be solid, and solidly attached to the body.

Next, crawl underneath the body, and look at the body mounts and floor supports underneath the car. Most old cars had some sort of reinforced sheet metal stamping for the body mounts, and many had stamped channels that reinforced the floor to keep it from "oil canning." These pieces are, unfortunately, good at holding dirt and moisture, and often rust out. Without them, you don't have a solid connection between the body and the frame, and the body will begin to channel itself as it settles, resulting in bad door fit and other problems (1947–54 Chevy pickups are notorious for this).

While you're looking at rockers and crawling around underneath the car, also inspect the floorboards. In any old car, you're almost guaranteed to find some floorboard rust, especially in footwells (more likely on the driver side) and in the trunk floor. While a car's floor is important to the structure, it's not as crucial as the structural members mentioned earlier, and it's relatively easy to fix. Floorboard rust by itself is not a big deal, as long as the underlying structures are solid.

Finally, there's cosmetic rust, rust that occurs when the outside body panels rust through (surface rust is also cosmetic, but it doesn't need repair, just removal). This kind of rust is usually in the bottoms of the doors and quarter panels, around the lip where the fender bolts on, and in the rear pan below the deck lid opening. Occasionally you'll find rust in the bottoms of rear fenders and deck lids, at the back edge of front fenders, and even on hoods. These parts are fairly easy to repair or replace, though.

Some cosmetic rust is to be expected, but if it's too extensive, it can seriously weaken the body. For instance, if a body is rusted out in the quarters, and has rust around the fender lip, and has a rusty rear pan . . . well, face it, there just isn't much holding the body to the floor pan, is there? Most cosmetic rust is fairly easy to repair, especially if you have a Chevy or a Ford. Reproduction patch panels for doors, quarters, and trunk lips are available for almost all Ford and Chevy products. For other brands, you're on your own. Some GM products (the smaller Oldsmobiles and Pontiacs, especially) can use Chevy patch panels, but for other makes you'll either have to fabricate patch panels or take sections from donor cars to make repairs.

Wood Rot

Even if the metal is good, there's another nasty surprise waiting for us old car buffs: dry rot. The earliest car bodies were simply wooden structures with metal (or even cloth) panels covering the framework. As time went on, manufacturing volumes grew and metal stamping

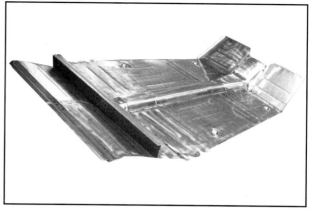

A common problem in any old car is a rusty floor. Replacement floors, rockers, floor supports, and other relevant parts are available for most Fords and Chevys, though. This is a complete floor pan set for a 1946 Chevy from Bitchin' Products. This floor is not for an accurate restoration, but it is fine for hot rodders.

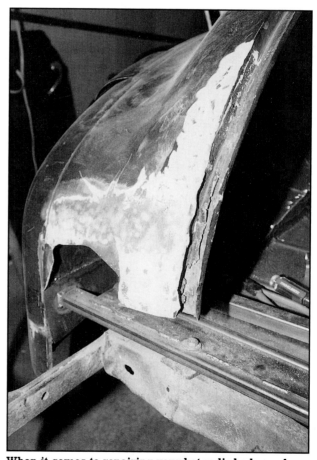

When it comes to repairing your hot rod's body, we hope you don't run into problems like this. On this 1947 Olds, everything on the tail pan below the taillights was rotten—nothing but rust-perforated metal and plastic filler. Note that floor repair is already well under way, with a piece of tubing forming a new rear body support.

That rusty rear pan was fixed with a new, stamped tail pan from Engineering & Manufacturing Services (EMS). EMS makes tail pans and other patch panels for a variety of cars. They require some good fabrication skills to install, but they're far, far better than starting from scratch.

technology improved, so it became cost-effective and easier to make bodies completely out of steel. (Incidentally, stamping technology is the reason old cars had a cloth top insert—a one-piece metal top couldn't be stamped until GM perfected the process with its "Turret Top" in 1935.) But this was a gradual process.

Ford used quite a bit of wood in its car bodies up until 1935. Prior to that, wood was used in door posts, around rear window openings, and to support the cloth top inserts mentioned earlier. Wood was used to a lesser degree in later years, and you'll find that the smaller a car's production run, the more wood there is in the body. For instance, 1939 Ford four-door convertibles are fairly rare for 1939 models in that they have a lot of wood framing the body.

GM used even more wood in its bodies, up until the 1937 models came out. In fact, a Chevy body built prior to 1937 without its wood is little more than a collection of sheet metal panels stacked together. Doors had wood frames inside them, and the door openings were framed entirely in wood, as were rear window openings, top inserts, and sometimes even body subrails! Even after 1937, some low-production bodies had quite a bit of wood. For instance, the 1939 Chevy sedan delivery's rear door opening was framed in wood, and some inner body structural members were wood as well.

Now that the interior is removed and the wood is exposed, you can take a close look at what repairs, replacements, or modifications need to be made. Almost all cars with wood will need some wood work done after all these years. In most cases, rot starts at the bottom and works its way up, so look at the bottoms of door posts, in the bottoms of doors, and at the lower sections of back-window framing—anywhere water would collect. Some wood damage will be easy to spot, but sometimes dry-rotted wood looks fine until you poke it with a

screwdriver and it crumbles. Don't be afraid to poke and prod a little bit to find out how solid that wood is.

Collision Damage

Most old cars have had at least one fender-bender in their lives, maybe even a severe accident. Oftentimes, repaired damage is difficult to spot from the outside, but on the inside of the body, there will be signs. Look for wrinkled or buckled floor pans, weld seams on one side of the body that aren't on the other (indicating a spliced-on body part), and uneven door gaps or seams. You can also look at the insides of panels for the backsides of dents that are filled on the outside.

Why look for collision repair? Because it could make your life difficult when it comes time to fit new parts or repair other damage. As an example, in this book are photos of Hendrickson's '47 Olds convertible. That car had been hit in the left rear corner at one point in its life, hard enough to bend that corner of the frame down an inch or so. The damage was fixed cosmetically, but the frame was never straightened. This made it very interesting when it came time to fit a new deck lid and reproduction tail pan to the car. We basically had to cut the trunk lid opening loose from the body and reconstruct the whole thing to fit the deck lid. It also caused problems when it came time to hang the bumper—the left bumper iron was about 1-1/2 inches lower than the right, and it was quite a bit of work to repair.

Dents

Most dents are not nearly as frightening as they look. Large, shallow dents in curved panels are actually relatively easy to pop out and repair, as are smaller dents in flat or slightly crowned surfaces. What you want to look out for are dents so severe that they have folded the metal and bent it beyond its built-in "memory."

Also watch for dents that go across moldings or through sharp factory creases. These will be much more difficult to repair.

AFTER ASSESSMENT, REPAIRS

OK, so now that you have a firm handle on what's there and what it needs, where do you start? The biggest job you face is making sure the car is structurally sound, with good floors, rockers, body mounts, and floor supports. If you were smart (or lucky) when you bought your project, you won't have to do much.

Fixing Floors

In the past, some ersatz hot rodders thought it acceptable to fix floors with anything from road signs to asphalt roofing shingles. No kidding! At one time, the aforementioned '47 Olds convertible had an awful assemblage of old car hoods, galvanized ductwork tin, and other miscellaneous scrap steel that passed for a floor. It was simply laid over the rusted remains of the original floor, then attached with whatever was handy at the time. We found sheet metal screws, pop rivets, arc welds, and brazing (along with some sort of gorilla-snot putty used as a sealer) holding the mess together. We also know another resurrected old hot rod that made extensive

use of shingles as a flooring material. Luckily, times have changed, and that kind of work is not nearly as common as it once was. Unluckily, we are now often faced with fixing those cars that were butchered years ago.

Like most hot rod chores, replacing an old car's floor is either a build or buy proposition. For Fords and Chevys, you can find reproduction-quality replacement floorboards and floor patches advertised in places like *Hemmings* and *Old Cars Weekly*. In the hot rod world, companies like Bitchin' Products and Direct Sheetmetal manufacture replacement floors for most popular Ford and Chevy hot rods. Their floors are not stock appearing, but they do the job well, and they're more in tune with a hot rodder's needs when it comes to things like transmission clearance, seat mounting, and so forth. Bitchin's products are also designed to work with their firewall kits. If you can buy a repro or replacement floor for your car, it's the way to go, because the engineering work and development are already done—you just have to read the instructions and install it.

If you have an off-brand car or limited funds, though, you might have to go it on your own—but relax, it's not that bad. Here's a brief rundown on how to plan a new floor installation in your car:

If nobody makes new floor panels for your car, you can do the job yourself, like we did on this 1947 Olds convertible. After installing new rocker panels, a stout piece of tubing was bolted to the frame and welded to the quarters. New floor supports were fabricated between the rockers and the body mount holes on the frame, and 16-gauge sheet metal was stamped with beads and cut to fit. Note the tubing braces in the door opening: they keep the body in shape during the work.

The Olds got the same treatment in the trunk; here you can see another piece of tube that forms the rear body mounts and supports the trunk floor. The tail pan has not yet been installed on the body.

First, identify the original body mount locations on the frame, either by looking at the remains of the original floor, or by checking out service manuals or another car of the same make, model, and year that still has a floor. Next, clear out any old rusted metal, and clean and sandblast the areas on the body that you'll be welding to.

Get the body situated on the frame, using blocks or tack-welded tubing braces to hold it in place. Make sure that both the frame and body are straight and square, that the doors and deck lid open properly, and that the door gaps are all even. It sometimes helps to fit the doors, then actually tack-weld them to the body with short pieces of tubing or sheet metal so the body and doors are one big, immobile chunk.

Where you go from there depends on what kind of car you're building, but the basics are the same. You need to first build some sort of structural framework that attaches to the body mounts. On that '47 Olds convertible, we used a stout piece of rectangular tubing bolted across the frame rails, just behind the door openings. At the bottom, it picks up the stock body supports on both sides. We then installed new rockers on both sides, then welded new floor supports to the rockers, and bolted the floor supports to their body mount holes on the frame. At the

very back of the body, another piece of rectangular tubing was bolted to the frame to serve as the rear body mount brace. Once the structure was in, it was a fairly simple matter to fill in the holes with sheet metal. On the convertible, I wanted a tall floor hump to give the body more torsional stiffness. The hump was formed on a press brake out of 16-gauge sheet metal. The 16-gauge floor panels were then stamped with 1/2-inch beads for stiffness before they were trimmed and welded into place. Wherever the floor panels overlapped each other or one of the body brace tubes, the panels were drilled with 1/4-inch holes along the edge, so that the pieces could be plug-welded together. When all the welding was done, every joint got a bead of NAPA seam sealer, then a coat of self-catalyzing primer, and a shiny coat of battleship gray Rustoleum. If there was a chance that the bottoms of the floors would be visible to observers, I might've painted it body color, but this car is a driver, and low enough that no one can get their head underneath it anyway.

Some hints for building floors: First, have the engine and tranny (or at least dummies) installed in the frame, along with the rear

(continued on page 47)

Sectioning a car's body is not for the weak of heart—it involves removing a vertical section from the body to lower its pro-file. Don Shaikoski is doing that to this 1946 Ford Tudor sedan. Note that the section is angled in the quarter so it joins two vertical faces at the wheel opening and door opening. *Don Shaikoski*

The nearly completed job. The tape marks on the front fender indicate where it will be sectioned so it matches the body's new lack-of-height. This car is also channeled (the body is lowered over the frame) and was later chopped.

These next few photos illustrate some important points when chopping a top. In this case, the car is a 1934 Ford five-window coupe. The job starts by bracing the inside of the body with steel tubing. This prevents the body from spreading or springing out of shape when the roof is cut loose.

The cuts are carefully planned and marked first with tape. The top is coming down 3-1/2 inches, the distance between the tape. The cuts are staggered to keep the chop in the most vertical parts of the window openings. Precision is everything in this job.

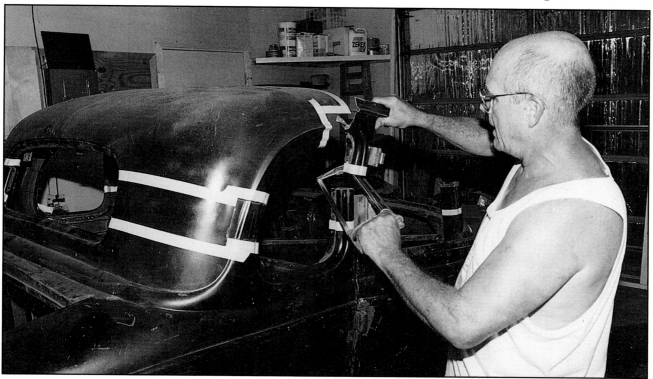

Chopping will change the shape of both the door opening and the quarter windows. To allow the B-pillar to drop straight down, it's cut free from the roof and from the bottom of the pillar.

After the B-pillar and the rear or the top is cut and rejoined, you can see how the shape of the rear quarter window is affected. Note also that the vertical cuts in the top of the quarter window were at the flattest point. This will make filling the resulting gap easier.

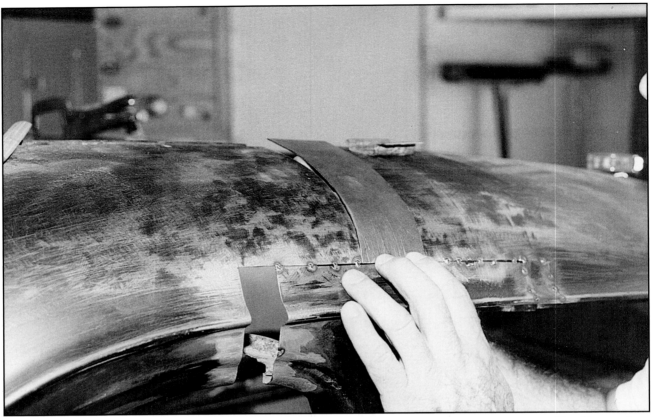

When the front of the top is rejoined to the windshield posts, there's another gap to be filled above the B-pillar. Here, a piece of 18-gauge is trimmed and formed to fit. Note the gap ahead of the B-pillar section that has already been filled.

The nearly finished chop. All that remains is to finish the door tops (they have to be stretched with pieces from another door) and cut the inside window moldings. Note that this top could've been chopped without lengthening the roof by tilting the windshield posts back, resulting in a "Bonneville"-style chop.

(continued from page 42)

suspension and drive shaft, so you won't have any clearance problems with the floor later on. If you're using a floor shifter, it helps to have it installed as well, so you can build the floor to suit it, rather than guessing and cutting later. Second, remember that weld beads shrink as they cool. If you make long, continuous weld beads lengthwise along the car, you can actually change the body dimensions as the welds cool. We know one rodder who did a great floor job, welded every seam its whole length, then found that his doors didn't fit. The bottoms of the door openings were almost 1/2 inch shorter than the doors when he was done. When attaching, say, floor panels to rocker panels, it's only necessary to stitch-weld them with 1-inch beads, about 4 inches apart. This reduces heat build-up and shrinkage, and you can run a bead of seam sealer later to prevent water from getting into the seam.

Repairing/Replacing Wood

If your car's body has rotten wood in it, you can either repair it, replace it with new wood, or tear it all out and replace it with steel. What you do depends on how rotten the wood is, how much work you want to do, and how strong you need the body to be.

For instance, I have a 1932 Ford three-window body sitting in the garage. The body is uncut, and every stick of wood in the car is rock solid. There's no need to mess with it, and as either a hot rod or a restoration, the car will be worth more in that original condition. The original wood identifies it as a low-miles, genuine, unmolested car. If the car had good sheet metal and rotten wood, though, I wouldn't hesitate to tear it all out and replace it with steel.

If you're faced with a lot of bad wood, your first option is to get a wood kit (available for most Ford and Chevy cars). This is not a bad option, but remember that a wood-framed body will flex more, and it's not nearly as strong, especially if the unthinkable should happen and you're involved in an accident. To find wood, we'd again recommend checking the ads in *Hemmings* in the section for your particular car.

If a wood kit isn't available for what you need, some pretty heavy-duty cabinet making and joinery skills will be required to produce new wood for your car. That leaves most of us with what I feel is the best option: replacing wood with steel. The best way to do this is to approach it much like a floor replacement. Bolt the body solidly to a straight, square frame, then adjust and shim it until the door gaps are all even and everything's square. Tack-weld some tubing braces inside the body to keep it stiff, and remove all vestiges of the old wood.

We've seen wood replaced with formed sheet metal pieces, with round or square tubing, or sometimes a little of both. For most jobs,

we'd recommend using 1/2-inch to 1-inch square tubing, along with sheet metal. The tubing can be notched and bent (or mandrel bent, if you have the equipment) to form curves, and sheet metal can be used to fill the gaps between the tubing and the original sheet metal. In this way, you can build a very strong framework for the body, complete with attachment points for upholstery panels, shoulder belts, and other interior necessities. Let the original wood be your guide for what to install and how to install it. The body should have flanges or other attachment points where the wood used to be installed. These points can now be used for the new steel framework.

Fixing Firewalls

An old car's firewall is an important piece, both structurally and esthetically. It supports the car's cowl on the frame, prevents the front of the body from flexing and twisting, keeps fumes, heat, and (god forbid) flames from entering the passenger compartment, and it provides a scenic backdrop for your hot rod's powerplant. Sometimes it also supports a car's master cylinder, pedal assembly, and other mechanical stuff. Unfortunately, old car firewalls are usually in sad shape, either through neglect, abuse, or both.

Holes in a firewall that are less than 1 inch in diameter can usually be patched fairly easily by welding-in a round sheet metal blank of the correct diameter. A good sheet metal shop will probably have a rotary index hole punch, and can make you a bagful of round blanks in a variety of diameters in the correct gauge metal. Hold them in place with a magnet from behind, and use a MIG, TIG, or gas welder to hammer weld them into place. Irregular holes from torchwork can be patched similarly. We started to use this approach on the Olds, but then realized that we were going to spend a week patching some 80 stock holes, and that it'd be easier to patch one big one.

Many GM firewalls of this age have the cowl formed over into a lip, and the firewall welds-in from behind. If you trim the firewall out about 1/4 inch from this lip, you get a nice ledge on which to weld a new, smooth firewall. For the Olds, we chose a chunk of 16-gauge steel, trimmed it to fit, and carefully welded it into place. Similar techniques will work with many other cars.

Finally, if you don't want to patch holes or build your own, replacement firewalls are available from Bitchin' Products and Direct Sheetmetal. They're smooth, new, and available with setbacks to accommodate modern powerplants where needed. Installation varies, but usually involves drilling out the spot-welds that hold the original in place, cleaning up and straightening the flange, then fitting and welding the new pieces in. As an added bonus, firewalls from these companies mate directly with their floor kits, with little or no fabrication involved.

Headlights can be frenched in a number of ways. This 1947 Oldsmobile used 1954 Mercury trim rings (Chrysler Cordoba headlight rings are another popular choice) to give the headlight a tunneled effect. The fender peak was extended; then the surrounding area was built up with formed pieces of sheet metal and smoothed with filler.

This 1947 Chevy uses a different approach; it looks like a stock headlight rim was welded to the fender, then an "eyebrow," similar to a 1955 Chevy fender, was built up over the top of the rim. It's a good look, reminiscent of the 1955 Buick headlight rim. The only downside to this type of headlight frenching is that it's difficult to change or adjust headlight bulbs.

Patch Panels

Once your car's structural issues are resolved, you can turn your attention to fixing the cosmetic issues. Again, if you have a Ford or Chevy body, you're in luck—patch panels are available to replace the bottom 6 inches of most of these cars.

If you have to make your own patches, choose steel that's of the same thickness as the original (usually 18 or 19 gauge). Gently curved panels can be reproduced fairly easily, but anything with compound curves or reveals will require specialized fabrication tools and techniques—something to consider when you're buying the car in the first place.

In general, installing a patch panel is a fairly simple affair. First, hold the patch panel in place on the car and use a permanent marker to mark the body where the edge of the patch panel is. Next, remove the rusted area of the body about 1 inch below that line, using a sheet metal nibbler or an air-powered cut-off wheel.

Now, this is the point where you make the decision if you want an OK car or a nice car. If all you want is an OK car, put the patch panel in place over the old body metal, and lap-weld the patch in. You can get a smoother joint by flanging the body metal with a special roller-type tool, but you'll still have a lap-weld. The resulting overlap will make it easy to weld, but the job will require more filler to get a smooth joint, and the overlap results in a water trap that will eventually cause the body to rust along the seam. It might take 10 or 20 years or more, but you can bet some future rodder will be cussin' you when he has to redo your work.

If you want a really nice car, do the job right—and here's how. Hold that patch panel in place, and scribe a line on the body right along the edge of the patch panel. Remove the patch panel, and use a snips or a cut-off wheel to cut right up to that line. Now, the patch should fit into place with its edges butted up directly against the edges of the body metal. You can then use a MIG, TIG, or gas welding torch (with a small tip) to tack-weld the patch to the body in three or four locations. As you make each tack-weld, use a hammer and dolly to knock the weld flat. Remember when we talked about a weld shrinking as it cools? By hammering it flat before it cools, it expands the weld outward and prevents the cooling weld from causing a low spot or pucker. That, in a nutshell, is hammer welding.

After the tack-welds have cooled, weld about a 1-inch bead along the seam, and hammer-and-dolly it before it cools. When that weld is cool enough to touch, move to another location along the seam and do the same. Keep welding, hammering, and cooling in succession, and you'll soon have a patch that's welded in solid. A light pass with a fine flexible grinding wheel and you'll have a splice that needs a minimum of filler.

Dent Repair

By now, most of the old tin that we're working with has collected its fair share (sometimes more) of dents, dings, and creases. Luckily, all but the most severely mangled sheet metal can be straightened, but it takes skill and patience.

If you want to do your own dent repair, we recommend checking out the Eastwood

Taillights can be frenched as well, as illustrated on this 1931 Model A roadster. What appear to be 1937 Ford taillight lenses are flush-mounted from the rear for a very clean appearance. The clean nerf bar bumper is a nice touch too.

Company's catalog (see the appendix for more info). They offer a body hammer starter set that includes a dinging hammer, a picking hammer, a general-purpose dolly, a toe dolly, a dinging spoon, a body file, and *The Key to Metal Bumping*, a great vintage how-to book. All the tools are excellent-quality pieces (mine are so nice they get their own drawer in the toolbox), made in the USA by the Martin Company, and Eastwood offers a complete line of Martin body hammers, dollies, and spoons to complete your collection. Whatever you do, don't buy cheap body hammers. We've seen sets of Chinese-made body tools that consist of cheap, cast dollies and even cheaper hammers that sell for $10 a set. They're essentially useless. Stick with the good stuff, and you'll get good results.

The secret to successful dent repair is understanding how dents are formed as the metal is stretched and pushed out of shape. When part of the metal gets stretched, it pushes and pulls on the surrounding metal, inducing stress and causing it to deform. Sheet steel has a memory, though, and it wants to return to its original stamped shape. By removing the part of the dent that's causing the stress, you can get the rest of the metal to pop right back into position.

For instance, the Oldsmobile's right front fender had a dent in the side behind the wheel opening. Something had pushed in on the side of the fender, causing a vertical, trough-shaped dent. As the dent got pushed in across the curvature at the top of the fender, a ridge formed in the shape of an inverted "V" at the top of the vertical dent (to illustrate this, take an aluminum pop can and press in on the side with your thumb—the same thing happens as the dent rolls across the curvature of the can). That ridge is what was holding the vertical dent in place. By hammering on this ridge with the dolly placed behind the vertical trough, we were able to knock the ridge down while pushing the trough out. When the ridge was knocked down, the vertical dent all but disappeared. The trick to this is to think about how the dent happened, then reverse the procedure, first taking care of the last damage that occurred.

Successful hammer-and-dolly work requires some research and some experience. We recommend you first read *The Key to Metal Bumping* or *Automobile Sheet Metal Repair* by Robert L. Sargent. The latter is a textbook published years ago by Chiltons, and is out of print. Copies can still be found, though, and it's an

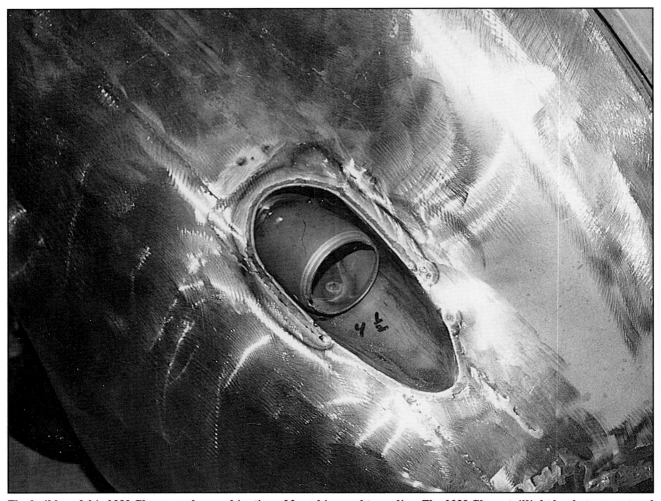

The builder of this 1939 Chevy used a combination of frenching and tunneling. The 1939 Chevy taillight bucket was cut and tunneled into the rear fender. Lots of work, but the effect will be unique and good-looking.

excellent reference. You can also get damaged doors and fenders from bodyshops, usually for free, to practice on. It's a good way to find out if you have the knack for banging tin.

Fenders and Other Bolt-ons

When the body is solid once more, you can begin fitting all the stuff that bolts onto it— fenders, doors, hoods, and deck lids. If you have to repair dents or rust in these pieces, the techniques are the same as outlined above. It helps, though, to have the pieces bolted solidly to the body so you can make sure they'll fit during and after the work. For example, let's take a look at the front left fender on my dear old '47 Olds convert. That fender was from a relatively rust-free parts car, but it had been picked up with a forklift and the rear of the fender was badly folded. In addition to that, there was a nasty "gonk" in the top of the fender just above the wheel opening. Looked like somebody had dropped a bowling ball on it. Well, when I had the bodywork done on the

car, the bodyman did a great job of straightening and saving that fender. After all, pounding dents is easier than welding up rust. Unfortunately, I didn't have the hood at the bodyshop at the time, so all the pieces weren't fitted together. Months later when the hood was installed, it was clear that the fender wasn't shaped quite right. It was straight and smooth, but there was a considerable gap between the hood and fender lip. It was my own fault. If I'd had the hood on the car, the bodyman would've known that the fender was out of shape and been able to fix it.

REPRO BODIES

Does all that sound like too much work, too much time, or too much money spent at the bodyshop? Fear not. As the supplies of available tin have dried up over the years, the hot rod aftermarket has done its capitalist best to fill that pent-up demand for hot rod bodies. At first, fiberglass bodies appeared, then when the demand for steel outstripped the supply, a few companies even began reproducing complete steel bodies.

Fiberglass Bodies

The first fiberglass bodies were 1923 Model T Ford roadsters, in both their turtle-deck and roadster pickup forms. Later, Model A roadsters and 1932 Fords came along, and today, fiberglass bodies are available for Model T roadsters; Model A roadsters, coupes, pickups and sedans; 1932 Ford roadsters, coupes, phaetons, and pickups; and a multitude of other Ford body styles all the way up to complete '40 Ford coupes and convertibles. There are even complete fiberglass '49 Mercurys available. As demand increased, some Chevy and Mopar bodies became available as well.

Most of these bodies are of good quality, but it still pays to do some research and ask around. For instance, some body manufacturers use steel tubing to frame their bodies, some use oak, some use a combination of the two materials, and all claim that their method is best. Personally, steel framework makes the most sense to me, both in terms of body strength, durability, and safety. But shop around, ask for other rodders' opinions, and look at some 'glass-bodied cars that have been on the street for awhile. You'll soon figure out which body is right for you.

Most modern 'glass bodies are so good that they have only one disadvantage: They aren't steel, and some hot rodders don't see them as "real" cars. For that reason, a steel 1932 Ford roadster will always be worth more than a comparable fiberglass car. However, that doesn't mean that a fiberglass-bodied car is any less fun, and when you get right down to it, that's what really counts. While most rodders would still prefer steel to glass, make up your own mind, and don't let the prejudices of others determine what you build.

New Steel

If you must have steel and you can't find or afford a gennie body, you're in luck if you're a fan of old Fords. For several years now, Brookville Roadster has been making exact replica Model A bodies—'29 roadsters and roadster pickups, and '31 roadsters and roadster pickups. About the only piece for those bodies they don't make is the gas tank, and all the parts interchange with originals. Then, a couple of years ago, they started making the ultimate hot rod body, the 1932 Ford roadster. Again, the Brookville bodies are dead-nuts original, down to every bead and reveal.

But they're not the only ones making real steel. Experimetal of Michigan has been making steel repro 1932 Chevy roadster bodies for a number of years. Rod Bods also started making 1932 Ford roadster bodies, but theirs have non-stock floors and firewalls, and more modern tubular bracing inside. Externally, they look absolutely correct, though. Finally, Steve's Auto Restorations in Portland, Oregon, is making 1933–34 Ford roadsters and cabriolets out of all-new steel. All of these bodies are high-quality pieces; the cost is more than a comparable fiberglass body, but in most cases they're much cheaper than an original steel body in comparable condition.

These new steel bodies, as well as new fiberglass bodies, will all require some preparation, fitting, and tweaking before they're ready for paint, but they're far better than trying to save a rusted, bent, original steel body. In the case of the repro Model A bodies especially, you're often money ahead buying repro steel instead of saving a roached and twisted original body.

BODY MODIFICATIONS:
Performance, Style, and Attitude

All great hot rods have a presence about them. It's a look, an attitude, and a style. Oftentimes it is easier to spot great attitude when it's completed than it is to visualize it during the construction process.

Hot rodders originally did things like channeling, chopping the top, and leaning back the windshield post as a way of cheating the wind. Less wind resistance meant more speed. The custom car crowd, on the other hand, removed trim, altered body lines, and smoothed things off in an effort to stylize the cars.

Today the top chop, channeling, removal of door handles, and body modifications are largely a function of style. The advent of the wire-feed welder and plastic body filler has made many modifications easily within the reach of the home builder. But before you grab that die grinder, Sawzall, or torch (listed in decreasing order of finesse) do some planning.

Look at cars similar to yours. Buy this book, look through it for ideas. Check magazines, old and new, and discover the look you want. Decide if a 4-inch chop is too radical or a 2-inch chop too conservative. Go to rod runs and cruise nights, meet the owners of cars that have the modifications you'd like for your own hot rod. Most owners are more than glad to discuss the process of building their cars.

Once you have decided on the look you desire, progress slowly. Make one body modification at a time, step back and rethink the project. Maybe a 3-inch chop is all that coupe needs, forget the channeling or sectioning. Resist the temptation to see how many body mods you can do to one car. Oftentimes you are simply creating more work than it's worth, and you can also modify a car to death. What was looking really good can turn to "overdone" in no time. Remember your goal is not to change the car, but to improve the car. Think of your car as a cup of coffee. Add cream and sugar to improve the taste. Add too much of either and it's no longer coffee. The same holds true to building a good hot rod. We love modifications, but oftentimes less is best, and you can always add another modification in the future.

In this section we'll take a look at the work required in some of the most popular body modifications in the hot rod world today. Armed with a die grinder, a MIG welder, and some patience, you should be able to perform many of them in your home shop. Let's start by defining some of the basic body mods that are common to hot rods and customs.

Chopping

Sounds brutal, but when done properly it is possibly the single most successful modification on any pre-1940 hot rod (be selective on post-1940 chops; they're more difficult to do, and more difficult to do well). Chopping is simply the lowering of the roofline. The process involves removing the roof by cutting through the vertical posts. Remove from 1 to 8 inches from the posts and reattach the top of the roof to the bottom. Lots of fitting, and lots of thinking before cutting is required. Remember also that chopping a top isn't just as simple as those last couple of sentences. Depending on the complexity of the roof, you may have to lengthen it when it comes down, or even widen it. You also have to cut the glass, the windshield frame, and the inside window moldings—and carefully cut and rejoin any wood bracing that the body might have. As mentioned before, we've seen plenty of aborted chop jobs that landed in the junkyard because somebody got in over their head. The chopping sidebars at the end of this article discuss the planning and execution of top chopping.

Channeling

Long before there was a psychic network, there were hot rodders channeling cars. Channeling is simply lowering the body down over the frame/chassis to reduce overall height. This involves removing the floor from the body, lowering the body down over the frame, fabricating new body-to-chassis mounts, and reattaching the floor to the body in its new location. In the past, this was done with widely varying degrees of crudeness, so be careful when buying an old car body that's been channeled.

Keep in mind also that channeling the body also means remounting the fenders, hood, and front sheet metal. It's a lot more work than it sounds like.

Sectioning

This modification separates the men from the boys. Sectioning a body means to remove a horizontal section of metal from the center of the body. Cut your car in half, remove a couple of inches, and reattach the top half to the bottom. Lots of thought, lots of fitting, lots of welding, lots of work. This job gets horribly complex when there are compound curves, door jambs, and body reveals involved. It is best to err on the side of caution and take a small amount out of the body, too much of a section removed can destroy the proportions of the car. Experiment on a photograph before actually cutting metal. That said, some of the greatest custom cars ever built were sectioned. Done right, it's a very effective modification.

Pie Sectioning

No, this isn't done at the local Perkins after the club meeting. Pie sectioning is usually done to just body panels such as hoods, quarter panels, and fenders. Basically, a wedge-shaped section is removed from the part to give it a visual "rake." This modification is especially effective on the hoods of some fat-fendered cars, such as 1946–48 Chevys. By removing about an inch of height from the front of the hood, you get a much more streamlined look to the car's nose.

Frenching

Add this to the list of terms that no one seems to know the origin of. Frenching is simply smoothing a body element into the body so it's faired in—most often the headlights and taillights of a vehicle. To french headlights, the headlight ring or bezel is welded solid to the body and the seam filled, and the headlight buckets are modified so the headlight can be removed and adjusted from the rear. In some cars, the stock headlight rim can be used, but in other cases, it's best to use a '54 Merc headlight rim (available in reproduction) or Chrysler Cordoba headlight bezels. On some cars, the Merc headlight rims can be welded directly to the body; in other cases, they must be modified to fit. To use the Cordoba rims, you must essentially extend the fenders outward to meet the edge of the rim. Both the Merc and Cordoba rims give the headlight a nice tunneled appearance as well. Taillights are treated similarly and are often sunk into the body in the process. Very traditional, very effective.

Shaving

Think of it as hygiene for hot rods. A good shave provides a nice clean look. Shave hood emblems, door handles, trunk emblems, and even side trim. Just as the term suggests, it is the smooth removal of stubble from your car. Almost every good hot rod has been at least partially shaved.

To do this work, you basically remove the offending trim, then fill and smooth the mounting holes. Just be careful that you don't remove so much trim that the car loses its character—most cars need at least some brightwork.

Suicide Doors

Simply put, suicide doors are hinged at the rear edge of the door. Ford started this trend with its 1932 Ford three-window, then used it on most '33 and '34 Ford models. It was thought that these doors would provide easy entry. True, but you have to crawl halfway back out of the car to close the door, you have to "back into the seat, and after you are seated you pray the door doesn't open at speed. They quit for a

Fuel filler caps or gas doors can also be frenched or flush-mounted. That same 1931 Model A roadster mentioned earlier has a motorcycle-style fuel filler cap flush-mounted in the top of the body just ahead of the deck lid. Note how it fits into the body reveal. Racy looking, smooth, and functional too.

good reason: If a suicide door pops open at speed, it folds back and smacks into the quarter panel and fender with alarming force.

Converting regular, intelligently designed doors to suicide operation involves installing new hinges at the rear of the door opening, and moving all the latch hardware to the front edge. However, this modification ranks way down on our list of body modifications. It makes little sense, requires lots of work, and you can't tell it has been done when the door is closed, which is 90 percent of the time. And most damning, it increases the potential for major body damage and decreases passenger safety.

Rolled Pans

One way to smooth the front or rear of a hot rod is to remove the bumpers and replace them with a rounded body panel that mounts to the bottom of the body and hides unsightly chassis rails. Rolled pans are best when they are pro-portional to the car, small, and neat. They look great, but running without bumpers is not a good idea—bumpers are there to protect the body from other motorists, remember? If you install a rolled pan, at least use nerf bars for some protection.

Nosing

Hot rodders have always had little use for hood emblems and ornaments. Removing them and filling the associated holes and seams is known as "nosing" your car. The smooth look of a hood sans emblems is one of the classic looks of hot rodding. A cheaper, easier alternative for some cars is to remove the emblem and replace it with a chrome "bull nose" strip. In the 1950s, you could buy bull nose strips from any speed equipment dealer. You might be able to find an NOS one, but chances are you'll now have to fabricate your own. Might as well put that work into filling the holes instead.

Decking

Same as nosing, only it's the removal of the trunk emblems, external latches, and so forth. Sometimes the lock remains in the trunk, other times it is removed too, which means some kind of remote latch assembly must be installed. All part of "decking" your car.

Nerf Bars

No, these are not watering holes for comput-er geeks. Nerf bars are tubular structures that replace bumpers on cars, especially early midgets, sprint cars, and track roadsters. Nerf bars can also be fabricated in front of the rear wheels on open-wheeled racers and street cars to prevent dreaded wheel-to-wheel contact. *Nerf* is another name whose origin is lost to history, but we have heard it used as a verb, too, as in "That sumbitch nerfed me coming out of turn two!"

The rear end of Jerry Johnson's 1948 Chevy roadster pickup has some great hot rod touches. The louvered tailgate is first—all good hot rods should have louvers, and the more the better. The rolled rear pan has some nice frenched taillights, a sunken license plate, and some exhaust cutouts. At least half-a-dozen techniques in one shot!

Tunneling

This is the act of sinking any appendage into the body. The most common applications include headlights, taillights, and antennae. A sleeve is formed and sunk into a hole in the body, then welded in place. The light (or other part) is then mounted in the tunneled opening. In the past couple of years, we've even seen side trim and emblems tunneled into a body side. Lots of work, but it gets a lot of cool points if done right.

Louvers

No, it's not an art museum, rather it is a set of stamped openings in a panel that permit air to enter or exit. Steel dies in a large press are used to both cut the opening and form the raised portion that covers the slot. Louvers were originally used mainly in hood sides, but hot rodders put them in hood tops, deck lids, belly pans, headlight buckets, and just about anything else that'll fit into a press. We've even seen louvers in a '34 Ford's top insert.

That covers most of the hot rod body modifications we can think of. Now for a few words of advice: Before you get out the torch and hammers, think about how the modifications will work with the car's original lines, and how the mods will work with each other. Often, subtler is better—we've seen a lot of late-1930s sedans especially that have been chopped 5 or 6 inches, when a 2- or 3-inch chop would've been a lot more effective. Think about the work before you do it, and plan the job well. Now let's take a look at some how-tos.

IN THE SHOP:

REMOVING RUST

We all know what sandblasting is: Using high-pressure air to shoot abrasive sand from a nozzle to remove paint, rust, and just about anything else from parts. It's a very aggressive stripping method, well suited to removing rust and paint from heavy parts like frames, cast-iron parts, forgings, and the like. You can do it at home if you have a compressor and a blaster, or you can get a commercial outfit to do it for you, usually for a very reasonable price.

We do not recommend sandblasting for sheet metal parts, though, because it can seriously warp or otherwise damage sheet metal. This happens two ways: First, heat is generated by friction between the sand and the metal being blasted, sometimes enough to cause warpage by itself. Second, the sand is hard enough to pit the surface being blasted. This causes that surface to have more surface area, in effect stretching it. When only one side of a flat panel is stretched, it warps. Sandblasting can also work-harden sheet metal, making it difficult to repair and weld.

1

This is plastic-blasting media. It looks like laundry detergent, but it removes paint without harming metal or fiberglass.

In addition, sandblasting does not get into all the nooks and crannies that other methods reach. Sometimes rust and dirt are left behind, and that can come back to haunt you after the parts are painted or plated.

The bottom line is this: For frames, axles, cast parts, or forgings, sandblasting is an inexpensive, effective way to remove rust and paint. But please don't try it on sheet metal!

PLASTIC-MEDIA BLASTING
How It Works

The technique is similar to sandblasting, except the blasting media is small beads of thermoset plastic. Each plastic bead has rough edges that abrade paint. However, the plastic is soft enough that it won't affect metal or fiberglass. The media is loaded into a large hopper and fed via a hose to a large blasting gun that the operator aims at the parts to be stripped. The process uses low pressure (25–40 psi) and high volume (150–175 cfm) to propel the media from the nozzle. Blasting creates a lot of dust, so the operator wears coveralls, gloves, and a blast hood with its own air supply. To help the operator see his work through the dust, a bright spotlight is mounted right on the blasting gun.

What It Does

Plastic-media blasting removes paint, primer, and thin layers of filler. Lead filler and brazing is unaffected. In some cases, a skilled operator can remove individual layers of paint, leaving filler or factory primer underneath. Most rodders will want it removed to bare metal, though.

Cost

This method is relatively inexpensive. Our test fender had one layer of primer and one layer of 30-year-old lacquer paint that was easily removed. Completely stripping the whole fender would've taken about 5 minutes, and the cost would've been approximately $10 to $20. The average price for stripping a full-size metal car (exterior only) is about $450. The average price for doing the exterior, underside, jambs, hood, and deck lid of a steel musclecar is about $650.

2 "We will not harm your planet!" Plastic blasting is dirty work and requires a full hood, coveralls, and gloves. Note the air supply lines and the light mounted on the blasting nozzle. For testing, we used a fender off my Deuce three-window. It has 30-year-old lacquer on it, a coat of Rust-oleum on the inside, and, we knew, some lead filler along the bead and in a filled taillight hole.

3 The paint comes off fast; doing half the fender, inside and out, only took about two minutes. Here you can see black paint at right, some lighter skin-coat filler in the middle, and bare metal at left. Thicker layers of plastic can be left intact.

4

Here's what we had after blasting. The dark patches are surface rust that formed under the paint over 30 years. The light patches are lead filler, which aside from a slightly roughened surface, was unaffected. If this was all there was, we could have sanded off the surface rust and proceeded from here. However, the entire inside of the fender was covered with a solid layer of surface rust that the previous builders simply painted over. On to the dip stripper.

Keep in mind, however, that these are ballpark prices. Newer urethane paints are tough to blast, as are basecoat-clearcoats; removing them is usually time-consuming and therefore more expensive. Likewise, if your car has several layers of paint, blasting time increases and the price follows. Strip-Rite has a meter on the blaster that measures actual blasting time for a job; that determines the price.

Pros

Plastic-media blasting is excellent for fiberglass parts and bodies. (Corvette restorers think it's the greatest thing since Zora Arkus Duntov.) It won't distort or work-harden sheet metal; even light-gauge aluminum aircraft parts can be safely stripped (in fact, the process was developed by the U.S. Air Force and is used by most airlines). It's also fast—most places can do an entire car body in one working day or less, depending on how busy they are. Plastic media is nonabrasive, so you don't have to worry about it getting into hinges and so forth. It also cleans up much easier than sand.

Plastic-media blasting is also environmentally friendly. The inert media can be reused a couple of times before it's too pulverized to be effective, and there are no solvents or toxic chemicals to dispose of.

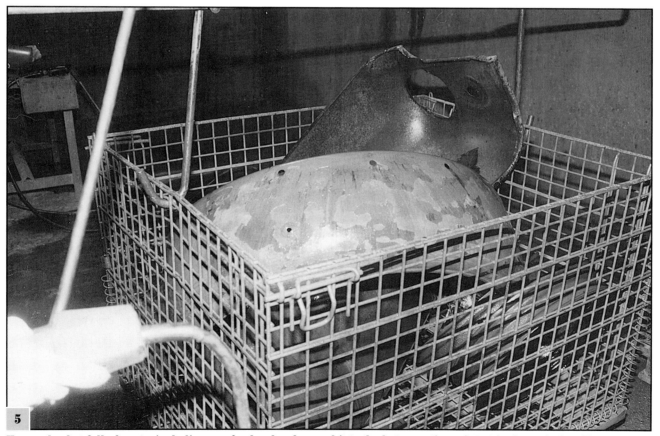

5

Here, a basket full of parts, including our fender, has lowered into the hot, caustic, paint-stripping solution. The parts sat in there overnight. When the parts emerge, the paint is still on them, but it's now a soft muck that's easily removed.

Cons

Plastic-media blasting does not remove rust; patches of surface rust appear as black splotches on the bare metal after a part's been stripped.

Best Applications

This technique is excellent for removing paint from finished cars and parts for repainting. For example, say your car is an older street rod that has two or more paint jobs on it, and you want to repaint the car to freshen it up. Plastic-media blasting is a good way to neatly and economically remove built-up layers of paint so you have a good, clean foundation for the new paint job. And, as mentioned before, it's perfect for stripping paint off of fiberglass bodies and parts.

DIP STRIPPING

There are two types of dip stripping available: acid-dipping and electrochemical stripping. Acid-dipping isn't as common as it once was, and we don't recommend it for sheet metal parts for several reasons: First, it removes healthy metal as well as rust, so it's possible to end up with holes where you didn't have them before. Second, acid-dipping can cause sheet metal to become brittle.

Electrochemical stripping doesn't remove healthy metal and it doesn't embrittle parts; it's the method of choice for most street rodders.

How It Works

Electrochemical dip stripping is usually a two-step process, one step for removing paint and another for removing rust. Typically it works like this: The parts are first immersed in a tank (large enough to take a whole body or frame) filled with a hot caustic solution that loosens and dissolves paint, grease, dirt, undercoating, and just about anything else that isn't metal.

Parts are usually left in the caustic paint-stripping tank overnight; this softens the paint into a sticky goo that a worker then blasts off with a high-pressure spray. (You don't want the paint to come off in the tank, or the solution would get used up too fast.) In most cases, one dip will do it, but if the paint is unusually thick or hard, it may take two or three dips.

Often, thick layers of filler will not be removed by the caustic dip. If it's really thick, some dippers will leave the filler in place until the customer sees it, so the customer won't think that the stripper dented the part. Usually,

A good high-pressure bath removes all traces of paint, dirt, and grease. This is probably the most important part of the job; quality strippers spend several hours spray cleaning a complete body to make sure all the caustic solution is removed.

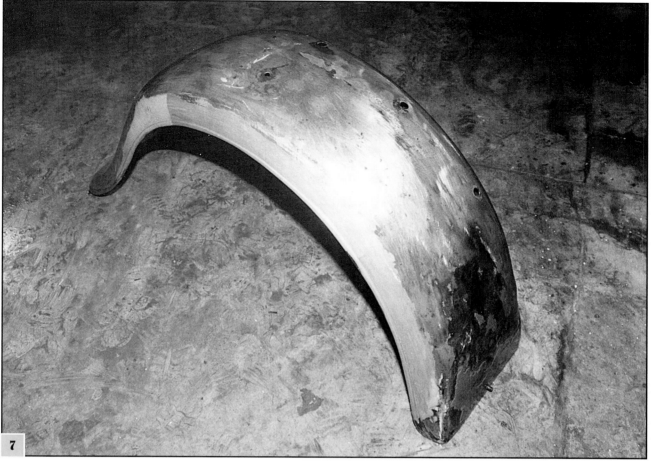

7

The dip-stripped side of the fender looks much like the blasted side, except that the lead surface is smooth. The other difference is that the paint is gone from inside the fender bead, where the blasting can't reach.

though, filler is loosened enough that it can be removed with a putty knife.

We should note here that due to environmental regulations, many dip strippers no longer use the caustic dip method to remove paint. Many have switched to plastic-media blasting to do the job, followed by electrochemical derusting. Plastic blasting is probably better than caustic dipping, as it doesn't leave any residue in cracks and crevices.

After all the paint and undercoating is off, the parts are removed and rinsed, and any stubborn undercoating or gunk is removed by hand. Once the parts are paint- and gunk-free, they're put into the derusting solution.

Rust is created by an electrochemical reaction between iron and oxygen that forms iron oxide, Fe_2O_3. The process is speeded up when water is present to carry the small electric current that produces rust, and it's greatly accelerated when that water contains salt, which increases the water's conductivity.

To remove the rust, the parts are immersed in an alkaline solution containing hydroxyl (HO) ions, and electrical current is run through the metal parts. When the parts are the positive pole, or anode, electrons from the HO are transferred to the iron oxide, allowing the bond between the iron and oxygen molecules to be broken. The resulting iron molecules are released into the solution, and the oxygen molecules form bubbles and rise to the surface. These bubbles also perform a scrubbing action that helps clean the parts.

Periodically, the current in the tank is reversed, so the parts become the negative pole, or cathode. This causes hydrogen gas to be released from the mixture, which also scrubs the parts, and the reversed polarity repels negatively charged dirt particles from the parts.

Note that only iron oxide is removed by the process. Unrusted steel or iron is unaffected, and emerges from the tank with zero rust. The clean parts are then coated with a phosphate solution that protects them from surface rust; this coating is easily washed off when it's time to paint the parts.

An overnight dip will remove most surface rust, but deeply pitted rust may take two or three trips to the derusting tank to get it all off.

Cost

While dip stripping is more expensive than other processes, it's still reasonable when you consider that the end result is a part that's completely free of rust and paint. The cost for dipping our test fender was $70; a similar front fender would've been $80–90 simply because it's bigger. Other ballpark prices: an older body shell costs about $650, whereas a unibody musclecar body will run $850, and a late-model body and frame goes for $1,200–1,500. Of course, these prices will vary from stripper to stripper and by areas of the country; these are presented for comparison only.

Pros

Electrochemical stripping is the most effective metal stripping method available, because it removes everything but the sound metal. All paint is removed, and all rust or corrosion completely disappears without harming the base metal. Even areas that you can't reach manually (between panels, inside rolled edges, etc.) are completely clean. For thoroughness, you just can't beat it. We recommend it for any part.

Cons

Electrochemical stripping is the most expensive of these processes, but it's still affordable, especially when you consider the results. Otherwise we see no drawbacks to the process. Some fairly nasty chemistry is involved, but reputable strippers like Carolina Chem-Strip and Redi-Strip have complex wastewater treatment systems and are required by law to dispose of their wastes in a responsible manner.

HOME STRIPPING

By far the cheapest method of stripping is to do it yourself. It may take some time, but you can realize significant savings. Basically, you have two choices: manual and chemical.

Manual stripping means sanding and grinding. On the plus side, it's cheap and you get the satisfaction of being able to say you did it yourself. On the downside, it's hard, dirty work, and you usually can't get everything off. For instance, if we had sanded or ground all the paint and rust off of our test fender, it would've taken several days (under the paint, the inside of

Next, the fender took two overnight trips through the de-rusting tank, with thorough spray cleaning between. When it was done, there was no rust or paint left, just bare steel and lead filler. They recommend that old lead be melted out and replaced, because it's porous and can hold moisture and chemicals. We did uncover a surprise at the front of the fender—plastic filler over a patch. Most strippers will scrape (not grind) small amounts of putty from a part; they leave thick plastic in place until the customer can see it. Otherwise, a customer unaware of the plastic might think the parts were dented at the shop. Sometimes stripping uncovers some unpleasant surprises.

9

Here's a Mopar fender that's ready to pick up at Carolina ChemStrip. Note the old brazed repair in the upper left; with all the paint, rust, and filler gone, a good metal man could metal finish this to like-new condition. Even if you just smooth it with filler, you won't have to worry about it lifting or bubbling from old rust or imperfections underneath the new paint. Dipped parts have a phosphate coating that inhibits new rust; when you're ready to paint, just wash it off with soap and water, dry, and paint. Larger dip-stripping facilities, like Carolina ChemStrip, do complete bodies and frames, too.

the fender was covered with a pretty thick layer of surface rust). And, we wouldn't have removed the rust from inside the rolled fender bead. Dip stripping got it *all* off.

Manual stripping does have its place though. For small parts or even big parts that are known to be relatively rust free, it works fine. And we did discover a tool that makes it go pretty fast: 3M makes a rust and paint removal wheel that you can chuck up in your drill and grind away. It looks like a very coarse Scotch-Brite pad with abrasive bonded to it, and it removes paint and surface rust very quickly. We used it to clean up some rust "scabs" that formed on our late-model winter beater and were amazed at how fast it produced a patch of

bare metal. Similar pads are also available for disc grinders from 3M and other suppliers.

Chemical stripping is also a viable home option. Eastwood and others sell aircraft paint stripper that works fairly quickly; it's a gel that you brush on, let sit, then scrape off. We tried it on some small parts and were pretty satisfied with the results, but it does have its drawbacks: It's messy work and you have to dispose of the paint/stripper residue. The stuff smells, so it's best to use it outside, and because it works best above 60 degrees Fahrenheit, wintertime use is out for many of us. On the plus side, a gallon costs about $30. Eastwood also sells a rust remover called Oxi-Solv and a rust neutralizer called Corroless. Both products are reputed to work

IN THE SHOP:

FIXING DENTS

Hammer-and-Dolly Work

My 1947 Olds convertible was one of the rustiest cars on the planet, and we probably replaced about 80 percent of the car in the process of rebuilding it. Many of those parts came from a cheap parts car that had a rust-free, slightly bent front clip on it. A friend of mine, Kurt Senescall at Creative Metalworks, said to have the parts stripped before I did any hammering on them, or the hammer blows would push the rust particles right into the metal, with unpleasant consequences later on. (Rust and dirt are also very hard on the working faces of body hammers and dollies.) So we had the parts plastic-media blasted to remove the paint, undercoating, and flaky loose rust; then the parts were electrochemically derusted at the same facility.

It was then time to hammer and bang on the parts to get them in shape. The hood was nearly perfect, but the fenders were another story. Decent parts for Olds 66–series cars are hard to come by, so we settled for these because they were 99-percent rust free (and cheap). But they are beat up. The right-side fender has a large, shallow dent in the side from being shoved up against another car in the junkyard. The left side is even worse; the rear section of the fender was folded upward when the car was lifted by a fork-loader. But neither is as bad as it looks; the damage is fairly simple, with no tears, crumples, or severe creases.

To accomplish the repairs, I needed tools, so I ordered Eastwood's 8-Piece Body and Fender Tool Kit (Item No. 1324), which consists of a general-purpose dinging hammer, a general-purpose pick hammer, a general-purpose dolly, a toe dolly, a dinging spoon, a flexible body file with holder, and a copy of *The Key to*

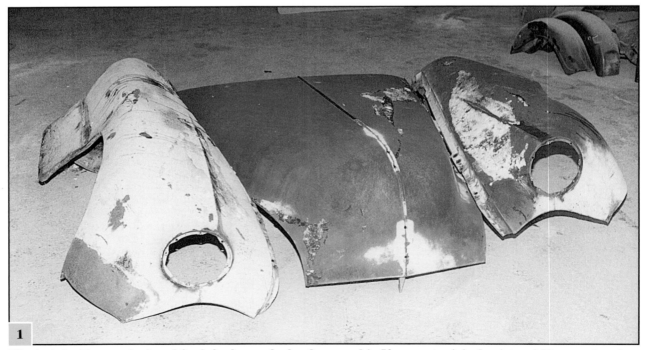

1

We started with some junkyard-fresh fenders and a hood, covered in 50-percent original paint and 50 percent surface rust. The hood is perfect. The fenders are bent but 99-percent rust free.

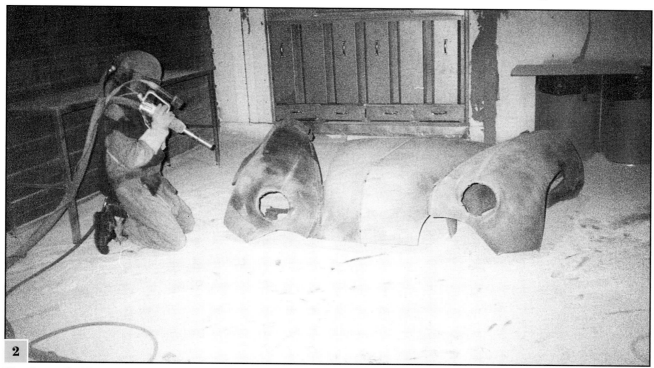

2

Plastic-media blasting was used to remove all the paint, loose rust, and undercoating. Dusty work, but it cleans the metal well without damaging it. The process even works for fiberglass cars and parts, and it's environmentally friendly.

Metal Bumping by Frank T. Sargent. These tools are made by Martin Tools in the USA, and they are top-quality stuff—probably the nicest tools I own. The book contains very good information on the tools and techniques for repairing dents, creases, and other sheet metal damage.

Here's a brief rundown on what the tools are, and a few tips on hammer-and-dolly techniques:

The general-purpose dinging hammer is a lighter hammer with two faces, one larger diameter than the other. The two faces also have different crowns, or surface curves; the large head is flatter and spreads the blow over a larger area.

The general-purpose pick hammer has one large-diameter, low-crown face, and a sharp pick on the other end that's useful in metal finishing. It's used to raise small low spots from behind the panel so the outside surface can be sanded smooth.

The general-purpose dolly is a heavy, shaped block of tool steel that you hold behind the panel. It has several different curvatures on its surfaces for working behind different shaped panels. Using different areas of the dolly behind a relatively flat panel will also change the rate at which the metal moves.

The dinging spoon is used to spread a hammer blow over a large area, useful for flattening long, smooth buckles in sheet metal; it's placed on the metal and hit with a ball-peen. Spooning out buckles is usually the last metal-bumping step, after the more severe damage has been worked out with a hammer and dolly.

3

To straighten sheet metal, the basic tools you'll need are included in this starter set from Eastwood. A dinging hammer, a picking hammer, a general-purpose dolly, a toe dolly, a dinging spoon, a body file, and *The Key to Metal Bumping*, a very good how-to book.

Some shallow dents in relatively flat panels (i.e., a kick-type dent in a door panel) can be worked out entirely with a dinging spoon.

The body file has very coarse, very sharp curved teeth, and is used after most of the rough hammer-and-dolly work is done. The file is run lightly over the area you've worked, and

4 Here it is, rust free but bent. You can see where the splash apron inside the fender is holding the rear of the dent in; you can also see the vertical trough that moved up the side behind the wheelwell (solid line), pushing that inverted-V shaped ridge ahead of it. That ridge (dashed line) will be the biggest challenge.

5 To get the rear pushed out, I placed a bottle jack between the cowl and the bottom of the crease; then slowly applied pressure while hammering on the crease in the inner fender panel.

the high spots get shaved down slightly. This helps you identify low spots that need to be raised. It's also used in metal finishing to achieve a smooth surface.

Now, how do you use this stuff? First, I learned (to my surprise) that the dolly should not be used as an anvil that you flatten metal against. It's a little-understood fact that if you hammer sheet metal on the dolly, you will actually raise the spot you're hammering on. This is because the hammer blow thins the metal, and tries to push the surrounding metal outward; when the hammer rebounds, the inertia of the heavier dolly, combined with the pressure you're exerting on the dolly from the rear, causes it to push the metal upward. The hammer-on-dolly technique is particularly effective for raising dents with a trough (the trough represents the path traversed by a rolled buckle).

You can also hammer off the dolly by placing the dolly under a low spot and hammering on a high spot adjacent to the low spot. On a typical curved fender side, you'd place the dolly under the low spot and hammer above and below the dolly, not on either side.

When working hammer-off-dolly, start by hammering the metal farthest away from the

6

When the ridge was lower and less pronounced, I used the dinging spoon to knock down larger areas. I used a small ball-peen for this work; you don't want to mar the faces of the body hammers or it'll transfer those marks to the metal you're working. Also, use light hammer blows from the wrist; lots of light blows will work better than one big one. Remember, you're not driving spikes.

dent, and work your way inward. Be careful that the hammer blows don't push the metal down too far: Remember, it's not backed by the dolly. Use a high-crown section of the dolly face.

Keep in mind also that the metal in a damaged area has been stretched, and hammer-and-dolly work stretches it further. If you overwork an area, you will probably end up with an "oil can" effect or even a part that doesn't fit. To solve that, you can shrink the metal with a shrinking hammer, or by using heat from a torch, along with a hammer and dolly.

Before you start whanging away, read either *The Key to Metal Bumping* or *Automobile Sheet Metal Repair* (see sources). They contain good information that you need to know before you start. It's also a good idea to first practice on a dented fender or door that you don't care about before you start on the real thing.

So, after doing my homework, I started the repair process by bolting the passenger-side fender to the car. This held it steady while I hammered and pulled on it, and also made sure that it didn't get distorted or twisted in the process.

When repairing dents or other collision damage, you essentially have to analyze the

7

With the big ridge knocked down and the trough starting to raise, I started hammering on-dolly to raise low spots. It takes practice to keep the dolly behind the hammer blow; there's a definite metallic "klink" when you hit it right. Hammering on-dolly actually raises the metal because the metal stretches, then reacts to the rebound of the heavy dolly from behind.

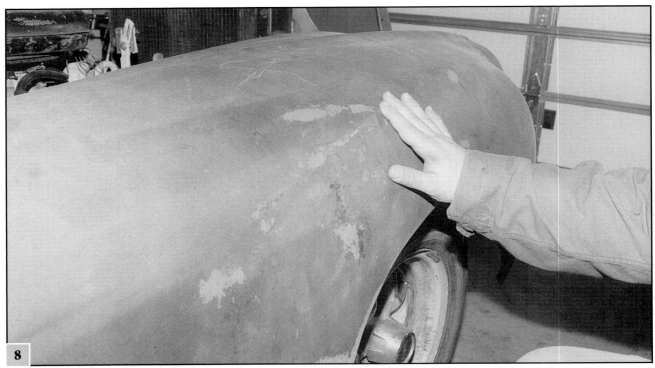

8

At this point it's in the right shape, but there are still some small ridges and low spots to contend with. After a while, you get good at finding low spots by "feel," simply by running your hand over the metal. Those light spots you see are pitted areas that were bare rusty metal before stripping.

9

When it's getting close, take the body file and run it across the worked area. This will shave off some of the highest spots and make the low spots that need raising much more visible. Note: I'm not showing proper technique here—the file should be held horizontally and moved along the length of the fender so as much of the file contacts the surface as possible. I should also remember not to photograph the top of my head; people will soon be mistaking me for Burger.

damage and figure out what metal was damaged first and how the damage proceeded. For instance, in our passenger-side fender, something pushed in at the center of the flat area of the fender; the potmetal side spear was strong enough to force the whole side of the fender in, buckling the inner splash panel in the process. This action also caused a vertical trough to form that caused a "rolled buckle" that traveled upward across the fender to the crown (see photos). The result is a vertical trough behind the wheel opening, with a kind of inverted V-shaped ridge at the top of it. This V-shaped ridge also made the curve along the length of the fender more square in this area.

I started by placing a small bottle jack between the cowl and the back of the fender where it was pushed in the farthest. By applying pressure and hammering (with a regular ball-peen) on the inner splash apron, I was able to get it back to its correct shape so it wasn't holding the fender in.

That done, I was able to concentrate on the more serious trough-and-ridge damage near the wheel opening. Starting at the ridge on top (because it was the last damage to occur), I placed the dolly below the ridge and started hammering (off-dolly) lightly on the ridge. The ridge began to flatten, and the surrounding metal was slowly raised from the dolly pressure from behind. I also gave the low spots an occasional "bump" from behind with the dolly. At one point, enough stress was relieved that a large area in the side of the fender "popped" back into its original position (this area was secondary damage that was held in place by the primary damage I was working on).

Eventually, the ridge was low enough that I could use the dinging spoon to knock it down pretty good. Then it was a matter of using the hammer-on-dolly to raise the low spots. When it got close, I made several passes with the body file. This shaved the tops off some peaks, and also made the remaining low spots easier to identify. A little more hammer-and-dolly work and the fender is definitely back into its original shape. Considering this was the first time I'd ever done this, I was pretty pleased with the results.

At this point, the Olds fender was ready for either metal finishing or a light skin-coat of plastic filler. Either choice is OK, it just depends on how much time and work you're willing to invest in your project.

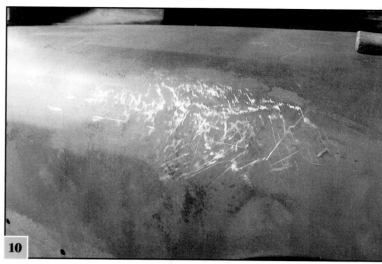

10 This masterfully lit shot shows the results of using the body file. Low spots are the dark areas between the shiny spots. Just a little more hammer-and-dolly work, and this fender will be ready for a skin-coat of plastic filler, or metal finishing if I'm real brave. Here you can easily see where the horizontal ridges in the fender were.

11 The worst damage is taken care of, and the fender is now close enough for plastic in most areas. There's still some work at the rear though—there's a vertical crease about 1-1/2 inches in front of the rear of the fender, where the outer skin got folded over the edge of the splash apron behind it. I can't get a dolly between the fender and apron, so I'll have to remove the apron to fix this.

IN THE SHOP:

HAMMER-WELDING A PATCH PANEL

No matter what kind of old car you choose to hot rod, the supply of original steel bodies is getting thin, and many rodders are beginning to use bodies and parts that would've been folded up and dumpsterized 10 years ago.

Luckily, this job is getting easier thanks to the large number of companies supplying patch panels. Installing patch panels isn't a job for beginners, but if you're reasonably handy with a gas, MIG, or TIG welder, you can do the job yourself with good results. In this example, Kurt

Senescall is installing a patch panel on the bottom edge of a Model A door. Keep in mind that patching Model A doors is relatively simple because the doors overlap the body. On later cars with flush doors, the job is trickier because the patch has to fit the door opening. The first thing you'll notice on this job is that the patch panels are flat, whereas the Model A door surface has a slight compound curve. Don't worry, after the seam is welded and the sides of the skin are folded over, the patch will be pulled so it comes pretty close to matching this curve.

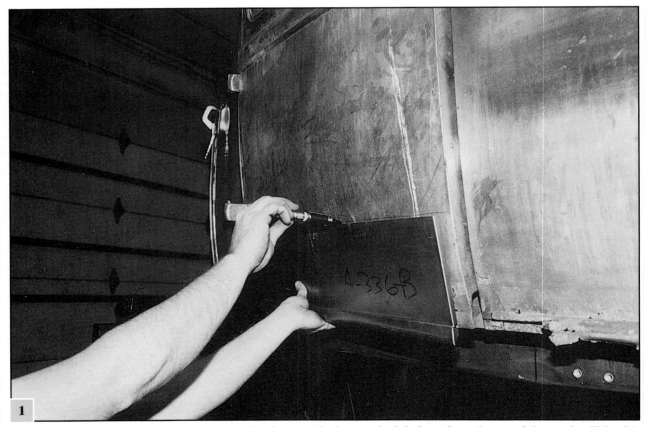

1

First, hold the patch panel up to the door and make a mark about an inch below where the top of the patch will be. It's best to keep the door on the body if you can.

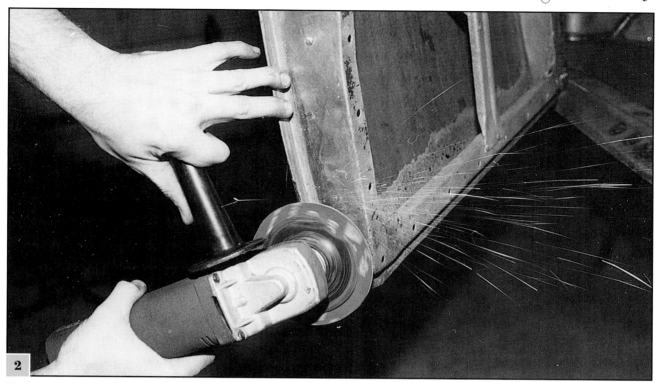

Next, use a grinder to buzz the edges of the door skin off below the mark. Be careful to only go deep enough to separate the skin—you don't want to grind off the edge of the door frame.

Next, trim off the rotten sheet metal with a snips or a nibbler. Don't remove too much!

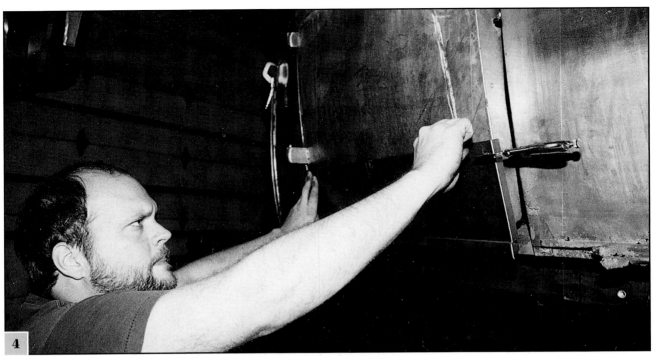

4 With the bottom of the door skin removed, you can now slide the patch up over the door frame for an exact fit. Make sure the door's bottom reveal lines up with the body reveal, and scribe a line on the door along the edge of the patch.

5 Next, carefully trim the door skin along the scribed line. Masking tape along the scribe line makes it easier to see what you're doing.

6

The straighter the edge, the better your weld will be. To straighten your cut, clamp a piece of angle iron along the edge of the door skin and use a grinder to remove any excess metal.

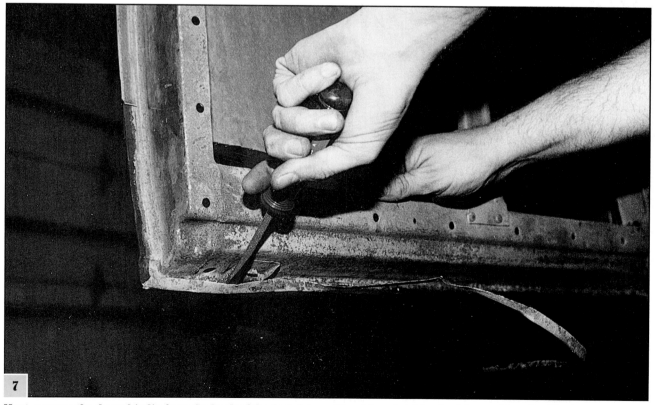

7

Next, remove the door skin lip from the back of the door frame. The old spot welds should pop off easily; it's also a good idea to smooth up the back of the door frame before installing the patch panel.

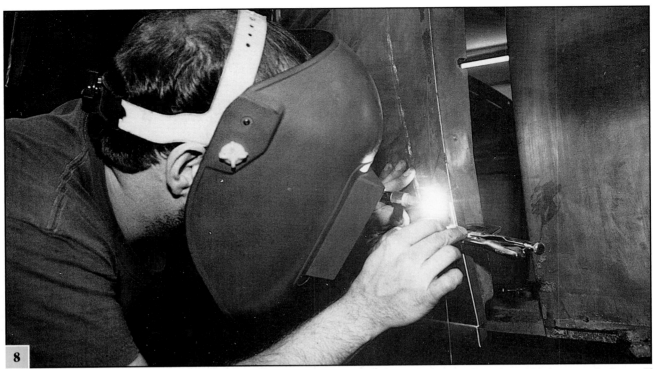

8 Clamp the patch into position, make sure the pieces are butted together with no gaps, and tack-weld it in several places. If you're gas or TIG welding, use 0.030-inch wire-feed wire as filler rod to minimize build-up.

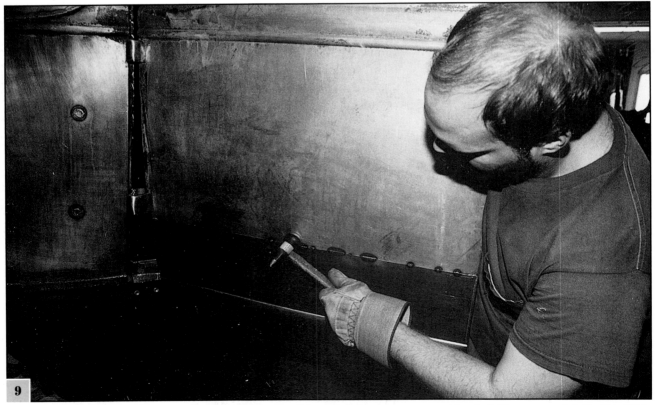

9 Begin welding short beads across the door, being careful not to let any one area get too hot. Hammer and dolly the welds flat before they cool. (If you're not proficient at hammer welding, have a pro do it.)

Start by holding the patch up to the door, then marking and cutting off the door skin about an inch or so below the top of the patch. Next, use a grinder to buzz the edge of the door skin off the door frame. Only grind deep enough to get the skin released—don't remove any of the door frame! After you get the front panel off, peel the folded-over portion of the door skin off the back of the door frame. Generally the spot welds are old enough that they'll snap off easily. Otherwise you'll have to drill or grind them out. Now, clean off any rust or crud and smooth off the back edge of the door frame so the new skin will fit snugly.

Slip the new patch up over the door frame so there's no gap between the bottom of the door frame and the patch, then clamp the patch to the door skin and scribe a straight line on the doorskin where they overlap. Remove the patch and use a snips or a nibbler to cut the door skin along this line; the cut must be absolutely straight so it butts against the patch for best results.

TIP: If you can't get the cut perfectly straight, clamp a piece of angle iron along the edge and remove the excess metal with a grinder to get a straight cut.

Now you can use a hammer and dolly to fold the edges of the patch over the door frame. By doing this after welding, it tends to put tension in the door skin and pull it into shape.

After some hammer-and-dolly work to get out the larger dips and bulges, use a flexible grinding disc to smooth off the weld bead. At this point, a light skin-coat of filler is all it needs to be perfect.

12

The finished product, ready for finishing. This procedure is much the same for any door skin, or for any patch panel for that matter.

Now, slide the patch into place, butt the edges together, clamp 'em, and tack-weld in five or six places.

TIP: If you're gas or TIG welding, use low heat and 0.030 MIG welder wire as filler rod. This'll minimize warpage and keep the material build-up as low as possible. If you're using a gas welder, use a small tip and a neutral flame (as opposed to an oxidizing or carburizing).

Don't fold the edges of the patch panel over the door bottom yet (an exception—you may have to fold one edge so you can close the door to check the fit). As you weld, the metal will pull in toward the center of the door. If the bottom edge is folded over, this pulling will suck the center of the door into a big dent that'll be a bear to fix.

Now, hammer-welding: If you're using a gas welder, you can do this yourself. If you're using a TIG setup, you'll need someone else to hammer and dolly the weld beads—TIG welds cool too fast for one person to do it quickly enough.

Weld about a 3/4-inch bead, then immediately work it flat with a hammer and dolly. If left alone, the welds will shrink considerably as they cool, pulling on the surrounding metal and creating warpage. By hammering the welds flat as they cool, you expand the metal again, and the forging process actually makes the welds stronger. Next, go to another cool spot on the seam and repeat the procedure. Keep working back and forth, being careful not to overheat any one area of the door skin. Eventually, the whole thing will be welded with a minimum of distortion.

After the welding is done, use the hammer and dolly to fold the bottom of the patch over the door frame. You'll find that as you do this, it should pull the door skin tight and cause the flat patch to follow the curve of the door. It isn't necessary or desirable to weld the folded edges. Also, don't hammer the folds too flat, or the door skin will "grow."

At this point, if you have the skill or the guts, you can continue the hammer-and-dolly work until the door is smooth. Then you can either metal finish the skin or just get it close enough so a bodyman can finish it off with a thin skin-coat of plastic filler. This procedure is basically the same for any lower-body patch panel.

IN THE SHOP:

REPLACING ROTTEN BODY WOOD

Up until 1936, almost all GM bodies were built using wood frames with the sheet metal panels nailed and bolted on. The first all-steel bodies made their debut in 1937 on popular models, but some low-production cars, such as sedan deliveries, had wood-framed doors into the early 1940s. This system worked well during the car's normal service life, but some 40 years later, most GM products have the telltale signs of Rotten Wood Syndrome: sagging doors, stress cracks in the sheet metal, and so forth.

We've taken pictures of two wood replacement projects: The first was in Ed Stulc's 1934 Chevy coupe, and the second is in a 1936 Pontiac coupe. Between the two projects, we were able to photograph all the necessary steps and put together a step-by-step outline of how the job is done.

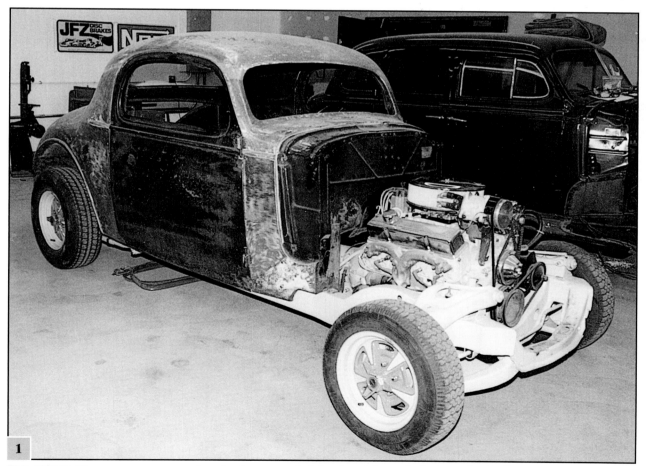

1

This 1936 Pontiac coupe was once a bunch of unsupported sheet metal panels that were basically leaning together. Now that the rotten wood's been replaced, it's as strong and square as any new car.

2 This before shot of a 1934 Chevy coupe door shows how bad the problem can get. The door itself is a wooden framework covered in sheet metal, and the door opening is framed in wood too. Both are rotten beyond repair.

3 The 1934 body is supported by a pair of wooden "subframe" rails that are also rotten. When this goes, the only thing holding the cowl to the rest of the body is the roof. The result is stress cracks and badly sagging doors.

4

When everything fits correctly, weld the doors shut like this, and weld cross braces inside the body to hold everything in position.

Start with the most basic structural elements. If the car's body had wooden subframe rails (like the 1934 Chevy in this case), build them first using appropriate-size rectangular steel tubing. Bolt them to a square, level frame, and bolt the body in the correct position.

Next, align the doors and deck lid so they have an even gap all around. You may have to use a Porta-Power or other kind of jack to get the body in position so everything fits well. Once everything fits to your satisfaction, tack-weld the doors and deck lid shut using small pieces of sheet metal to bridge the gaps.

Now, while everything fits, cross-measure inside the body to make sure that it's not leaning to one side or the other. For instance, measure from the bottom of the left door jamb to the top of the right door jamb, and vice versa. When the body is square, the measurements will be equal. Once it's square, weld some cross-braces inside the body to hold it that way.

Now that everything's in place and securely braced, remove what's left of the original wood.

Rebuilding the door frames can be done in two ways. On the 1934 Chevy, square steel tubing was cut with a chop saw so it could be formed to the desired curvature. Tack-weld the tube pieces in and continue in this manner until the door is completely framed.

5

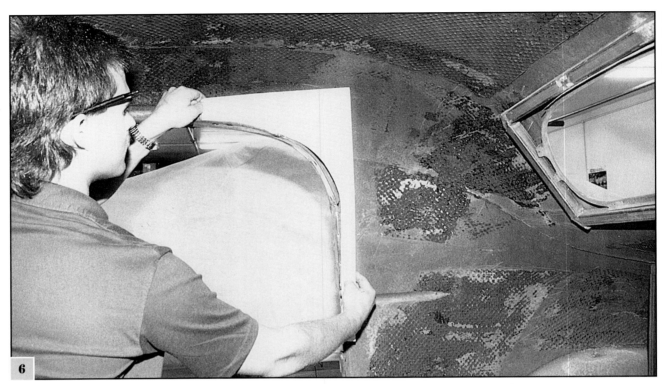

6

The second method was used in the Pontiac. Cardboard templates were made of the door opening.

7

A brake was used to make some 90-degree sheet metal angle pieces, and an Eastwood shrinker/stretcher formed the desired curves. The resulting pieces are very stiff and strong.

By using the shrinker/stretcher and a few cuts in the angle, the builders ended up with a brace that fit like this. Once welded in, this boxed section will be very light and strong.

If there's enough there, save it and use it for patterns. Otherwise you'll just have to wing it.

Start the reconstruction process with the doors. In both of these cars, once the wood was removed, all that was left were the outer skins and the edges. With no inner skin, the doors will flop and twist all over the place if you remove them from the car now. To prevent this, you can go one of two ways:

- **First,** you can build a new inner door skin and install it while the door is still welded in place on the body. When you pop those welds and remove the door, it'll maintain the correct curvature.
- **Second,** you can weld a tubing cross-brace to the *outside* of the door to prevent it from twisting or changing shape. Then remove the door and install your new inner door skin.

If possible, we recommend keeping the door welded to the body while you install the new

The inner door skins can be installed either on or off the car — we recommend leaving them on the car if possible. If you're going to do it off the car, build a brace on the outside like this so the door doesn't twist. If you don't, it may not fit properly when you reinstall the door.

The new door skins are cut out of sheet metal and welded into the door. For extra strength, take the skins to a sheet metal shop and get some beads rolled in them. Remember to leave a big enough opening so you can work with the door and window mechanisms.

With the doors out of the way, it's time to frame the trunk area. On both example cars, this was done using thin-wall 1-inch square tubing, curved to fit by slicing it with a chop saw. Frame the opening; then brace it to the floor with more tubing. You may also have to build a new water channel inside the trunk lid opening.

12

Window openings are done the same way, with square tubing, welded to the window lip.

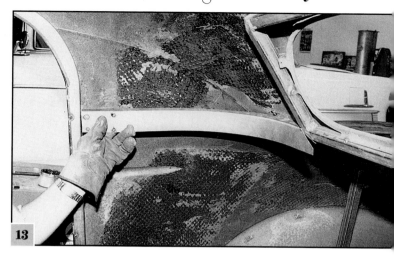

13

The final touch is to tie it all together, either with tubing or sheet metal. This formed sheet metal piece links the door frame with the rear window; another will link the rear window frame with the trunk opening.

inner skin—it's more foolproof. Whichever way you choose, get some beads rolled into the inner skin panels to improve their stiffness, and leave some kind of an opening so you can get the door latches, window cranks, and windows into the door. Remember, in some doors, the glass can't be installed through the window opening—it has to go in from the bottom. Check *before* you weld in a solid skin!

After the inner door skins are built and installed, you can remove the doors and concentrate on what's left of the body. Basically, you have to put a new piece of steel in to replace every stick of wood you took out. Start by framing the door openings. In the Pontiac coupe shown here, the builders started with a piece of 18-gauge sheet metal about 4 feet long and 5 inches wide, braked to a 90-degree angle. They then trimmed one edge to fit the curve of the body and welded it to the door jamb. Later on, they went back in and cut out recesses for new latch pins and so forth.

With the doors framed, they took thin-wall 1-inch-square steel tubing and used it to build frames for the back window and deck lid opening. To form the curves, he used a chop saw to cut through three sides of the tube, making these cuts every couple of inches. The tubing could then be bent to fit the desired curve and welded solid. More square tube braces were then built between the deck lid opening and the floorboards.

A pair of curved braces were also needed to go between the rear window frame and the door openings. The builders took some sheet metal, put a 90-degree bend in it, and used an Eastwood shrinker/stretcher setup to get these angled pieces to fit the desired curve. (We only had to watch the construction of one of these pieces to realize that a shrinker/stretcher is a necessary tool if you plan to do sheet metal work.) Once they were formed, the pieces were welded in, and the wood replacement was finished.

Hinges for the doors and deck lid, door latches, and new window regulators will finish

14

The last step is to work out the door latches and hinges. Stock hinges were attached to wood members in the body and door; these hinges can be used by welding heavier threaded plates into the doors and body. This is also a good time to install hidden hinges and late-model or aftermarket door latches.

the job. These steps will vary with each application, but we've included a few detail shots to give you an idea of how it can be done. Using these ideas, you'll find it relatively easy to save a body that's already served as a termite's mobile buffet.

INSTALLING "BEAR CLAW" DOOR LATCHES

How many times do you suppose the original door latches have been opened and closed on your latest street rod project? Let's face it, 40 or 50 years of hard use have probably taken their toll on these outdated mechanisms, and they're probably due for repair or replacement.

Repair is OK in some cases, and parts for most door latches are available through the better restoration supply companies. But if you're after the smooth look, your old latches may be too stiff to operate by solenoids. And, some of those old latches aren't designed well and aren't repairable. For example, the latch assemblies in 1947 to 1954 Chevy pickups are poorly designed and prone to wear; the result is that the doors will only close with repeated slamming, and sometimes they fly open when you turn corners. And, once they're worn out, they aren't repairable.

If you need to replace your latches, your first option is to head for the salvage yard and get some late-model latch assemblies (we've heard that Ford Escort and some VW latches work well). However, finding a latch that will fit in your early doors can be a problem. First,

modern car doors are often 4 to 5 inches thick. Doors on a Model A or 1932 Ford are only a couple of inches thick. Second, most late-model door latches extend too far into old doors and interfere with the window channels. This brings us to a second solution, aftermarket latches.

Several years ago, hot rodders discovered some neat aftermarket double-action latches that are strong enough to do the job, and small enough to fit in just about any street rod door. They're commonly called "bear-claw" latches, or burst-proof latches. The latches used in this

2

Here's where the latch's thinness is important. When mounted, the latch won't interfere with the window channel, which runs just on the inside of the window opening.

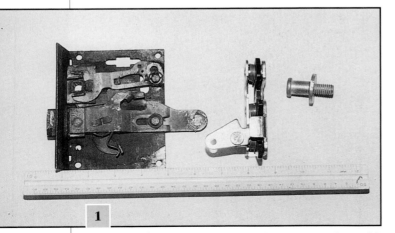

1

The new latches are compact and come complete with the latch pin. Notice how much smaller they are than the stock Buick latches.

3

The first step is to fill the stock latch receiver location on the door post; then drill a hole and mount the latch pin. Make the hole slightly oversize so you can move the pin for final adjustments.

4

Tom makes a plate with mounting holes and a notch for the latch. This'll make it easier to mount the latch in the door.

installation are 1-1/4 inches wide, 3-7/8 inches tall, and just over 3/4 inch thick. The latches are double-acting types and include the jamb pin; cost is typically less than $40 a pair.

This particular installation was done in a 1933 Buick four-door that has had most of the wood replaced with steel.

Before installing any latch, make sure that it'll fit within the door's thickness and that it won't interfere with the window channels. (We know of at least one rodder who went to install windows in a finished, painted door, only to find out that he couldn't because his late-model door latches were in the way.)

On the 1933 Buick, we first filled in the receiver location on the door jambs by welding in a patch, then drilled a hole and mounted the latch pins in the stock location. We then drew a horizontal line from the center of the latch pin to the outside of the door jamb, closed the door, and transferred the horizontal line to the

To locate the latch, we drew a horizontal line on the door-post at the centerline of the latch pin. We then transferred this line to the door and lined up the mounting plate. Here, we're marking the outline of the mounting plate on the door.

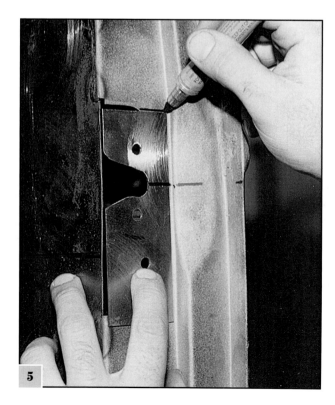

5

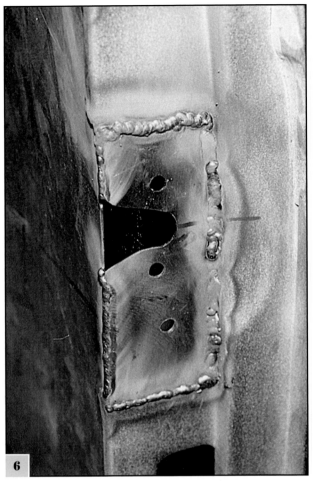

6

We then trimmed the opening and tacked the mounting plate in place. After mounting the latch and checking the alignment with the pin, we finished welding the plate to the door.

7

The last step was to cut an opening in the inner door panel. This makes it easier to install the latch and hook up the linkage. The arm at the bottom of the opening is the actuating arm; it can be hooked to a solenoid or to a regular door handle by mechanical linkage.

door. This line will help locate the latch assembly in the door.

To make installation easier, we made a sheet metal mounting plate that has predrilled mounting holes and a cutout for the latch pin. We then marked the centerline of the latch, aligned it with the mark on the door, and tacked it into place on the door frame. Then we installed the latch and checked to make sure everything worked before finish-welding the mounting plate.

After the plate was welded solid, we cut an opening in the inner door panel so the latch will be easier to mount. Later on, this will make it much easier to hook up the door handle linkage to the latch's actuating arm. The latches can be operated by solenoids or you can devise a mechanical linkage.

The only downside to these units is that they don't have an internal lock mechanism. However, this shouldn't be a problem if they're in a roadster or if you're going to operate them with a solenoid. And if you want to use stock door handles, some older cars have a lock tumbler in the door handle; this type of lock doesn't have anything to do with the latch, it just prevents the handle from turning.

These latches, or similar ones, are available from a number of hot rod parts suppliers in a variety of sizes and configurations, and they come with complete mounting kits. Shop around until you find one that fits your needs.

IN THE SHOP:

CHOPPING AN F-100 FORD PICKUP by Doug Jones

1

Here the back window is marked with reference marks and outlined for the cut to remove it as one piece. These marks will serve to relocate the window, which will remain at stock height. This kind of planning makes for a successful chop. *Doug Jones*

I liked my 1953 F-100, but one thing was for sure: It was too tall. To remedy that, I decided to chop the truck 2-1/2 inches in front and 2 inches in the rear, and to raise the stock rear window 1-1/2 inches for a more modern, proportional look. The 1/2-inch difference front to rear helps eliminate the "slant-cab" look without moving more metal around or slanting the posts, although I would have liked to totally square up the side windows. I'd like to point out that this was my first attempt at chopping a top. Also, except for some practice and minor rust repair, this was my first attempt at MIG welding. This should provide some incentive to a few folks—good tools and determination will help even dummies like me (a pharmacist) do some fairly complicated jobs.

I started the process by studying numerous books and magazine articles on chopping. Once I had an idea of how I wanted to proceed, I carefully measured the truck's top and marked guidelines for reference. On the back of the cab, I made several reference marks for the rear window, as it was going to get completely removed and remain stock height after the chop. In the windshield opening, I measured out five reference points from the center toward each side, top and bottom. Five rods were cut to fit the stock opening, then tagged to correspond to the reference points. These were later cut the same amount as the front chop and tacked into the windshield opening for alignment.

Then the cut points were chosen where both vertical sections were as parallel as possible, and marked out with tape equal to 2-1/2 inches in front, and 2 inches in the rear. With the tape in place at all cuts, the areas were outlined in permanent marker and the tape removed.

The cut for the rear window was marked, then cut and removed. There's a brace inside the cab running from the rear of each door across the back of the cab under the rear window. I cut

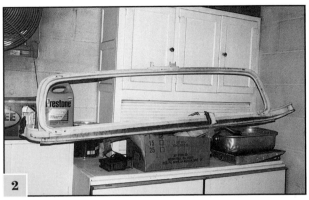

2

The rear window has been removed; notice the inside brace that goes under the frame. This piece is spot-welded to the rear of each door jamb. Cut out the spot welds and take it out with the rear window frame. *Doug Jones*

the spot welds and removed this brace with the rear window in one piece.

To avoid cutting across the middle of the top, I then cut the center of the roof out in one piece using a saber saw. The cuts were made approximately 6-1/2 inches up from the drip rail, just beyond the curve of the top.

I was also lucky enough to have a complete second top; this gave me a complete second turret, both door tops, gap filler pieces for the sides, front, and rear, and inside braces for the headliner and dome light.

The actual chop process began with the doors. We cut them (2-1/2 inches in front, 2 inches in the rear) with a power circular saw and a metal cutting blade at the marked points. The circular saw was used because the large saw base makes it much easier to keep the cuts parallel through the multiple layers of metal. The door tops from the second top were then cut to fill the resulting gap and reduce the number of welds.

With both doors cut and the new pieces tacked on, the top was marked in quarters and cut off, one quarter at a time, starting with the left front. (Note: Before you start cutting the top off, it's a good idea to either tack-weld the doors shut or weld tubular braces inside the

3

Here the cuts are marked out all around the cab, and five numbered 1/4-inch rods are placed in the windshield opening to ensure that it keeps the correct shape during the chop. The mark on top above the door is where the front top quarter will be cut. All cuts are made with a circular saw with a metal-cutting blade to ensure straight cuts all the way through. *Doug Jones*

Luckily, I had a second top and door frames from a junk cab. After the door was cut 2-1/2 inches in front and 2 inches in the rear (to eliminate some of the slant in the roof line), the top of the second door was cut so only one weld in the door top was needed. *Doug Jones*

truck cab so it doesn't "spread" when the top's off.) We used the circular saw for this process also, as it cuts easily through the double panels and makes nice straight parallel cuts all the way through.

To strengthen the windshield posts, we placed a piece of heavy angle iron inside the post, then rosette-welded it to the lower post so it protruded about 3 inches. This was slipped inside the upper half of the post and rosette-welded to it for extra strength. We then tacked the rest of the front quarter on. Also, at this time we used the round rods in the windshield opening. They were shortened 2-1/2 inches and spot welded to the top and bottom of the windshield opening to hold the top in the correct position.

Next, the left rear quarter was cut, dropped, and spot-welded, followed by the right rear. Small scrap pieces were tacked between the sections to hold them in place where the gaps were. Finally, the right front corner was cut and dropped, using the same angle iron reinforcements inside the posts and windshield rods for location.

Sections were then cut from the second top to fill all the gaps between each quarter section. Also, the rear window was repositioned

The first door is put back together with only three seams. After removing 2-1/2 inches from the front edge, it was reattached; then the second door top was cut to fit the remaining opening. This shows the gap between the chopped door and the stock top. Now the top will be cut and fit around the door. *Doug Jones*

6

Before cutting any posts, we marked the turret top and cut the middle out with a saber saw. Be sure to remove the inside brace that attaches the headliner and interior light. The cuts were made about 6 inches above the drip rail, just above the curve. *Doug Jones*

7

The scary part. Three cuts with the circular saw and the first quarter is off. I rosette-welded a piece of heavy angle iron inside the windshield post with about 3 inches sticking out. It was inserted into the upper part of the post and rosette-welded when reattached, both for strength and alignment. *Doug Jones*

8

Here the front quarter is attached, and the wire rods (now shortened 2-1/2 inches) are lined up to their reference marks and tacked on to hold the correct windshield opening. *Doug Jones*

9

Next, the left rear quarter was cut and reattached. Notice that the front portion of this quarter needed to be bent down slightly to join the front quarter. This was no problem. *Doug Jones*

10 The two left quarters are tacked up with filler pieces from the second top, including the rain gutter and a piece at the very top. The broom handle inside the cab is keeping the top straight across the rear. *Doug Jones*

11 The rest of the wire rods were reinstalled to make sure the windshield opening was correct. Now all the filler pieces will be tacked in (note the gap in the middle), everything checked for alignment, and finish-welded. And as long as we were in the neighborhood, we welded up the cowl vent, too. *Doug Jones*

12

After everything else was solid, the rear window was reattached. In moving it around, I discovered the cab looked best when the window was moved up about 1-1/2 inches. I trimmed 1/2 inch off the bottom and tacked it in. Only two small filler pieces were needed in the upper corners. Inside braces were also reattached, and a reinforcement was added where the roof sections meet in the top center. *Doug Jones*

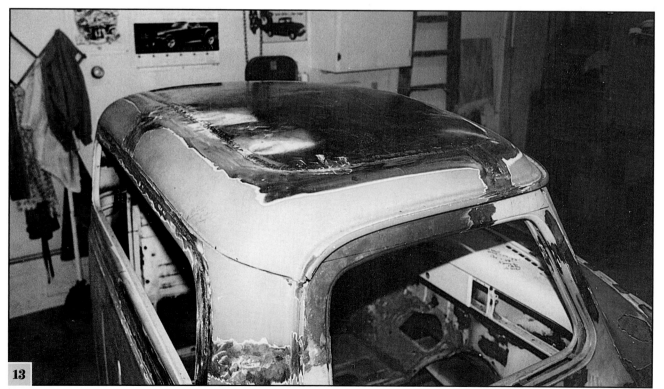

13

All filler pieces are in, and the turret's been cut from the second top. This piece was cut 1/2 inch larger than the hole, then lap-welded inside and out at intervals, until it was completely welded in. *Doug Jones*

14

Here, the truck's mocked together. Top looks almost stock, especially from the rear. Note the extended wheelbase. The chassis was built by Rick Talbot with the Cordoba front suspension moved ahead 4 inches from stock. The front wheel openings were then moved ahead 3 inches in the fenders, eliminating the heavy front overhang common to these trucks. *Doug Jones*

and moved up 1-1/2 inches from stock. We trimmed 1/2 inch off the bottom of the rear window section. Then it was reattached. Small pieces had to be trimmed and welded in to fill the gaps that resulted between the rear window and the cab in the upper corners.

Finally, the turret from the second top was carefully measured and cut so it was 1/2 inch larger than the opening in the chopped top, then carefully positioned and lap-welded inside and out. That done, it was time to take the cab outside, carefully sandblast the welds, and use some filler to begin the smoothing out process. A little thinking went a long way in this case. Check out the photos and think about it—is your car too high?

IN THE SHOP:

Top Chop Techniques

How difficult a top chop is depends on what you're chopping. Obviously, cuttin' the lid on a "T" coupe is going to be much easier than lowering the top on a 1940 Ford four-door. The number of doors and the number of curves add to the difficulty, but the biggest problem encountered in chopping a top is the need to lengthen and sometimes widen the top once it's lowered. Why is this? Well, beginning in the early 1930s, most carmakers started slanting the windshields back and the rear of the roof forward, making the profile of the roof into a trapezoid. When you take a slice out of the middle of that trapezoid, the bottom of the upper half is going to be shorter than the top of the lower half. Move a little later in automotive history, and automakers began slanting the sides of the car toward the middle, too, a characteristic known as "tumblehome." This makes it necessary to widen the top as well as lengthen it when you chop it.

There are several ways to get around this problem. First, you can slant the windshield posts back so the bottom meets the top; this is usually known as a "Bonneville chop." Good examples are the Pierson Brothers Coupe and Lance Sorchik's "Jersey Suede" 1934 Ford coupe. Speaking of Lance, he also used this technique to chop his 1948 Chevy pickup, which we'll be showing you soon. He even went so far as to slant the sides of the truck in so he wouldn't have to widen the top.

If you're chopping a coupe or sedan, you can simply bring the roof forward until the windshield posts line up, slant the B-pillar, and add a section between the back of the roof and

1

These illustrations (of a 1948 Chevy truck, but the principle applies to most cars built after about 1932) show what happens when you chop a top—the top half of the roof needs to be lengthened, and sometimes widened, to meet up with the body again. If you don't want to stretch the top, you can tilt the windshield posts back so they meet up; this results in a fairly radical-looking chop that looks cool on a hot rod, but may not be appropriate for some cars. Otherwise, you're going to have to split the roof and add sections from a second roof or patch pieces to make up the difference. _Eric Aurand_

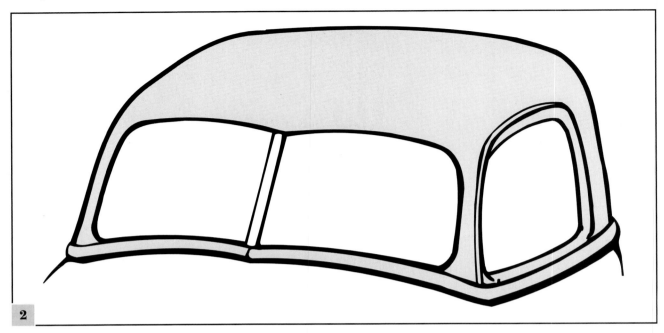

2

To solve the problem, your options are: Leave it stock (yawn!), or . . .

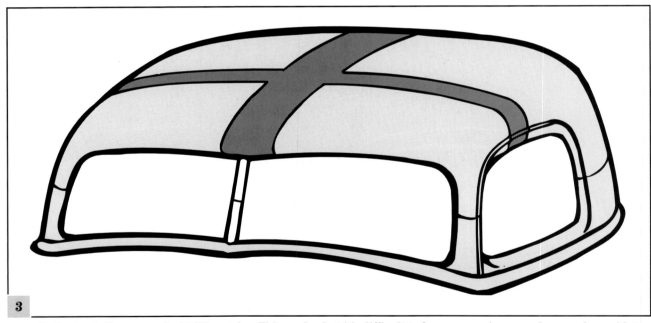

3

. . . split the top both ways and add filler strips. This works, but it's difficult to form some pieces, and you end up with two weld seams across and two weld seams fore and aft. That's a lot of weld, a lot of heat, and a lot of warp potential. To do this, you'd better be good with a TIG welder or good at hammer welding, or you'd better be willing to use lots of filler. *Eric Aurand*

the deck to make up the difference. Be careful, though, to keep the proportions right. You might want to try cutting up photos first, to get an idea of what the finished product will look like.

Elsewhere in this book you saw how Doug Jones approached the problem on his F-100; by cutting the center of the roof out, he only had to add filler pieces around the edges, then set the

center of a second top over the now-bigger hole and weld it in. This reduces the amount of welding and keeps you from having to weld across the flat middle of the top, minimizing warpage.

Yet another technique is illustrated on this page, and was used by Darrel Bernloehr on his 1948 Chevy truck. Many rodders use the back half of a second top when chopping a top; by

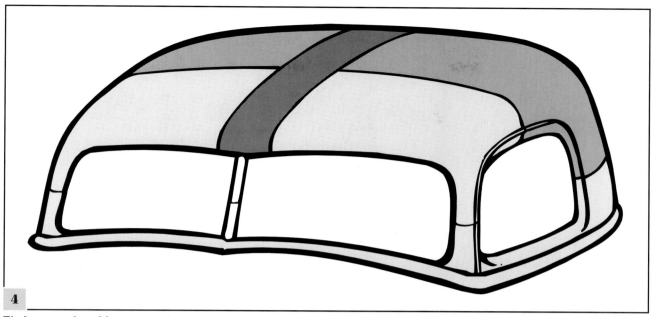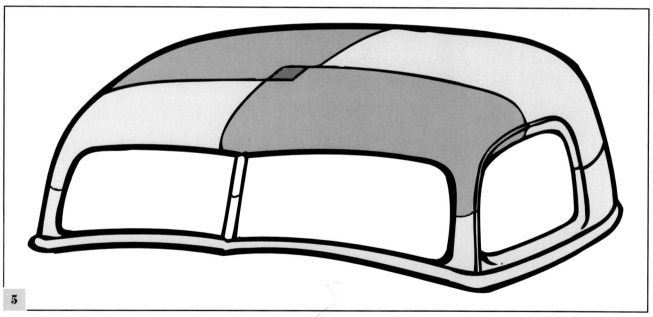

4

Find a second roof from a wrecked or very rusty parts car. Use one half of it, and cut it long enough so it takes the place of the crossways filler strip. You still have to add a section down the middle (in some cases), but you've cut the welding across the top in half. This is a very common procedure. *Eric Aurand*

5

Darrel Bernloehr also used a second top, but he used opposite corners to eliminate both filler strips on his 1948 Chevy pick-up. Because the opposite corners are both longer and wider, he ended up with a small square hole in the middle where they used to overlap (no big deal to fill it). This technique allowed him to cut the welding in half, with one seam across and one seam front-to-back. The results are less distortion, a minimum of filler, and a very nice chop. *Eric Aurand*

cutting it a little longer, they can get by with just one weld seam across the top. Unfortunately, this does nothing to widen the top, and two lengthwise seams are often required. Darrel used an approach that, as far as we know, is unique. By using the right front and left rear

quarters of the second top, both cut oversize, he was able to put it back together with one seam across and one seam front-to-back, cutting the amount of welding in half. This technique left a small square hole in the center that had to be filled, but it was no big deal.

IN THE SHOP:

INSTALLING DZUS BUTTONS

It's funny; although lots of rodders know what Dzus buttons are, a surprising number of us don't know exactly how they work or how to install them. That's a shame, because Dzus buttons are among the most basic hot rod components—like quick-changes, louvers, and dropped axles, they're almost necessary if you want to call your car a hot rod. For quick-release hoods, belly pans, interior panels, access panels, and who knows what else, they're the quick ticket.

Here's how they work: A Dzus button assembly consists of an aluminum button and a metal "S" spring that the button hooks on to. The spring goes behind the inside panel and is held in place by pop rivets. So, say we're going to fasten a hood side to a car body. First, we figure out where we want the buttons installed, then we punch a 13/32-inch hole for each one. We then hold the panel in place, and mark

1

Here are some different Dzus components and tools you might need: **A** – mounting tabs, both purchased and homemade; **B** – self-ejecting button; **C** – buttons and springs; **D** – reinforcing plates; **E** – dimpling dies; **F** – 82-degree countersink tool for making dies; **G** – regular Dzus button and S-spring.

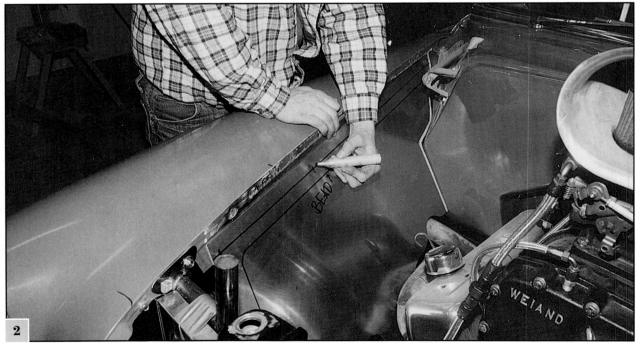

2

First, you have to figure out where they go. Here, Kurt Senescall at Creative Metalworks has made an aluminum inner fender panel for a 1953 Chevy and has marked the locations for beads and Dzus buttons.

Prior to this, he welded a small strip of steel onto the inner fender lip (arrow) to serve as a mounting surface for the Dzus buttons.

Once the button locations were marked, he drilled the necessary holes and dimpled them with a homemade die (you can buy them, too). The dimple ensures that the button will be flush with the sheet metal surface.

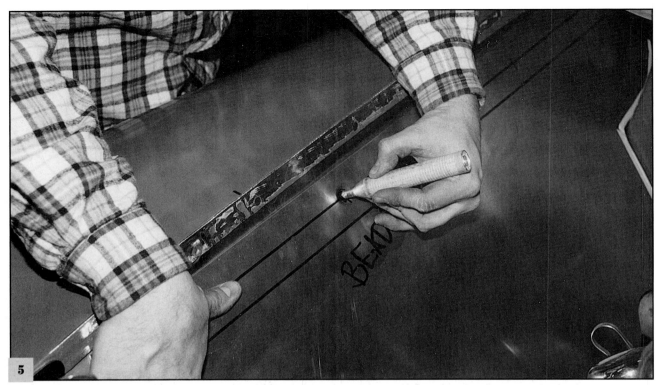

With the panel held firmly in place, he then transferred the hole location to the mounting flange on the fender.

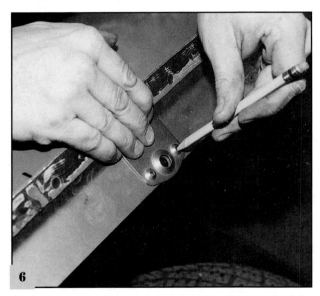

Using a purchased tab as a template, he then marked the pop rivet holes in the mounting flange. Remember that the slot in the button will always align with these holes, so keep 'em level.

those hole locations on the car. Punch another set of 13/32 holes in the car where we made the marks. Then, using a template, mark where the pop rivet holes go on the car, two to a button. Drill 1/8-inch holes (or whatever size rivets you're using) for each of them.

Now, to make the buttons fit flush with the outside panel, you have to dimple those holes. You can buy dimpling dies from just about anybody who sells Dzus fasteners, or you can make your own on a lathe using some bar stock and some 82-degree countersink cutters. Dimple the holes in the hood, and dimple the button holes and the rivet holes in the car body. Pop rivet the spring to the backside of the body panels, and you're in business.

A couple of notes: The screw slot on the Dzus button will always be aligned with the spring holes when the button's installed. Neatness counts, so make sure all your springs are going the same way. Also, when you're riveting the springs on, get one rivet started, install and tighten the second one, then go back and finish the first. You'll find it's much easier to keep the spring aligned this way.

Once the spring is installed, you can adjust the tension. If the panel is too loose, just pry the spring back from the inside panel. If it's too tight, squish it in closer to the inside panel with a pliers.

If you don't have a sheet metal panel to fasten your hood to, you can buy or make tabs that you can weld to other panels or tubes. If you're attaching fiberglass body parts, small reinforcing panels are available (and recommended). And, the flush-mount flat-headed variety (technically it's the FJ-style head) commonly used on hot rods isn't the only one available. Dzus fasteners are available with rounded heads, wing-nut-style heads, hex heads, Phillips heads, with rings, knurled knobs,

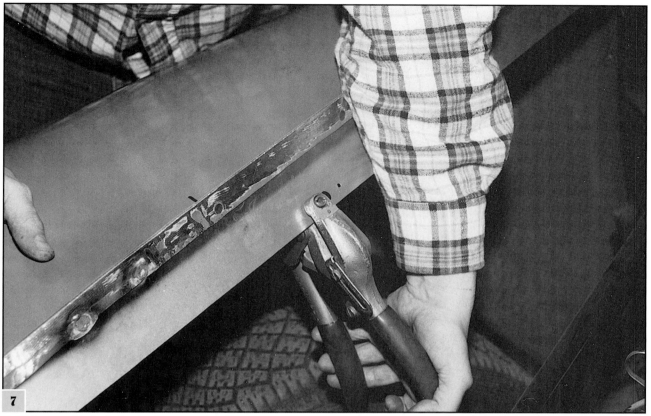

Drill (or punch) the holes in the mounting flange and de-burr them.

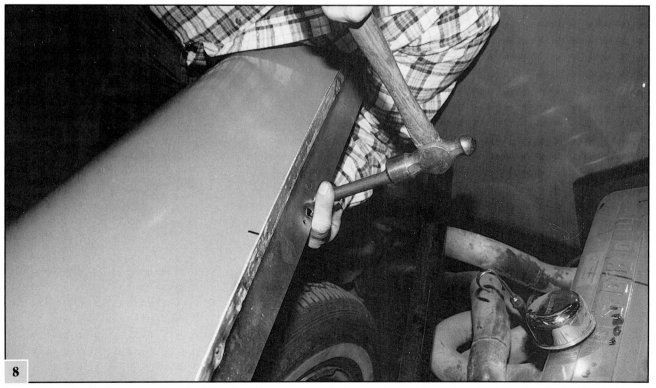

Dimple the rivet holes too, or the rivet heads will cause a gap between the panels and make it tough to install the buttons.

9

Pop rivet the S-spring to the back of the mounting flange; it helps to get the first rivet started, install the second, then finish the first.

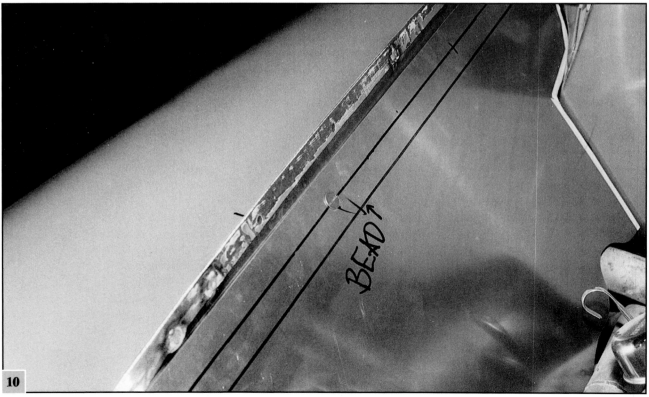

10

Put the panel in place, stick the button in, and give it a quarter-turn. That's it!

and in a neat self-ejecting model, all in different sizes. These latter styles aren't as common and may be more expensive, but if you can find them they're really slick for the right application. You can also get grommets that fit into the panel hole to prevent wear and protect the finish, and Full Bore Race Products (424 W. Rowland Ave., Dept. RD, Santa Ana, CA 92707; 714-436-0822) sells stainless washers that do the same thing.

11

If the panel's too loose, adjust it by prying the spring out slightly; if it's too tight, flatten the spring a little with a pliers.

Where to Get 'Em

Dzus deals mainly with manufacturers who buy fasteners by the thousands. Consequently, their pricing structures are such that it's not to your advantage to buy directly from them. For starters, you'd have to buy buttons by the carton, and you wouldn't get a quantity price. You're better off buying them directly from one of their authorized distributors. They buy 'em by the truckload, so they get quantity discounts that they can pass on to you. Most local rod shops or racing fabricators also have a supply on hand, or you can check your Yellow Pages under "Fasteners." Dzus' list of official Performance Automotive Stocking Distributors is:

Behrent's Speed Center
36 Vandervort Street
Florida, NY 10921
(914) 651-7389

S&S Engineering
1537 McKinley
Azusa, CA 91702
(818) 334-6018

Summit Racing
P. O. Box 909
Akron, OH 44309
(216) 630-0255

Speedway Motors, Inc.
P. O. Box 81906
Lincoln, NE 68501
(402) 474-4422

H. Edward Quay Welding
Rt. 100 and State St.
Pottstown, PA 19464
(215) 326-8050

Moroso Performance Products
P. O. Box 1470
Guilford, CT 06437
(203) 453-6571

12

If there isn't a sheet metal panel to fasten to, buy or make one of these weld-on tabs. Kurt will use this one to attach the bottom of the panel to a roll bar.

HAMMER FORMING

1

Start by building your buck. We made ours from 3/4-inch plywood, cut with a band saw. We then used a belt sander on the edges to make sure they were square.

Hammer forming is a quick and easy way to make strong, good-looking parts, but it's a technique that few street rodders are acquainted with. Basically, the process consists of building a form called a buck, then clamping the sheet metal to it and hammering the metal over the edges of the buck to form a lip. It's easy, it's fast, and it's cheap, but the results usually look like an expensive, professional, time-consuming job. In other words, it gives a lot of bang for the buck.

This technique can be used to make air cleaner tops, lids, or covers, or parts of more complex, welded-together pieces. For instance, when building wheel tubs, make a formed lip on the flat inner panel and weld it to the curved piece. You'll get a better-looking, stronger edge.

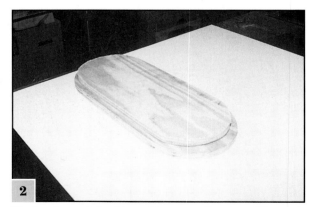

2

The buck consists of two pieces, one the size of the part, the other about 1/2 inch smaller. The size and finish of the smaller one is less important.

To show you how to do it, we asked Kurt Senescall to do some hammering. Kurt is a first-class metal shaper, and in about an hour he built a buck and formed a tri-power air cleaner base. With a little practice, you can get results just as good.

Normally, you can form a 3/8-inch lip with no trouble. Any larger and you're trying to shrink too much material. And, if you don't want a

3

Carefully scribe the outline of the larger buck on the sheet metal you want to use, then use a dividers to mark the trim line. For instance, if you want a 3/8-inch lip, make the trim line 3/8 inch from the edge of the buck. You may want to add a little extra just in case.

straight 90-degree edge, you can also use a router to put a curved edge on the buck so you can do rounded corners.

For tools, you'll need at least four large C-clamps or welding-type locking pliers, a rubber or nylon hammer, and a hammer and dolly. You can make a buck out of plywood, aluminum, or steel. If you're only making one or two parts, a hard plywood buck will work fine. If you need to make a few more, use aluminum. If you're going to make 10 or more parts, use a hard steel buck.

Start by making a posterboard pattern of the piece you want to make. Transfer the pattern first to a piece of sheet metal, then to your buck material. In this case, we used 3/4-inch plywood; a good chunk of hardwood would work even better. Using a band saw or jigsaw, cut one buck to the exact shape of the part you want. (Note: If you're doing precision work, make the buck two material thicknesses smaller than the outside dimensions of the finished product. In addition, metal bucks will give more precise results than wood.) Then cut a second buck that's about 1/4 inch smaller than the first. It's a good idea to use a belt sander to smooth the edges.

Now, cut the sheet metal that'll form the part. Start by scribing the outline of the top of the part, then, if you want a 1/4-inch lip, simply cut the piece 1/4 inch larger on all sides.

4

Clamp the sheet metal between the buck halves—the more clamps the better. Make sure the sheet metal is centered on the large half of the buck—use the scribed outline to check.

5

Use a rubber or nylon mallet to begin bending the sheet metal over the edge of the buck. Work back and forth around the form. Don't go too fast, or you'll get some sharp "puckers" that'll be tough to work out later.

6

You also want to check regularly to make sure the sheet metal isn't shifting between the bucks. Even if you're 100 percent careful, you'll still end up with some wrinkles, like these. As long as they're not too big or folded, you'll be OK.

Once the lip is fully formed, use a body hammer to start shrinking the wrinkles out. Go lightly, and you'll be surprised at how fast they flatten out. Be careful not to pound the metal into the edge of the buck, though.

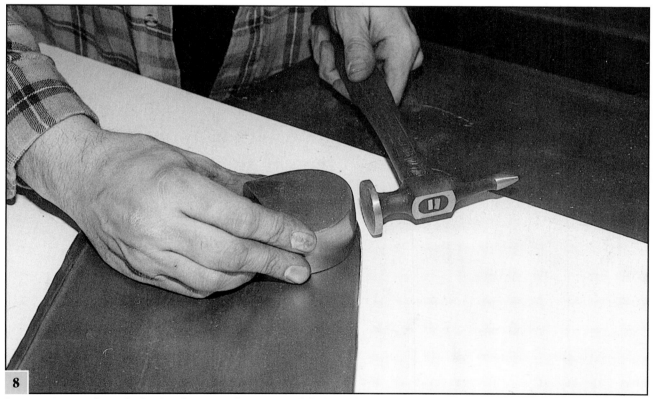

Remove the part from the bucks; then use a hammer and dolly to sharpen up the edges. This'll also remove any "lift" from the top of the part and flatten it out.

9

Chances are the edge won't be perfectly straight, due to the metal stretching and shrinking at different rates around the curves. Clamp a couple pieces of 3/8-inch stock to the piece to use as guides, then use a disc grinder to finish the edge.

10

You can also form lips on inside holes, but it's tougher. Kurt uses a piece of bar stock with a machined rounded end to work the metal inside the hole. In this case, he's building a demo piece using a couple chunks of aluminum as a buck.

Clamp the sheet metal tightly between the two bucks, with all three pieces centered. Now the fun part starts. With a rubber or nylon hammer (a metal hammer leaves nicks and scratches on the part), start hammering the sheet metal over the buck. Work all the way around, just going a little bit at a time. If you hammer one area too far too fast, you'll end up with large puckers in the sheet metal that can be difficult to remove. Something else to watch for: Check regularly to make sure the sheet metal isn't shifting or sliding between the bucks. If it does, your part won't be shaped correctly.

As you work around the part, you'll be surprised at how fast the metal moves. Once the lip is formed to the full 90 degrees, you'll probably have some small puckers. Start tapping away on these until the sheet metal shrinks enough to make them flatten out. Be careful not to hammer the sheet metal into the edge of the buck, though.

When the lip is formed, unclamp everything. If you used plywood, you'll notice that the edges of the buck are kind of rounded and beat up. If

you need to make a second part, just use the other side.

Now you can use a hammer and dolly to finish flattening out the lip and make sure it's a true 90 degrees. If the bottom of the edge isn't straight (and it often isn't when the metal is stretched like this), you can trim it with a belt sander, a grinder, or a coarse file.

You can also form edges in openings, but it's a little more difficult. You make the buck in the same way, and you can use a hammer if you're working with a large enough hole. For small openings, Kurt uses a piece of bar stock with a rounded end and taps it with the hammer. In this case, you're stretching the metal instead of shrinking it, so you can't form as large a lip. But you can still get good results if you take your time.

That's all there is to it. You probably have the tools already, so the next step is to get out in the garage and start hammerin'! Start with a couple of practice pieces, and before long, you'll have some trick parts that look a lot more expensive and time-consuming than they really are!

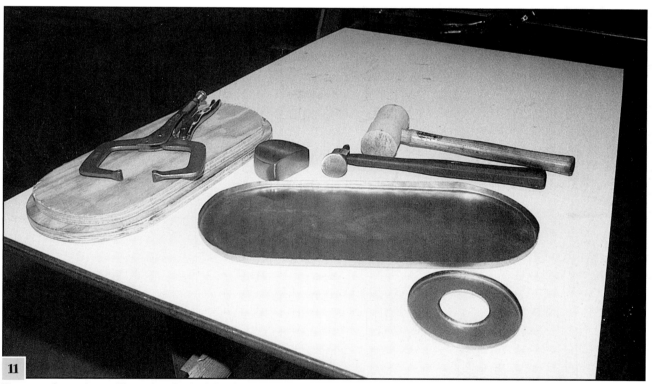

11

Here are the tools you'll need to do the job, along with two of the finished demo pieces we made. It goes surprisingly quick; the air cleaner top only took about an hour to build, and that includes time out for photos. You can get just as good a result with a little practice. So get out in the garage—it's hammer time!

The Hot Rod Frame

STOCK FORD FRAMES 109

STOCK GM FRAMES 110

STOCK MOPAR FRAMES 111

OTHER STOCK FRAMES 112

AFTERMARKET FRAMES 112

EVALUATING AN ORIGINAL FRAME 112

EVALUATING AN AFTERMARKET FRAME 116

FRAME SWAPS 117

FRAME REPAIR 118

FRAME MODIFICATIONS 118

IN THE SHOP:

    CUSTOM TUBULAR X-MEMBERS 125

    CUSTOM MOTOR MOUNTS 133

    INSTALLING A SUBFRAME FRONT SUSPENSION 137

Seems like every hot rod chassis article that's ever been written tells how a good frame is the foundation for a successful hot rod, and as cliché as it may sound, it's still true. You can't have a good car without a good frame. Today's hot rodder has a lot of choices when it comes to frames, though. First, there's a huge variation in original frames, depending on the make and age of the car. Second, the aftermarket has created new frames in all kinds of configurations for all kinds of cars.

STOCK FORD FRAMES

First, let's look at the types of original frames out there, starting with a brief chronology of Ford chassis. Way back when, Henry gave us the Model T, and it was good. The T frame was a flexible, lightweight affair, just a hair more sophisticated than a ladder. The rails were small steel channels with a puny 3-inch sidewall. Only two cross-members held it together, one at the front, one at the rear. It did the job for a stock Model T, but it isn't suitable for much else, and we don't recommend using a stock T chassis for a hot rod.

In 1928, Ford introduced the Model A, which was bigger and more powerful than the T, and it had a stouter chassis to meet those needs. The rails were beefier, with a 4-inch side rail, and now there was a third cross-member in the middle.

The A frame also had gracefully curved and tapered front frame horns that were esthetically pleasing. In its stock form, the A frame is probably too weak for most modern hot rodding. Early hot rodders knew this, and if they added a flathead V-8 to an A frame, they often added a modified 1932 Ford K-member (a stamped steel cross-member with two diagonal reinforcing legs) to strengthen it. Today, a stock A frame can be used if it's properly reinforced, with boxing plates, cross-members, and other refinements.

That brings us to the classic hot rod frame, the 1932 Ford. Henry built a sturdy frame that followed the body's curves, this time with a full 6-inch sidewall on the frame channels. In addition to the front and rear cross-members, there was a center K-member that served as a mount for the tranny and the pedal assembly. As an added bonus, the frame side rail was exposed on a stock 1932 Ford, so the rail was painted and sculpted with a distinctive character line for appearance. This makes the Deuce frame one of the best-looking hot rod chassis for high-boys or full-fendered 1932s. A stock 1932 frame is adequate for a mild flathead Ford, and it can also be upgraded for more power by boxing and adding X-members or tube cross-members. Its popularity (for both 1932 Ford and Model A bodies) has made it scarce, but original frames and rails are still available in the hot rodding community.

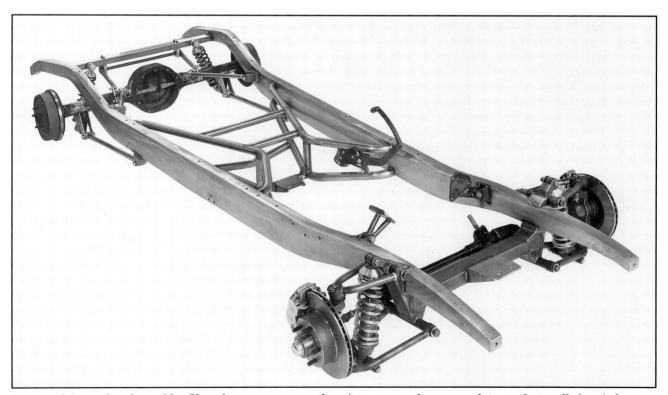

It's a good time to be a hot rodder. If you have more money than time, you can buy a complete, ready-to-roll chassis for your hot rod. This Roadster Shop 1934 Ford chassis uses new rails, a tubular X-member, a 9-inch Ford rear end with coil-overs and a triangulated four-link, and a Mustang II–derived independent front suspension. Bare frames without suspension are also available.

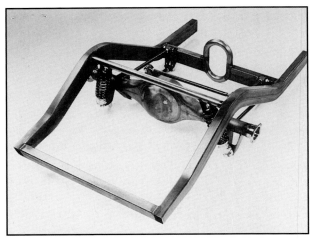

If you're building or modifying a frame, some companies offer chassis subframes that have the front or rear suspension completely set up. These subs, from Chris Alston's Chassisworks, feature a custom-made independent front suspension with rack-and-pinion steering up front, and a coil-over suspension with unequal-length four-links in the rear.

For 1933 and 1934, Ford beefed up their frames further, with the company's first integral X-member. While not as graceful as the 1932 frame (none of the 1933–1934 frame was exposed to view), it's a good hot rod foundation that'll easily stand up to mild flathead power, and perhaps even mild small-block power with little modification. However, for more power, some boxing is recommended, and in many cases the stock X-member interferes with modern transmissions. In those cases, tubular X-members and boxed rails are often the best ways to modernize a 1933–1934 Ford frame.

In 1935 Fords changed dramatically, gaining mass and size, and the frames grew to fit. The frame rails still had a 6-inch wall, but the X-member was larger, and fit inside the side rails for double-wall strength at the front and back ends of the frame. In addition, lateral side braces were added between the center of the X-member and the frame rails. These frames need little to strengthen them for hot rod use; the biggest problems occur when the X-member interferes with newer transmissions, particularly automatics. This same frame was used from 1935 to 1940 on passenger cars, and until 1941 on pickups.

The last generation in Ford's hot rod chassis development was the 1942–1948 Ford frame. Except for dimensions, it's very similar to the previous generation of frame, and offers the same benefits—and the same challenges regarding transmission clearance.

Amazingly, all these Ford frames used essentially the same suspension arrangements. Up front was an I-beam axle with a transverse leaf spring attached to the center of the front cross-member. A wishbone connected to the ends of the axle; the back end of the wishbone was a ball that was held captive in a socket in the center frame cross-member. In back, a torque tube-style rear end was suspended with another transverse leaf spring. Both setups were elegant in their simplicity, and served Ford customers well for years. These suspensions are still the basis for traditional-style Ford hot rods today.

These Ford frames are easy to modify yourself, and they're well supported by the aftermarket as well. A variety of front and rear suspension kits are on the market, everything from complete independent setups to traditional wishbones and hairpin radius rods. Precut boxing plates are available from a number of manufacturers, as well as new channel and tubular X-members.

STOCK GM FRAMES

Up to 1936, Chevrolet cars had a channel-style frame, and models from 1934 to the 1936 Master had a channel X-member very similar to a 1934 Ford frame. These frames make good hot rod material—they're strong, relatively light, and they accept suspension and drivetrain modifications easily.

However, in 1936 on the Standard models, Chevy introduced its "top-hat" style frame. On these frames, the rails consisted of an upside-down U-shaped channel with flanges—in profile, this piece looks like a top hat. This channel was made of relatively light material (as light as 10 gauge), and a flat piece of heavier stock was spot-welded to the bottom of the rail to enclose it. The resulting rail was light and strong, but somewhat flexible. This frame design was used on Chevrolet cars all the way through 1954, and on Corvettes through 1962.

For rear suspension, all Chevys from the 1930s to the 1950s used parallel leaf springs in the rear. Up front, an I-beam axle with parallel leafs was standard through 1940, but Chevrolet offered its "knee action" independent front end on Master or Master Deluxe models from 1934 through 1938. (Knee action was a truly bizarre setup based on the French Dubonnet suspension;

the spindle was attached to a trailing swingarm, which operated a vertical coil spring inside an oil-filled can. The whole assembly steered with the wheels.) In 1939, the troublesome knee action front end was replaced with a more conventional coil-sprung, kingpin independent front end, which was used in basically the same form all the way through 1954.

The Chevy top-hat frames from this period (1936 to 1954) are good in their stock form, but according to some experts they don't take kindly to some kinds of modifications. The reasons for this are that the frames are somewhat flexible, and the top-hat section is made of relatively thin material, compared to more conventional channel-type frames. This causes problems when these frames are subframed, or when structural members such as cross-members or motor mounts are welded to the sides of the rails. In many cases, subframed top-hat frames develop stress cracks near where the subframe joins to the original rails, because the subframes are much stiffer than the old rails. And when suspension cross-members or motor mounts are welded to the thin top-hat sections of the rails, the stresses can eventually cause cracks and tears around the welds.

For these reasons, some manufacturers recommend bolt-on modifications for these frames. Most bolt-on kits use the strength of the entire top-hat frame rail, including the heavier plate on the bottom. This approach makes sense when you look at how Chevrolet designed their suspensions for these frames—even the independent front ends bolted onto the heavy flanges on the bottom edge of the frame.

In the 1930s and 1940s, Buick, Olds, and Pontiac generally used heavy channel-type frames, usually with equally heavy X-members. X-members for closed cars were often channel-type, while convertible X-members were sometimes made of I-beam-like material for extra stiffness. In the late 1930s, Buick and Olds began offering some pretty good coil-spring rear suspensions, using long trailing arms that angled to the center of the chassis X-member, Panhard bars, and anti-roll bars. These suspensions can be upgraded with the addition of a late-model rear end fairly easily. All three divisions also used different independent front ends starting in the mid-1930s. Some of these suspensions can be rebuilt, but it's expensive, and they're difficult to lower. The frames, however, are usually easy to upgrade to other late-model or aftermarket front suspensions.

STOCK MOPAR FRAMES

Through the 1930s and 1940s, Dodge and Plymouth products had some of the best frames on the market, using heavy channel

If you want to use your stock chassis, like this 1939 Chevy frame, you can buy bolt-on suspensions and mounts to bring it up-to-date. This frame uses a bolt-on Mustang II front suspension and leaf spring rear suspension from Chassis Engineering. The motor mounts, tranny cross-member, and master cylinder mount are also C. E. pieces.

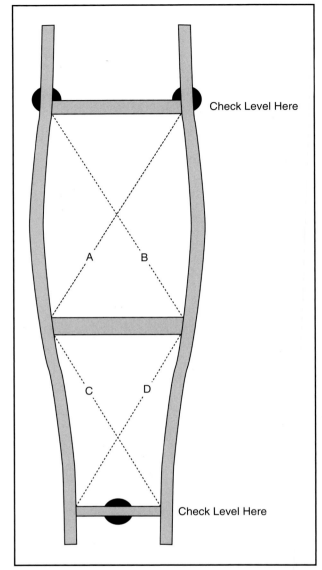

Before you start working on your frame, you have to make sure it's straight and square. Set the frame up on three jackstands (black circles in the illustration); then use a 4-foot level to make sure the rear of the frame is level. Then check for level at the front of the frame. If the frame is twisted, you'll need to take it to a frame shop or put it on a jig for straightening. To check for square, cross-measure as indicated. Measurements A and B should be equal, and measurements C and D should be equal. If they aren't, the frame can be pulled into shape with a come-along, or you can put it on a jig.

rails and X-members, with stout front and rear cross-members, sometimes stamped with really cool lightening holes. Mopar products used parallel leaf-spring rear suspensions, and decent independent front suspensions (IFS) were available as an option as early as 1933. IFS became standard in 1939, and all of these Mopar frames are easy to modify.

OTHER STOCK FRAMES

If you're building anything outside of the big three auto manufacturers, you're pretty much on your own, with a few exceptions. Anglia and Willys frames and components are available through the aftermarket, and manufacturers such as Fatman Fabrications make Mustang II front-end kits for a dizzying array of makes and models, but when it comes to deciding if that frame is hot rod material, it's your decision. Just make sure that decision is an informed one.

AFTERMARKET FRAMES

In the past 20 years, the aftermarket has jumped into the frame business with both feet, making hot rodding easier and more accessible for the masses. Simple Model T and Model A frames were probably first, then in the late 1970s the Deuce Factory made a substantial tooling investment and started stamping out accurate reproduction 1932 Ford frame rails. The Deuce Factory discontinued production some years later when the stamping dies wore out, but that torch was picked up again by American Stamping Company in the late 1990s, and their Deuce rails are the basis for hundreds, maybe thousands, of 1932 chassis today.

Today, all other Ford frames up to 1948 (as well as 1953–1956 Ford F-100 pickups) have been manufactured by a whole mess of manufacturers all over the world. In addition, reproduction 1934–1938 Chevy car frames, 1948–1953 Chevy truck frames, 1933–1934 Dodge and Plymouth frames, Willys frames, Anglia frames, and now even 1955–1957 Chevy frames are available. Most of these chassis are available in nearly any stage of completion, from a basic perimeter frame to a complete rolling chassis, with a variety of front and rear suspension designs. Take a trip through the ads in the leading street rod magazines to get an idea of what's available, or check out the manufacturers' displays at any of the major street rod events.

EVALUATING AN ORIGINAL FRAME

Evaluating an original frame is a pretty easy job. It has to be straight, square, and strong. It's easiest to inspect a frame if it's bare, with no body, but most of these inspections can also be done with the body on the frame.

First, look for obvious damage from past collisions or other accidents. Bent flanges, broken brackets, and bent frame horns are the obvious things to look for. Keep an eye out also for damage related to age and fatigue, like cracks and sagging frame horns. For instance, early-production 1932 Ford frames are especially susceptible to sagging and cracking behind the rear cross-member. The weight of a full gas tank would eventually pull the rear frame rails down, causing them to buckle and crack just behind the cross-member. Many original 1932 frames have

(continued on page 116)

If you're going to build a chassis yourself, it's best to have the frame rails bolted solid to a frame jig. This jig was built by Jim Zahn, and consists of a sturdy table with bolt-on frame "stations." Jim has several sets of stations for different Ford frames—one for 1932s, one for 1933–34s, and one set for 1935–40s. In this shot, a 1934 Ford frame is taking shape.

Once the frame is boxed, the backside of the rails will be inaccessible. This particular frame is going to be under a full-fendered car, so Jim welds nuts inside all the fender mount holes on the frame. If it was going to be a hi-boy, all the holes would be filled.

Once the rails are straight in the jig and all the nuts are welded in, Jim cuts and welds in full-length boxing plates to strengthen the rails.

After welding in the front and rear cross-members, he then positions a dummy engine and transmission. Note the simple piece of flat plate that holds the engine up. With the engine supported like this, it's easy to build motor mounts between the engine and frame rails.

With the engine, tranny, and rear end in place, a string is run down the frame and driveline's centerline for reference. Jim then begins cutting, bending, and welding in tubular cross-members.

In a relatively short time, the chassis is down off the jig and rolling on its new suspension. Jim builds cars for a living, but he uses relatively simple tools—a band saw, a drill press, a grinder, and a MIG welder. The point is, workmanship like this can be done in your garage.

(continued from page 112)

blacksmith-style repairs in this area, consisting of hunks of angle iron arc-welded in place over a crack. Late-production 1932 frames have an additional brace installed to prevent this, but it's still something to watch for.

Rust generally isn't a major concern in hot rod frames, but it's still something to watch for. Most old frames will have some rust pits in them, where water and dirt were trapped by frame webbing or other porous materials. While it may take some work to make these frames look good, the strength usually isn't compromised. Be wary of rust only if frame members are rusted through, or if the entire surface is pitted deeply. One special note for Chevrolet top-hat style frames—because of their construction, these frames could get dirt and water trapped inside, and have been known to rust out from the inside. If possible, take a look inside the ends of the rails, or inside larger holes to look for signs of rust inside the rail.

Your frame might also have been the victim of hot rodders in the past. Early engine swaps could be very tough on old car frames—anything that got in the way of that Chrysler Hemi would simply be removed with a torch. Look for torch cuts in the rails, and in the K- or X-members that stiffen the chassis. Other early hot rod tricks involved moving steering boxes to clear exhausts—my 1932 Ford frame has a small boxed section built onto the side of the frame rail so the steering box can be moved outward to clear headers. It's ugly, and it also weakens the frame in a critical area. This frame also has some small slices taken out of the top of the passenger-side frame rail to clear header tubes—not as serious, but it is something that must be fixed to make it right.

Bent, diamond-shaped, or twisted frames pose serious problems, but this kind of damage is tougher to spot. The best way to check a frame for these kinds of problems is to put it up on three jackstands—two in the rear, and one in the center of the front cross-member. Use a large level and some shims to get the rear of the frame perfectly level, then check the front of the frame for level as well. If both ends are level at the same time, the frame isn't twisted. If one end isn't level, the frame will need straightening.

While the frame is still on those jackstands, you can also check it for squareness. To do this, find some body mount holes that are the same on both frame rails. Then, measure diagonally from one corner to the other, then repeat that measurement going the other way. The diagonal measurements will be the same (or at least within 1/8 inch) if the frame is square. If the measurements differ, the frame has a diamond shape, and must be pushed or pulled into squareness before modifications can begin.

It used to be that we just worried about frames that had been butchered in the 1950s. Now enough time has passed that we also have to worry about frames that were butchered in the 1970s and 1980s, as these cars are either being updated or brought back into hot rodding. Watch also for bad workmanship, especially bad subframe jobs on some cars. Some chassis manufacturers maintain that any subframed chassis is junk; we won't go quite that far, but inspect any subframed chassis carefully. Make sure the sub is installed square with the frame, that the wheelbase is correct, and that the welding and fabrication is done well. If the sub has been narrowed, inspect that joint carefully, and look to see how the steering linkage was narrowed as well. If possible, have the car or chassis checked out on an alignment rack.

Check the fabrication work, too. Look for good weld penetration, reinforcing plates over the frame-to-subframe joint, and just a general neat appearance. Look also at the track width, and be sure it's appropriate for the car; otherwise the tires will stick out of the fenders, which is never cool. If there are any questions about the subframe's installation or integrity, look for another chassis or another project.

So, what do you do if that chassis is junk? Well, you can first search for an original replacement, but that often means buying a whole second parts car. That leaves us with aftermarket chassis.

EVALUATING AN AFTERMARKET FRAME

If it's in the budget, an aftermarket frame may be the way to go for your hot rod project. Checking out an aftermarket chassis is a much simpler job than checking out a stocker—generally, the hot rod industry does a good job of producing new frames. Before buying, shop around, look at what the magazines have to say (just keep in mind that they support their advertisers for a reason), and above all, ask questions. Talk to other hot rodders you know, and if you see a car at an event that has a chassis you're interested in, talk to the owner. Hot rod events are also a good chance to see aftermarket frames firsthand in the manufacturers' displays. Larger manufacturers will usually have at least two or three frames on display at one of these events, and the guys who work the booths are generally pretty knowledgeable about their products.

So what to look for? Quality materials, good welds, and strength. Some aftermarket manufacturers build their brackets and components out of lighter-gauge materials than others do, perhaps because they're located in parts of the country that don't experience frost-heaved and potholed roads. However, in all our years of hot rod magazine work, we've heard almost no negative feedback on hot rod chassis parts. Companies that sell inferior products don't tend to last long.

The great thing about buying an aftermarket frame is that they're available in almost any stage of completion. Most manufacturers will

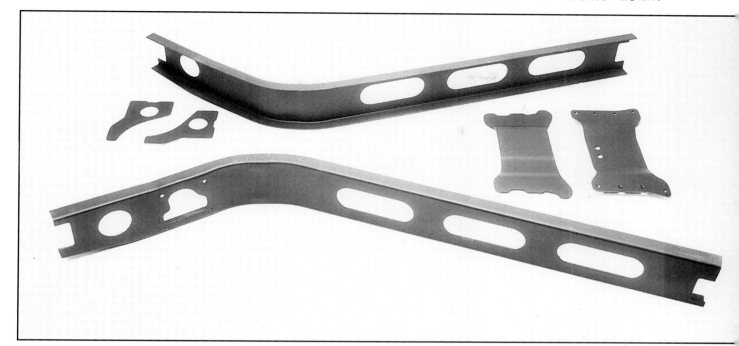

If you don't want tubular X-members, the aftermarket also has channel-type X-members available for 1932–34 Fords, like this set from Chassis Engineering. While they look heavy, a channel X-member is often lighter and just as strong as a comparable tube X-member.

sell you anything from a bare perimeter frame with no brackets, to a complete rolling chassis with plumbing, brakes, wheels, and tires. Many suspension options are available, so what you get depends entirely on your budget and your wants and needs.

In addition to aftermarket chassis, there are countless small rod shops around the country that will build or modify a frame to suit your hot rod project. Most are good, but like any basket of apples, there are a few rotten ones. Know whom you're dealing with before you commit money or parts to a shop. Ask around for references, and make several visits to the shop, both to check on the quality of the work, and to see how projects are moving along through the shop. If projects are getting dusty, you may want to shop elsewhere.

FRAME SWAPS

"Is there a late-model chassis that will fit under my '38 Kinnardly body?" It's a question that comes up all the time, and on the surface, this looks like an easy solution. Take that neat old sheet metal off its original tired frame; plop it down on a new chassis with modern suspension, brakes, and power; hook up some wiring; tighten some bolts; and head off down the road. Unfortunately, it's not that easy, and novices who try this often accomplish nothing more than ruining two cars.

But before we tell you not to do this, we do admit that there have been a dedicated few who have successfully swapped old bodies onto late-model chassis. Typically, these guys start with a late 1940s or early 1950s body that has a severely rusted floor. Then, they hit the junkyards with a tape measure to find a donor car that has the same wheelbase and track width. The donor car is then stripped of its body, but often the floor pan and part of the firewall are left intact. The old body is then hoisted above the frame/floor, and the old floor is trimmed away until the body fits down over its new frame and floor pan. At this point, the body is tacked in position, and the gaps between the old and new are painstakingly filled with pieces of sheet metal.

It doesn't sound easy, and the reality is even harder than that. One combination is the late 1970s Cutlass/Malibu under a 1946–1948 Ford, but in this case, the Cutlass' perimeter frame rails need to be removed and replaced with shorter frame rails further inboard, and all-new body mounts need to be constructed. Hardly a simple fix.

The best example of a frame swap we've seen is a 1949 Merc on a 1977 Olds 98 four-door chassis, built by Al Kopecky in 1991. The rusty body was channeled over the frame 4 inches, then Al chopped it 3 inches and smoothed it off. The Olds floor pan was mated to new rockers, and the bottom of the Olds firewall was mated to the top half of the Merc firewall. The car looked great, and Al used the car as a year-round daily driver for quite a while, but even he admits it was a mountain of work to build the car this way.

With that info in hand, we'll say this: The best frame for your 1938 Kinnardly body is the 1938

Kinnardly frame that came under it. It has the right body mounts, the right shape, the right length, and the right width; and unless it's dangerously rusty or otherwise damaged, it can be easily modified to accept a modern drivetrain with a hot rod stance. In other words, just say no to frame swaps.

FRAME REPAIR

Assuming you've decided to go with an original frame, what's a guy gotta do to get it in shape for hot rod use? Well, repair is the first order of business, followed by strength-improving modifications.

The best way to start working on an old frame is to bolt it to a frame jig—something that, unfortunately, most of us don't have. Basically, a frame jig is a solid, immovable table that works as a reference surface for building a chassis. We've seen a number of different styles of jigs in different rod shops. When Greg Fleury was building Pro/Stock chassis, his chassis tables consisted of a heavy steel tube framework with a huge 1/2-inch steel plate welded to the top. The tables had six or eight legs, each with adjustment bolts so the table could be leveled very accurately. Precisely cut stanchions were tack-welded directly to the table to provide an accurate jig for laying up frame tubes. Neat, but impractically large and heavy for us garden-variety hot rodders.

Simpler jigs also work well. Jim Zahn has a frame jig that's welded up out of heavy square tubing, and the whole thing is also on wheels so it's mobile. He has built several sets of "stations" that bolt to the table—one set for 1932 Ford frames, one for 1933–1934 Ford frames, and one for 1935–1940 Ford frames. These stations are set up to bolt to the frame rails in four or five known, stock locations on each side, to ensure that the rails are set up correctly in relation to each other. He can then start adding boxing plates, cross-members, and the various brackets necessary to build a complete chassis.

But what if you don't have the room, resources, or talent to build a frame jig? You can still build a chassis, if you take extra care to make sure the frame rails are correctly located. You'll also need a good set of dimensioned chassis drawings for your frame. Accurate drawings for Ford frames (Model T, A, 1932, 1934, and 1935–1940) are provided in every Wescott's Auto Restyling catalog. For other makes, you'll have to find copies of original chassis service manuals.

Start by making sure the frame is straight and square, as discussed earlier. The frame should also be cleaned of all grease, paint, and rust, which usually means that it should be sandblasted. Mount it on three jackstands and make sure both ends of the frame are level, then measure some key chassis widths and compare them to the factory drawings. If everything checks out, you can tack-weld some stout tubing braces across the top and bottom of the rails to

hold them in place. If the chassis doesn't measure correctly, you'll have to push, pull, or otherwise coerce it into the correct dimensions before you weld on any bracing. Keep in mind also that the bracing has to be placed so it won't interfere with your chassis work—plan ahead.

Once the frame rails are held tightly in their proper place, either on a jig or on the floor, you can start working on repairs. Common repairs include replacing bent or torched frame horns (reproductions are available for many frames), welding up holes, replacing torched-out sections of frame rail, or straightening dents and welding up minor cracks. If you're replacing metal, make sure it's of the same grade and thickness as the original. In addition, make sure your welder is up to the task; you probably need an arc welder or a 220-volt MIG or TIG system to do this kind of work. Most 110-volt MIGs aren't powerful enough to do structural welding on frames—they don't generate enough heat to get good penetration.

Anytime you do welding on a frame, don't weld long beads in one area of the frame. Alternate from one side of the frame to the other. Otherwise, you can build up too much heat in one location, which can lead to warping. Having the frame secured in a jig can help minimize warping, too.

FRAME MODIFICATIONS
Boxing

The easiest way to stiffen up a channel-style frame rail is to box it; that is, weld in a plate on the open side of the channel to form a box section. You can cut your own boxing plates out of 1/8- or 3/16-inch cold-rolled steel, or for some frames you can buy precut boxing plates from several manufacturers. Model A and 1932 Ford frames are often completely boxed, front to rear, but 1934 and newer Ford frames, which had an X-member from the factory, are usually just boxed in certain sections. For instance, if you're adding a Mustang II cross-member or newer motor mounts, boxing plates are often added forward of the X-member to stiffen the frame in that area. And, if you're installing a parallel-leaf rear suspension in one of these cars, the rear section of the frame is usually boxed to stiffen the rails. Remember, with the stock buggy spring, the frame behind the rear cross-member only had to support the body, not suspension loads, so strengthening them is a good idea in this instance.

Boxing plates are typically cut so they fit flush with the top and bottom of the frame rail. This way, the edge of the plate can be chamfered so very good weld penetration is achieved. However, the So-Cal Speed Shop recently began offering what they call a "step boxed" frame, where the boxing plates fit inside the frame rail, stepped back from the edge. The resulting frame rail is just as strong as a conventionally boxed frame, but the small frame lip looks more traditional and provides a small recess in which to

This is the rear section of a 1955 Chevy pickup frame built by Barry Larson. Note that it uses partial boxing plates in the rails, a rectangular tube cross-member over the quick-change rear end, and round tubes to triangulate the frame and keep it stiff. The cross-member at the right is an aftermarket part that incorporates a drive shaft loop. Note also the diagonal Panhard bar.

run brake and fuel lines. This looks better and protects the lines from road damage.

Cross-Members

Most hot rod frames will need some kind of new cross-members to support new suspensions and drivetrains. Let's start at the front. Almost all old car frames have a front cross-member. On Fords, this cross-member acts as a mount for the buggy spring, and carries most of the front suspension load on the car. On most all cars, the front cross-member supports the radiator, and is therefore very important for mounting and locating the grille, hood, and associated front-end sheet metal. In most cases, stock front cross-members can be reused if they're in good condition.

It's worth mentioning that on Fords with a buggy-spring front end, the front cross-member is also instrumental in determining ride height, as that's where the suspension mounts. Model A cross-members are often installed in 1932 Ford frames because the A cross-member is flatter, which lowers the car. Nice quality repro A cross-members are available from the aftermarket. In other Fords, the front cross-members

can be modified to lower a car, but it's usually not necessary.

A new front cross-member is also necessary if you plan on installing a Mustang II or comparable independent front suspension (IFS). If you can find a good, stock Mustang II cross-member, it can be modified to fit most early cars, but they're big, clunky knobbly lookin' things that are best hidden under fat-fendered sheet metal. If you have any esthetic sense at all, under no circumstances should you use a stock Mustang II cross-member or A-arms under a car that has open fenders, like a 1934 or earlier Ford. They're just plain too ugly.

Having said that, the street rod magazines today are choked with ads for companies that make aftermarket IFS setups based on the Mustang II suspension. In fact, the Mustang II front end is so popular that original-style control arms and spindles are being reproduced by several manufacturers, along with springs and new dropped spindles.

The typical Mustang II suspension kit consists of a welded-up steel cross-member, two shock towers, new spindles, either stamped or tubular A-arms, and either coil springs or coil-over shocks. Most kits now do away with the rear strut rod by making the lower control arm into a conventional A-arm, and either standard or power rack-and-pinions are also available. Kits are available in widths and degrees of lowness to suit nearly any hot rod that you can think of, and for those that the manufacturers missed, there are Mustang II subframe kits, where a Mustang II front end is hung on a pair of replacement front frame stubs. These kits are also available in a variety of prices, with the cheapest using stock or repro stamped steel control arms, and the most expensive using polished stainless tubular A-arms.

In most early cars, the center cross-members will need to be removed and replaced or drastically modified to make room for mounting a modern transmission. This is one case where we recommend looking to the aftermarket first, especially if you have a Ford or Chevy project car. There are probably dozens of companies out there making cross-member kits and X-member kits for most popular Ford and Chevy hot rods. The prices are right for these parts, and the engineering work is already done.

Rear cross-members on old cars usually support either the springs (buggy springs on old Fords, coil springs on later GMs) or at least the shock absorbers. They're usually pretty stout, and can often be used as is, modified to suit, or replaced with a new cross-member. For instance, on almost any 1932 to 1948 Ford, if you want to use the stock buggy spring out back, the stock cross-member will do the job just fine. If you want to switch to longitudinal parallel leaf springs, the cross-member can still be left in place and used as a place to mount the shocks. If you want to substitute coil-over shocks for the rear suspension, it's usually best to replace the rear cross-member with a beefier tube cross-member that can better support the stresses involved.

X-Members

In the early 1930s (1933 for most of the big three), most manufacturers started using X-members in their frames. Most of these X-members were made of channel stock (some were made of bridge-like I-beam) and were strong and lightweight. If you can use the stock X-member in your car, do so. However, some modern automatic transmissions won't clear the front legs of the X, so the X-member needs to be modified or replaced for clearance.

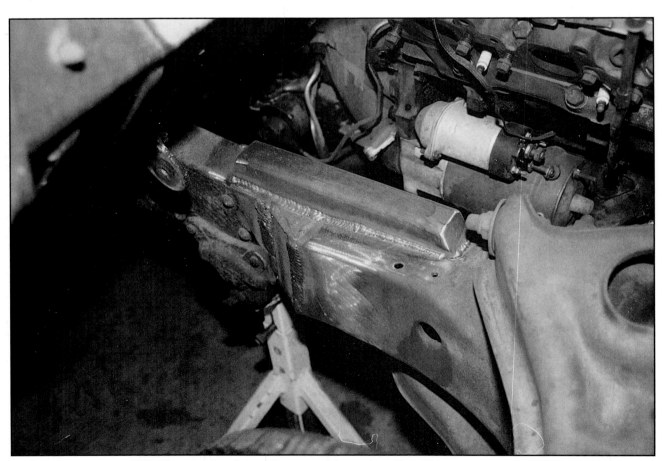

The other end of that 1955 Chevy pickup has a Camaro subframe installed. This view shows the joint between the 1955 Chevy frame and the sub—solid welds, no gaps, and a nice piece of reinforcing that spans the top of the joint. Subframe grafts have to be this strong.

Cars that didn't have X-members, such as Model As and 1932 Fords, can also have one added. In fact, the tubular X-member is almost a standard feature on modern aftermarket Ford frames. Some are built of round tubes, and some are made of rectangular tubes—that's strictly a matter of builder and buyer preference. Chassis Engineering also makes a channel-style X-member for 1932 Ford frames; it has a more traditional look to it, and they claim it's stronger and lighter than a comparable tubular X-member.

When modifying an X-member, keep in mind what it was designed to do—support the transmission and keep the frame from twisting. Anytime you remove material from it, you weaken it, and that strength has to be made up somehow. Transmission mount kits are available that bolt on to most stock X-members, and most X-members can be easily made to fit Ford C4 or C6 automatics, or GM Powerglide, Turbo 350, and Turbo 400 transmissions. Later Ford AOD automatics and GM 700R4 automatics are wider at the rear, though, and may require additional work to get them to fit.

If your X-member is really butchered, or if it requires too much modification, you can simply replace it with a tubular X-member, either bought or built. Tubular Dynamics, Pete & Jake's, and others manufacture tubular X-members for many cars, and these X-members are already set up with the proper mounting brackets, transmission mounts, and often rear suspension mounts already built in. Tube X-members are also good looking and very strong. Because they stiffen a chassis so well, they are highly recommended for convertibles, roadsters, or any fiberglass body.

Installing a tube X-member is as simple as putting it in position and welding it into place. Building your own is a little more work, but it's easier than most rodders would think. Look at the how-to sequence elsewhere in this chapter to get an idea of how it's done.

How stout should a tube X-member be? Mild steel DOM (drawn-over mandrel) tubing is adequate for street use (chrome-moly tubing is overkill, and it must be TIG-welded, so that rules out most home builders). The tubes in most X-members are usually 1-3/8- to 1-3/4-inch diameter, with a 0.120- to 0.125-inch wall thickness. Generally speaking, the more tubes you use, the smaller the diameter can be. If round tubes are too difficult for you to work with (fitting them together can be time-consuming), square or rectangular tubing is an option. Most manufacturers use 1-1/2-inch square tubing with a 0.120-inch wall thickness.

"C"ing

Everybody wants their hot rod to sit low, but there comes a point when the laws of physics get in the way—axles and frame rails simply can't occupy the same space at the same time. To remedy this, hot rodders long ago found that they could simply notch the bottom of the frame rail to gain clearance (it worked a lot better than notching the axle). To do this, a heavy steel plate is bent into a "C" shape, then the profile is marked on both sides of the frame rail. The sides and bottom of the rail are cut out, and the C-shaped plate is welded in to fill the resulting gap. It's recommended that the rail be fully boxed for strength where the frame is C'd, and the C should not be deeper than 1/3 of the frame rail's height at that point.

Front frame rails are also sometimes C'd to get more spring clearance on a Ford buggy-spring front end. These notches are usually rectangular, though, and quite a bit shallower than a rear-suspension C.

"Z"ing

Related to "C"ing by more than just the alphabet, "Z"ing was a technique widely used in the 1950s to lower the back end of a hot rod or custom. The frame was cut at an angle just ahead of the rear end, and the rear section of the frame was raised, usually so the bottom was even with the top of the front section. The joint was then boxed in with reinforcing plates to bring it all back together. Some cars were even Z'd up front to lower the front end as well, but that wasn't as common.

Pro/Street

In the 1950s it was wide whites. In the 1960s it was five-spoke mags. In the 1970s it was panel paint. And the 1980s brought us—Pro/Street: big-ass tires on huge aluminum rims, all stuffed under the wheelwells in an effort to look like a drag racing Pro/Stock competitor. It was pretty cool, too, until somebody actually tried to drive one more than 1/4 mile. Big, soft, bouncy tires with sometimes iffy quality control when it came to roundness, combined with a low stance and a limited suspension, made for an extremely cool-looking but very bad-driving car. In addition, these steamroller-like tires turned into skis at the slightest hint of moisture, causing more than one Pro/Street pilot to hydroplane his car into a muddy freeway ditch.

However, the techniques used to stuff all that rubber under the rear end are still useful to hot rodders today. Typically, the Pro/Street car required a narrowed rear frame section, kind of like a lateral "Z"ing. Usually, the stock frame was cut off ahead of the wheelwells, and a heavy lateral cross-member added. A new, narrowed frame stub was then added on to this cross-member. Usually, a roll cage of some sort provided extra stiffness. Now, most of us have gotten over the need to stuff 16-inch Mickey Thompsons under the back of our car, but a 10- or 12-inch street tire is no longer out of the question, and a mild Pro/Street treatment can still do the job. You can plan and build it yourself, or again, the aftermarket has come to the rescue with Pro/Street rear frame sections, ready to weld on to the chassis of your choice.

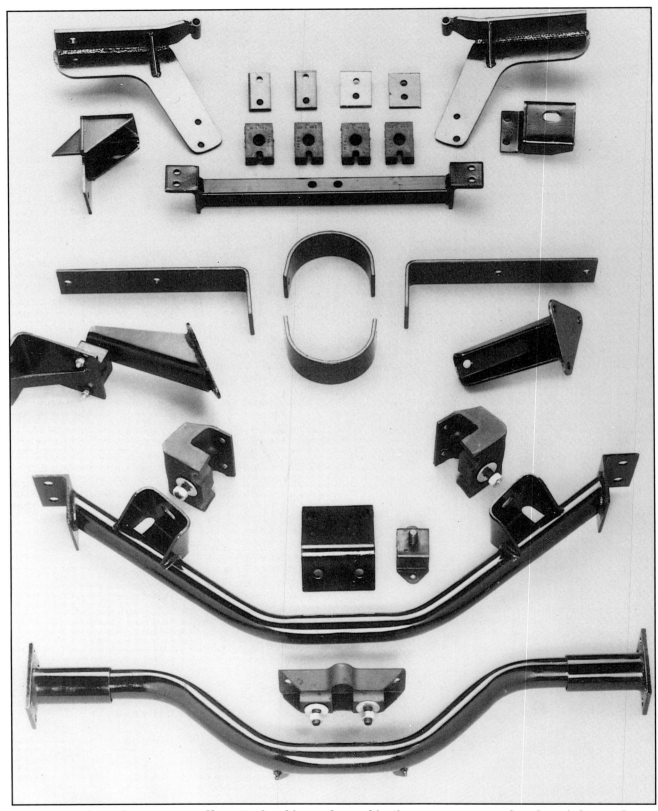

Name any engine and name any car. No matter how bizarre the combination, someone, somewhere has tried to put the two together. The aftermarket has responded by producing engine-swap kits for many of those combinations. This shot shows some of the engine and tranny mounts available from TD Performance.

Subframes

We can just about imagine the first time a hot rodder stumbled across a Nova subframe. . . It's the early 1970s, in a junkyard (they weren't automotive recycling centers yet), and there, lying on the ground, is a complete independent front suspension with disc brakes, power steering, and motor mounts already built in. The wonder of it all. Must've seemed like an answered prayer in those days.

And for many, it was. Subframing caught on big in the early 1980s (the earliest articles we can find are in *Custom Rodder* in 1982 and *Rodder's Digest* in 1982), with the early Camaro and Nova rear-steer unit being the most popular piece, often with Chevelle disc brakes swapped in. Later Camaros and Firebirds also gave up their front ends for hot rods, and today we see a lot of 1979–1983 Cutlass and Malibu and even Chevy S-10 pickup sub grafts going on (technically, these last two aren't subs, but frame sections).

Like any modification, subframes have their pros and cons. On the plus side, a subframe does give you modern brakes, steering, and suspension, with easy-to-find rebuild parts. Subframes are also relatively inexpensive, with prices ranging from free to a couple hundred bucks, and probably another couple hundred bucks to get everything rebuilt.

But there are several disadvantages to subframes. First, it takes top-notch welding, planning, and fabrication skills to do the entire job. This leaves many would-be hot rodders out of the loop. Second, although you save cash, you spend more time doing a subframe. The sub has to be cleaned and prepped; the old car frame has to be stripped, cleaned, and prepped; and all measurements have to be checked and rechecked. In addition, most subframes are now old enough (and used enough) that they'll also need to be rebuilt with new bushings, ball joints, tie-rod ends, and perhaps even springs. This is a job that requires a quality spring compressor, a press, and a fair amount of know-how to do the job right. Finally, subframes are ugly. They were designed to be functional, not pretty, since they resided under modern cars and were completely covered by sheet metal, inner fender panels, and so forth. This makes them unsuitable for any hot rod where they'll be exposed; that's why we only recommend subs for fat-fendered cars.

So, how to do a subframe job right? Well, the first job is to measure, measure, measure. Measure your future hot rod's ride height, its wheelbase, the width of the frame, and the car's track width. Make notes on where the engine can and will go, and note especially how the sheet metal is mounted to the front end. Often, you'll find that it's mounted to the radiator cradle, which is bolted to the front cross-member in one or two locations. Take photos, take notes, and start the planning process.

Next, figure out what subframe is going to fit best. The popular options are: 1967 to 1979 Camaro and 1968 to 1974 Nova (rear steer, meaning the steering box is located behind the axle centerline); 1970 to 1981 Camaro and 1975 to 1979 Nova (front steer); 1979 to 1983 GM G-body (Olds Cutlass, Chevy Malibu and Monte Carlo, Pontiac Grand Prix, etc., front steer); and Chevy S-10 pickup (front steer). You'll need to measure the track width, the position of the steering box relative to the axle centerline (some front-steer steering boxes are mounted too far forward and interfere with grilles and sheet metal), and the width of the frame stubs.

You'll also need to make a bunch of measurements on a subframe that's at its stock ride height, when it's still under a complete donor car, with engine. You need to know the clearance between the cross-member and the ground, and the clearance between the frame stubs and the ground. You also need to know the distance from the lower A-arm pivots and the lower ball joints to the ground. Further, these measurements need to be taken with good tires that are equally inflated.

Why is all this information needed? Well, pretty soon you're going to end up with a bare subframe sitting on the garage floor, next to a stripped-down old car. Without this information, you have no way of knowing how to attach the subframe to the old frame and get the ride height you want. Basically, what you'll need to do is strip the old suspension off the old car frame, then set the car on jackstands at what you want to be the finished ride height. Then you need to compress the springs on the subframe and set it up exactly as it sat when it was under its donor car (the springs can be compressed by using lengths of 1/2-inch threaded rod in place of the shocks; large washers and nuts can be used to squeeze the springs down). Only then will you be able to figure out where to join the two frames. For more info on this process, see the how-to sequence located elsewhere in this chapter.

One other important—and often overlooked—item on a subframe swap is sheet metal mounting. Once you cut off the front of the old frame, all your stock sheet metal mounting points are gone forever. Before you do that, you MUST figure out a way to locate the sheet metal mounting points after the sub is in. The easiest way to do this is to build a simple locating fixture or jig. With the sheet metal removed, build a sturdy jig that bolts to several locations on the car's firewall, and maybe even to a tranny mount. After the subframe is installed, you can reinstall this jig on the car's body; then it's a fairly simple matter of building a bracket that goes between the subframe and the jig. This reestablishes the stock mounting location so the sheet metal can go back on.

Now, should you subframe your car? The answer is, probably not. In the 1980s, a subframe was often the only answer if you wanted a modern independent front suspension.

Subframe grafts are now almost unnecessary, thanks to the hot rod aftermarket. For many of us, though, economics don't allow us to go out and buy off-the-shelf components, and a subframe may be the only viable upgrade. In these cases, consider first what it will do to the value of the car. If it's a Ford or a Chevy, a subframe may actually devalue that chassis. Otherwise, go ahead. Next, consider your abilities. You have to be a talented fabricator, a little bit of an engineer, and a fully qualified welder to tackle a subframe graft. Remember, the lives of yourself, your family, and other motorists are at stake—a busted frame on the highway could kill people. Beyond the considerations of value, esthetics, and such, that's the biggest concern—if you can do the job safely. If you have any doubts, find another way, or find someone else to do the job for you.

Lots to look at here. Kurt Senescall's Model T coupe has a chassis made from round chrome-moly tubing, all built to NHRA specs. Here you can see a frame rail, the drag-race style motor mount plate, the four-bar front suspension, and the tubular shock mount. One of the shock mount bolts also serves to mount the steering box on the inside of the frame rail. One part doing two jobs keeps it light.

IN THE SHOP:

CUSTOM TUBULAR X-MEMBERS

BY ERIC HENDRICKSON

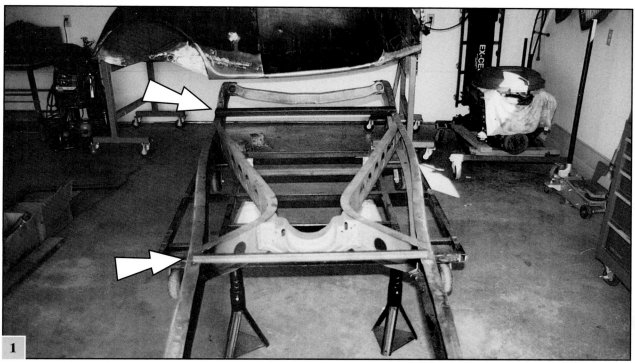

1

I started with a good stock frame that'd been jigged and straightened. I then tacked on two tubular cross-braces (arrows), welded my frame cart to the bottom of the chassis, then leveled the whole assembly using jackstands and shims. This'll keep the rails from spreading or bowing when the stock X-member is removed. *Eric Hendrickson*

The first decision that I had to make in the chassis design was what kind of car I wanted to build. I already had a nice original frame that had been jigged and straightened by Jim's Rod Shop; it also had a new Chassis Engineering dropped front cross-member installed. Starting with a frame that had been previously jigged was a big advantage and worth the cost. As it turned out, one of the rails needed a fair amount of massaging at the front to get it back to the original 1934 shape. Then along came a nice 1934 five-window body, and the ideas started coming together.

The picture that gradually formed in my head was of a chopped 1934 Hi-boy with a big-block Chevy, Turbo 400, quick-change, roll bars, and so forth—in other words, a basic, kick-ass

hot rod. Knowing the original X-member would have to be heavily modified to accept a big-block and TH 400, I ruled out using it right away. A stock X-member would also have caused exhaust clearance problems, as I planned to use 3-inch pipes. I wanted the car to sit very low (it now has a dropped front cross-member, a Durant mono-leaf front spring, and a Vintage Chassis Works dropped tube axle), and I didn't want the cross-members or exhaust to hang below the bottom of the frame, both for clearance and appearance. I also wanted a rear suspension that would hook up well at the drag strip, and that meant creating an adjustable, unequal-length four-link.

After reviewing a whole stack of catalogs, and checking out quite a few tubular X-member designs, I decided that to get exactly what

125

2

A Sawzall was used to very carefully remove the stock X-member. You can see here why the braces were so important—at this point there's not much else holding the frame together. *Eric Hendrickson*

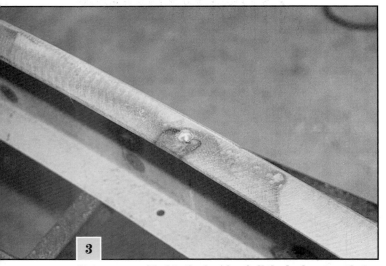

3

Nuts were welded to the inside of all the body mount holes before any boxing plates were added. I also filled all the extra holes in the sides of the rails because this car won't have fenders. *Eric Hendrickson*

I wanted I'd have to come up with my own design. That decision led to one more consideration—the tools I had at my disposal. My garage is probably similar to a lot of street rod garages—I have a drill press, a band saw, a 110-volt MIG welder, a compressor, and the usual assortment of hand tools. Maybe better

equipped than most, but nothing fancy—no mills, no lathes, no plasma cutters.

The next decision was material. Square tubing would be easier to work with, but in my mind, round tubes are nicer looking and have a racier look. The extra work would be worth the effort, so I bought some round tubing to get the project started.

Before cutting the original X-member from the frame, I tack-welded two braces across the frame (in front of and behind the X-member). I also tack-welded the frame directly to a rolling frame-cart that I had. The frame was then leveled on four jackstands. This gave the frame enough support and allowed me to carefully cut out the original X-member with a Sawzall.

With access to the inside of the frame, the next step was to weld nuts inside the rails under the body mount holes. And, since the car would be a Hi-boy, I also filled all the holes in the sides of the rails.

Using a grinder, I flush-ground the front and rear portions of the frame rails that were double-wall. This provided a nice flat surface to weld the front and rear boxing plates onto. The boxing plates were also from Chassis Engineering, but I had to modify them slightly as I wasn't using the original X-member.

The boxing plates were then clamped in place and tack-welded every 4 to 6 inches, taking care to weld to both wall thicknesses of the frame rails and to ensure the rails were free from excessive gaps. I used C-clamps to

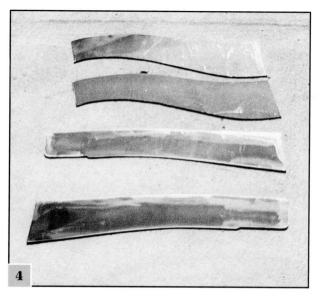

4

The Chassis Engineering boxing plates are designed to be used with a stock X-member; to use them on this application, we just had to trim the "kicked" portions of the plates off. *Eric Hendrickson*

squeeze any gaps shut between the rails and the plates.

Since I didn't feel it was necessary to box the rails fully, I had to make some short boxing plates that the tube cross-members could weld to. These were made from 3/16-inch cold-rolled plate, with the ends dressed up using a drill and a band saw.

Instead of stacking the tubes one above the other, I decided to offset them to provide more strength and more clearance between the tubes for exhaust tubing. I then clamped the plates to the drill press and used a hole saw to drill 1-1/2-inch-diameter holes in the plates for the tubes to weld into. Two sets of plates were made, one for the front ends of the tube X-members (they go near the tranny) and one set for the rear of the tubes (ahead of the wheelwells).

These plates were then tack-welded to the inside of the frame rails. (Where you place your boxing plates will depend on where you want your cross-members to attach to the rails; that in turn depends on what kind of chassis you have and what kind of engine and tranny you'll be using.) The plates' position relative to each other was determined by measuring from the

5

Here, the front boxing plate is being stitched to the frame. Vise-grips hold the plates tight with the frame; a C-clamp is used to close the gap between the rails and the plate. Stitch welds are placed about every 4 to 6 inches. The same procedure was used on the rear boxing plates. The stock rear cross-member and rails will later be removed and modified because the car's going to have a quick-change, coil-overs, and bobbed and "C"ed frame. *Eric Hendrickson*

6

I opted not to box the entire length of the rails, and instead built short boxing plates from 3/16-inch cold-rolled mild steel that the tube cross-members will fit into. Here, one pair of plates has been clamped together and a hole saw is cutting 1-1/2-inch holes in them to accept the tubes. *Eric Hendrickson*

front X-member back to the plates. I also measured diagonally between the plates to make sure they were located squarely in the frame.

The rear plates were basically eyeballed for distance between the front plates and the rear cross-member. I also had to keep in mind that their position would determine the length of the rear unequal-length four-link setup that I intended to use.

With the plates tacked in, two 1-1/2 x 0.120-inch wall tubes were cut to run the width of the frame at the top and tacked in. On the rear tube, the upper brackets for the adjustable four-links were slid onto the tubes before the tube was installed. They'll hang loose until we're ready to set up the rear end.

The lower bars needed to be bent. After making some measurements and determining the angles, we took a couple lengths of the same tubing to the local oval-track fabrication shop and had them do some distortion-free mandrel bends for $2 a bend, which is very reasonable. The bottom tubes are one piece that come off

the rear of the frame at a right angle to the rail, then they turn and run forward, parallel to each other at about 14 inches apart. A 45-degree bend brings them back into the frame rails up front.

Before welding, we slid the lower four-link brackets onto the tubes, then trimmed the tubes to length and tack-welded them in place.

I then started fitting the smaller lengths of tubing that joined the main tubes together—some required that the ends be "fishmouthed" for a snug fit to the other tubes. On straight cuts, I did this by clamping the tubes to the drill press (vise-grips and C-clamps), then carefully cutting the notch with a hole saw. With steady pressure and a little WD-40, it worked surprisingly well. If an angle cut was required, I just cut the tube flat with a band saw, then used a 4-inch grinder and a hand file to fit the tube as needed. Tedious work, but the results were worth it.

After fitting the bottom rails and tacking them into position, I put the big-block in place to see how everything was going to work. Once

7

After carefully measuring their position (measure from the center of the front cross-member, and cross-measure to make sure they're square), the boxing plates are welded to the frame rails. The next step was to cut two 1-1/2-inch-outside-diameter tubes and slip them into the upper holes between the plates. Before the rear ones were welded in, I slipped the brackets for the adjustable, unequal-length four-link that will later support the quick-change rear. *Eric Hendrickson*

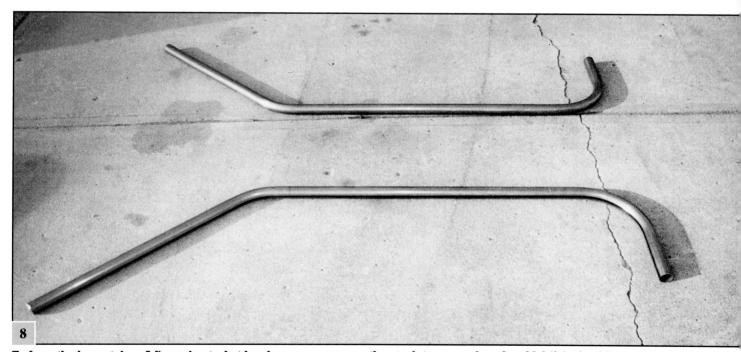

8

To form the lower tubes, I figured out what bends were necessary; then took two more lengths of 1-1/2-inch tubing to the local roundy-round fabricator for some mandrel bends. Eight bucks later, we had these. *Eric Hendrickson*

9

The lower tubes are mocked into position, with the back ends slipped into the boxing plates. The front ends aren't cut yet. Note how the frame cart also acts as a support for positioning and measuring the lower tubes. *Eric Hendrickson*

10

Square tubing clamped to the frame cart holds lower tubes in position while they're trimmed and clamped; this keeps the lower tubes parallel to the centerline of the frame. At the front end, they weld to short extensions added to the Chassis Engineering boxing plates. Note also the string that marks the frame's centerline as a reference mark. *Eric Hendrickson*

11

Joining the upper and lower tubes required fish-mouth cuts on short sections of tube. To do this, the tube was clamped to the drill press and center punched; then a hole saw made the cut with steady pressure and a little WD-40. Worked well for our purposes, but any more than this and we might've purchased a fixture. *Eric Hendrickson*

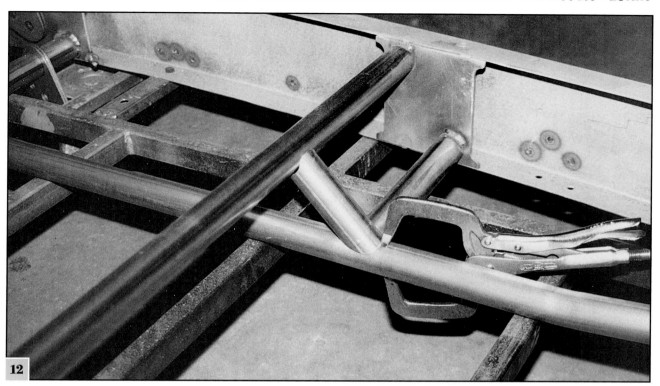

12 This shows the middle boxing plate with the sideways brace joining it to the lower main tube. Here, a brace between the top and bottom tubes is being fitted; the fish-mouth at the bottom end is at an angle and tough to do on a drill press. Instead, I cut it on an angle with a band saw, and then used a 4-inch grinder and a hand file. *Eric Hendrickson*

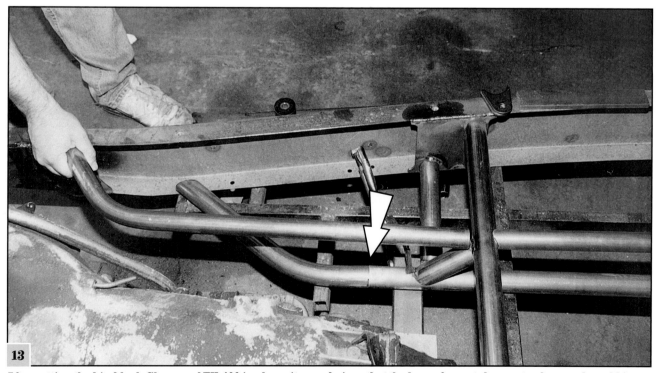

13 After setting the big-block Chevy and TH-400 in place, it was obvious that the lower frame tube was too long and would interfere with headers. To shorten it, it was cut square; then a sleeve was slipped in and the two pieces fitted with an 1/8-inch gap (arrow). The seam was then welded. Here, you can also see the angled upper tube being fitted to the front, and the tube that runs behind it between the two upper cross-tubes. *Eric Hendrickson*

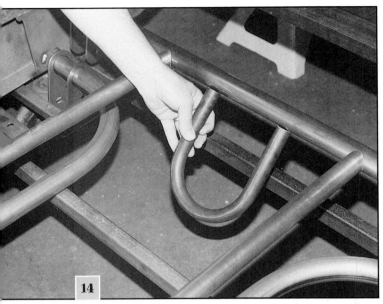

14

The last step was to install the two drive shaft hoops, which were mandrel-bent out of 0.090-wall 1-inch tubing. They'll attach to the upper cross-tubes at an angle, and I'll add some braces between them and the lower tubes as well. *Eric Hendrickson*

the motor was in position, it was pretty clear that the bottom tubes would have to be shortened, or I might run into clearance problems with the headers and exhaust. To make sure the resulting joint would be strong enough, I cut a sleeve to fit inside both ends of the tubes, then assembled it with a 1/8-inch gap and welded it all around.

At this point, a third set of plates was fabricated and added between the front boxing plates and the middle X-member plates (about where the firewall will be).

It was now time to build and install the top tubes, which are made of 1-1/4-inch x 0.090-inch wall tubing. The top tubes go from the front top cross-tube forward, then turn out at a 45-degree angle to meet the frame rails. Then another pair of 1-1/4 connector tubes run lengthwise to connect the front and rear cross-tubes at the top. With all the main tubes fitted and tacked, diagonal brace-tubes were fitted and tacked between the upper and lower tubes to add strength.

At the same time I was having the mandrel bends for the main tubes done, I had two drive shaft hoops bent out of 1-inch x 0.090-inch wall tube. These are attached to both upper cross-tubes and will soon be braced to the bottom tubes with sections of 1-inch tube.

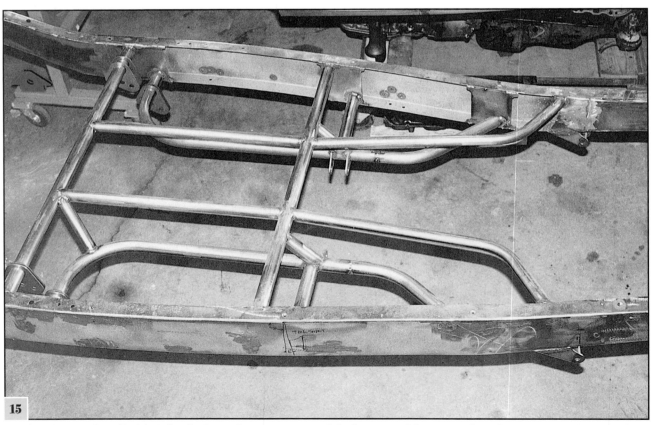

15

The finished product. At this point the frame is very strong and the braces and frame cart have been removed. Note the four-bar brackets hanging loose at the rear and the ears welded on the lower tubes for the tranny mount. Those pieces came from Chris Alston's Chassiworks. *Eric Hendrickson*

IN THE SHOP:

CUSTOM MOTOR MOUNTS

After we had the chassis cross-members set up on our 1934 frame, it was time to get that big-block Chevy and Turbo 400 jockeyed into position. The first step was to figure out where the engine should go. We did this by measuring a friend's 1934 Ford, from which we learned for sure where the firewall and radiator were, and where other components like steering boxes would be. It was then a pretty simple matter to bolt a radiator to our frame and set the engine in place on blocks. After getting the engine down, we decided to set it back an extra 1-1/2 inches, both for fan clearance and for weight distribution.

Then it was simply a matter of setting the chassis at ride height and deciding how high we wanted the engine to ride in the chassis. The engine was then centered from side to side, and we made sure the carb base was level from side to side and front to back. Due

1

After getting the engine sitting at the correct height and setback, and making sure the carb base was level, we started by building the drop-out tranny mount. First, a mounting plate with ears for mounting to a tube was fabricated and bolted to the tranny. Next, we bolted mounting tabs to our bushing sleeves and tacked the tabs to the lower X-member tube so the sleeves will line up with the mount's cross-tube. The cross-tube is 1-inch-diameter heavy wall tube. A shorter piece was clamped to the tranny side of the mount to determine where to mount the bushing sleeves. Once the mounting tabs were tacked in place, we measured the length and cut a piece of tube to fit. Here, it's clamped into place, ready to be welded to the tranny plate and the bushing sleeves (don't forget to remove the bushings from the sleeves first!).

2

The finished tranny mount. Here you can see where we split two narrower mounting plates and joined them together to make one wide enough for the tranny's mounting block. Now, if that massive big-block should thrash the tranny too bad, we'll be able to drop it out for service easily.

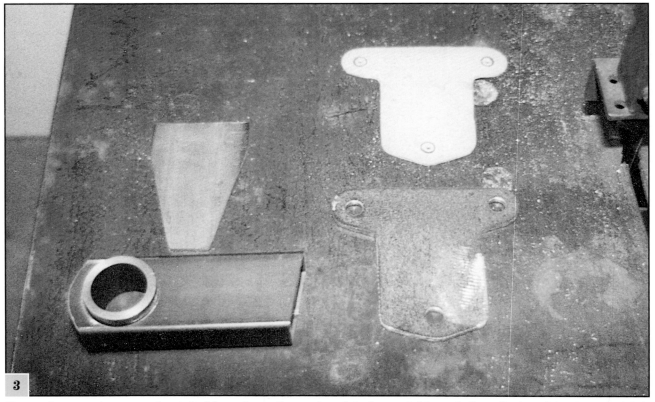

3

Our engine mounts are constructed of four pieces: the engine plate (lower right, made from the template at upper right), the mount tube and bushing sleeve (shown here assembled), and a stiffening plate (upper left). To make the mounts, the engine plate was bolted to the engine. The angle of the cut on the mount tube and its length were determined by holding it in position so the top edge aimed at the top of the frame rail. The tube is made of 1 x 2-inch, 1/8-inch wall stock.

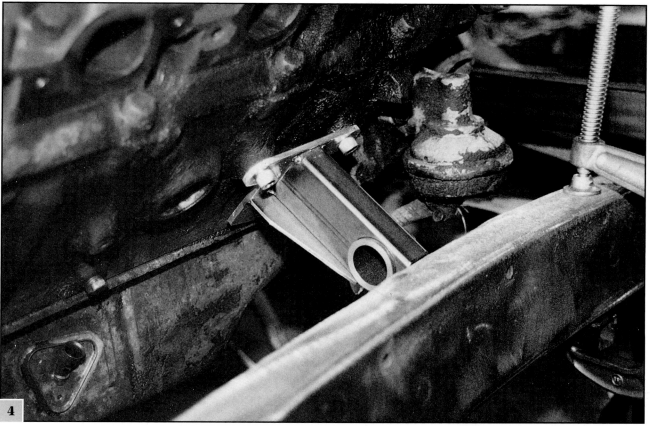

4

At this point, the mount is tacked together and bolted to the block. Note how the top of the tube is even with the top of the frame rail.

5

The finished mount with the bushing installed and all joints welded. A little cleanup and it'll look just like downtown, but with a down-home price.

to the chassis' low ride height, the engine sits about 1-1/2 inches higher than a small-block would. This will give us extra room for headers and steering shafts later on. We would've used aftermarket mounts from Chassis Engineering, TCI, Pete & Jake's, or any number of other advertisers, but the engine position we wanted meant that we would have had to modify the mounts; it's just as easy, in this case, to start from scratch.

To start the mounts, we ordered some heavy-duty urethane bushings from Pete & Jake's. These bushings have a 1-1/4-inch diameter that slips into a weld-on sleeve with an outside diameter of 1-5/8 inch and a 3/16-inch wall; the sleeves are 1-5/16 inches long. These are available from Pete & Jake's, but we had the tubing available and cut our own.

With the engine in position, we started by building the drop-out tranny mount, which will attach to the tube X-member. We had two mounting tabs from another project that were too narrow; both were split and the two larger pieces were welded together to make one that was wide enough. We then drilled holes in it to match the tranny mounting block, and bolted both pieces to the tranny. We then mocked a 1-inch tube into place to determine where the

6

We then bolted the mounts back on the engine and made cardboard templates of the ears that'll attach the mounts to the frame. These were then cut out of 1/4-inch plate, bolted to the bushing, and welded to the frame.

bushings would need to attach to the frame. Some premade tabs were bolted to the bushings and sleeves, and tacked into place on the X-member. Then it was a simple matter to cut a piece of 1-inch tube with a hole saw so it fit between the bushings. This tube was then welded to the tranny mount plate, and that part of the job was done. If the tranny ever needs service, we just have to remove two bolts from the bushings and the entire mount will drop out, making tranny removal and replacement easy.

The engine mounts were almost as simple. To begin, we made cardboard templates of the mounting faces on the engine block. These were transferred to 1/4-inch mild steel plate, the holes drilled, and the shape cut on a band saw. We then took two pieces of 1 x 2-inch, 1/8-inch wall tubing and bored holes through each piece

so the bushing sleeves fit in. The sleeves were tacked in place, and the ends of the tubes were trimmed at an angle so the top edges were aimed at the tops of the frame rails. The tubes were tacked to the motor plates, and a triangular reinforcing plate tacked to the bottoms of the tubes (this is, after all, a BIG block). We then installed the urethane bushings in the sleeves and used cardboard templates to build the tabs that went from the frame rails to the mounts. Those were cut out of 1/4-inch plate also, then tacked to the frame. Everything was then assembled to make sure the position was right. When everything checked out, all the joints were finish-welded.

We now have engine mounts that are strong, decent looking, and give us the engine position that we want.

INSTALLING A SUBFRAME FRONT SUSPENSION

In this book, you've seen quite a few jobs done on the author's 1947 Olds convertible. After most of the major body repair and fabrication was done, it was time to start in on the chassis, specifically the front suspension. Here are the options we had:

• **Install a Mustang II or other aftermarket independent:** Possible, but not easy. At the

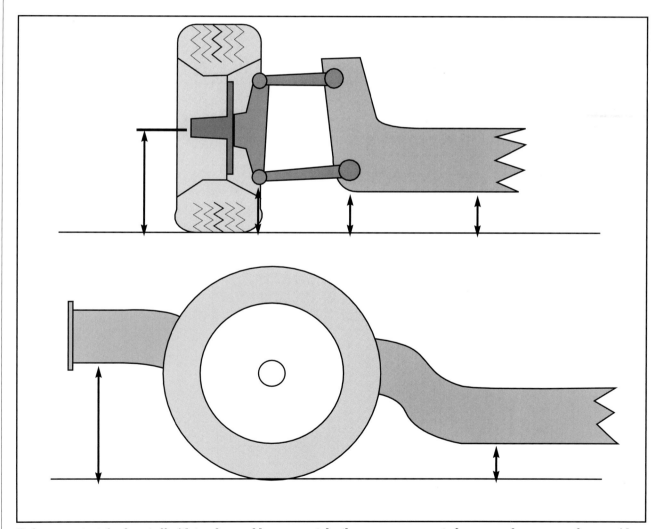

Before you start the fun stuff with torches and hammers, take these measurements from your donor car or from an identical donor car. Park it on a level surface, make sure the tires are aired up, and record each measurement. This will allow you to get the subframe set up properly for ride height and caster when you put it under your street rod.

2

Here's what we started with—the front half of a 1982 Olds Cutlass frame. Not exactly pretty, but it does provide modern IFS, disc brakes, and power steering in one fell swoop.

time, nobody made kits for this job, and the Olds frame is a massive, knobbly thing with spring pockets built into it, so installing a stock Mustang II cross-member would be an ugly job (in all senses of the word) at best.

- **Rebuild stock suspension and install dropped spindles:** No, No, No. First off, I drove this car with the stock front end, and know that the front end was, well . . . scary, and rebuilding the front end would've been expensive. Second, I just plain don't care for kingpin independent front ends. Third, the front end apparently sat in a bog, and the rust was so severe that parts of the main front cross-member were rusted through. So, the best solution was . . .

- **Hack it all off and start over with a subframe:** In this age of pre-engineered, relatively inexpensive kit suspensions, this isn't something I normally recommend; but in these circumstances, it was the best and least expensive option. We decided that Nova/Camaro subs were too wide (see table), and we didn't care to narrow one. In addition, they're getting tougher to find. We decided to go for a newer sub from a 1979–1983 Malibu/Cutlass. We'd seen this swap done under Jerry Wheeler's

1946 Chevy convert (which started life as an Olds), so we knew the width was good and that it could be done.

This family of subs (not a true "sub" frame, in that it doesn't unbolt from the donor car like a Camaro or Nova—it's actually the front section of a perimeter frame) has several things going for it: They all have disc brakes, and they're considerably narrower than a Nova/Camaro unit. It's a front-steer unit, which is good for some applications, bad for others; in our case, there'll be plenty of room for everything, and we're installing an Olds 455.

As you can see by that comparison, this sub is up to 3-1/4 inches narrower than other disc-brake subframes. Not bad. Now, there are a few more things you should know about choosing one of these subs. Beginning in 1980, GM began using metric fasteners. If you break out in a rash at the sight of a 14-mm open-end wrench, get a 1979 or earlier model. Also, two types of steering gear boxes were used on these subs, one with a bolt-on top cover (like the one in our photos) and one with a top cover held in by a big snap ring. We've been told that the model with the bolt-on cover is much better. And finally, these cars were available with V-6s or V-8s; we're assuming that V-8 models had heavier springs.

3

After recording the position of the radiator mount and determining where to splice the frames together (see text), we torched off the old front suspension. Definitely the point of no return. Note the location of the cut. It's about 13 inches ahead of the firewall, just ahead of where the X-member and the frame rail join; in other words, a very strong part of the frame. And a little cleaning of the torched frame end with a grinder never hurts.

4

We replaced the sub shocks with threaded rod and compressed the new suspension to ride height, then set it up for correct caster and so forth. We then wheeled it under the Olds frame and set the new wheelbase to 119 inches, stock for the 1947 Olds.

In this case, the 1947 frame was directly over the sub; we marked the sub and cut a notch in the top of the rail for the '47 frame to drop down into. We also had to slightly notch the bottom of the '47 frame so it'd drop down all the way.

We then dropped the Olds frame down to its ride height and jostled the sub into position. At this point, measure everything—wheelbase, sub height, caster—and cross-measure (as shown) to make sure the centerlines of the sub and 1947 frame line up.

Armed with this information, we spent $100 on a 1982 Olds Cutlass with a horrendous engine knock in its V-8; we then spent an enjoyable weekend tearing it apart, sold a bunch of pieces, kept some others, and broke even on the deal. One piece we saved was the front half of the frame, from about the middle of the front doors forward.

Popular Subframe Widths
(mounting face to mounting face)

Rear steer:
1967–69 Camaro and 1968–74 Nova with drum brakes: 60 inches
1967–69 Camaro and 1968–74 Nova with disc brakes: 61-1/2 inches

Front steer:
1970–81 Camaro and 1975–79 Nova (all disc brakes): 61 to 62 inches
1979–83 Olds Cutlass, Chevy Malibu, El Camino, etc. (all disc brakes): 58-3/4 inches

HOW IT'S DONE

Here's where you benefit from our mistakes: before you do any disassembly on the donor car, take measurements of the car's suspension

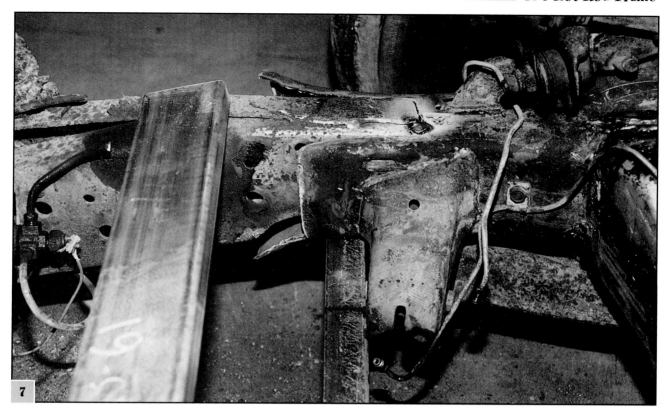

After measuring twice, tack it and measure again. Here's what our splice looked like at this point. First, the driver side from inside the frame, and second, the driver side from outside the frame. Lots of overlap will mean a strong joint; note the tabs sticking out on the bottom and outside. The top of the sub lines up with the top of the frame; this will give us a low but live-able ride height.

9

Note the struts clamped to the front of the frame horns; these maintain the correct caster angle. Also note the level on the car. Make sure the stock frame and the subframe are level side to side before anything's welded. Note also the blocks under the cross-member; this ensures that it stays at ride height.

10

Remember those tabs of metal at the splice? Heat and bend (or hammer) them until they are flush with the frame rail. This will increase the strength of the joint immensely. Then measure again, check your levels, and you're ready to weld. We used an arc welder for maximum penetration (our other choice was a 110-volt MIG, not powerful enough for this sort of thing).

when it's at ride height. Park it on a level surface, make sure it has stock-size tires on all fours and that they're aired up properly, make sure the tires are pointed straight ahead, then take the following measurements:

• ground to center of cross-member
• ground to both lower A-arm pivots on both sides
• ground to center of spindle
• ground to front bumper mount
• ground to bottom of frame

You may also want to place an angle protractor on the upper A-arm bushings and record that reading. These measurements will allow you to put the subframe back to its stock ride height and configuration after it's cut out of the car.

We didn't take these measurements before the sub was removed. We tried getting this kind of information from alignment shops and frame shops, but couldn't find one that was interested in helping. But we were lucky. We had seen a 1947 Olds four-door for sale last summer that had a 1979 Olds sub. We called the owner and builder, Tommy Shaw, and asked how it was, if he had photos, and so forth. He said it was easy, he had photos, and he also had scaled and dimensioned engineering drawings if we were interested. A week later we got an envelope full of photocopied drawings and photos. Thanks, Tommy!

OK, you have the sub figured out. Now to set the ride height on your street rod. We started by consulting Tommy's drawings and figuring in our own tastes, then we removed the Olds' tires and set it down on blocks where we thought it should go. The lowest point on the frame (at the cowl) in front was about 5 inches off the ground, and the rear was about 1-1/2 inches higher for a mild rake. This should put the front bumper 3-1/2 to 4 inches off the ground when it's all done (if you can, do this step with the sheet metal on so you know for sure). Before you go any further, measure and record the wheelbase on both sides.

At this point, you also have to take measurements so you can relocate your radiator/sheet metal mount after the sub is in. If the car isn't going to be moved, you can measure from a marking on the floor. You can also build a tubing jig that bolts to the firewall and to the rad mount; this will locate the position of the new mount after the original one is gone. Or, you can do like we did: take straight-line measurements from three marked holes in the firewall and record them. After the sub is in, these measurements will accurately locate the mount again.

With the Olds frame at its final ride height and leveled side to side, we went back to the subframe. We removed the shocks and inserted two lengths of threaded rod in their place, then tightened them until the suspension was compressed to its ride height. We then blocked the sub up so it was at the correct caster angle, and

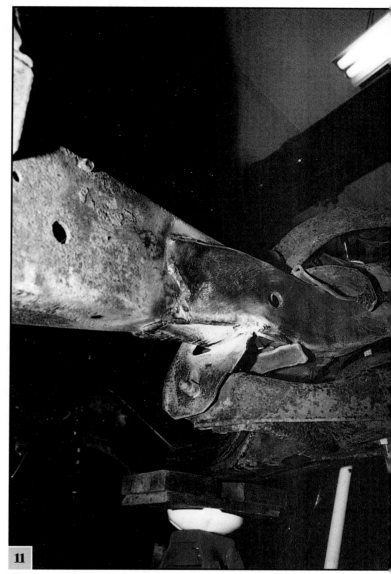

11

We did have to fabricate a few pieces to fill gaps in the bottom of the joint; other than that, it went very smoothly. This view is from the bottom on the outside of the passenger side.

set it next to the Olds. It was time to decide where to splice. What you need to do is compare the width of the street rod frame with the width of the sub at different distances from their front axle centerlines. Find a place where they're close to the same, then see if that location will work height-wise, and if a splice there will cause any interference problems. About the only thing to worry about is the lower A-frame mounts on the subframe; they can't be cut into.

Our cut was made just ahead of where the 1947 Olds frame and X-member intersect. At this point, the subframe rail begins to turn out and down, where it originally ran along the rocker of the donor car. (As an aside, the Olds frame is 33-1/2 inches wide at this point. This may help you

12

Another passenger-side view, from outside top. With this much overlap and such nice alignment, we felt boxing plates and reinforcements were unnecessary. If your application doesn't allow as much overlap, or if the rails don't line up as well, you'll have to add reinforcement plates on all four sides to strengthen the joint. Note that the reinforcing tube is still in place. It's the last thing to go.

determine how this sub will work in your car.) The subframe rail is also about 3/4 inch wider than the Olds frame rail, so we decided to cut a notch in the sub rail and drop the Olds frame down into it. We also decided to leave a long, curved "tongue" of metal on the outside edges where the subframe rail curved out and away. You'll see why in a minute.

Before cutting, double-check all measurements to ensure that you'll end up with the same wheelbase when you're done. The frame cuts and the sub cuts should be the same distance from their respective axle centerlines.

That done, we fired up the torch and cut off the excess parts of the subframe. Before cutting the Olds frame, we first welded a stout piece of rectangular tubing to the frame rails to keep them from shifting, spreading, or otherwise getting tweaked when the frame was cut. That done, we torched off the front of the frame and rolled the old suspension out into the driveway. Scary moment, but it felt good.

Before we moved the subframe, we clamped a couple of angle iron "struts" to the front bumper mounts to keep the caster angle from changing. The subframe was then rolled into place in its new home and shoved (it was a tight fit) into position.

After some minor trimming, fitting, and grinding, the sub was where it was supposed to be. We double-checked our wheelbase measurements, our ride height measurements, and cross-measured to make sure the subframe's centerline was aligned with the Olds' centerline. When we were satisfied that everything was right, we tack-welded the sub to the frame. Now, remember those curved "tongues" of metal we left hanging out the side? We heated and clamped them so they were flush with the Olds frame rail (actually, I started to heat and clamp them, until my less patient and more practical relations proved that a big hammer did the job just as well) and tacked them on too. This creates a good overlap between the subframe and the Olds frame; long lengthwise welds will create a strong joint. You'll note that we're using a good old-fashioned arc welder for the job. Our only other alternative was a 110-volt MIG that's a fine machine, but it doesn't have

(continued on page 161)

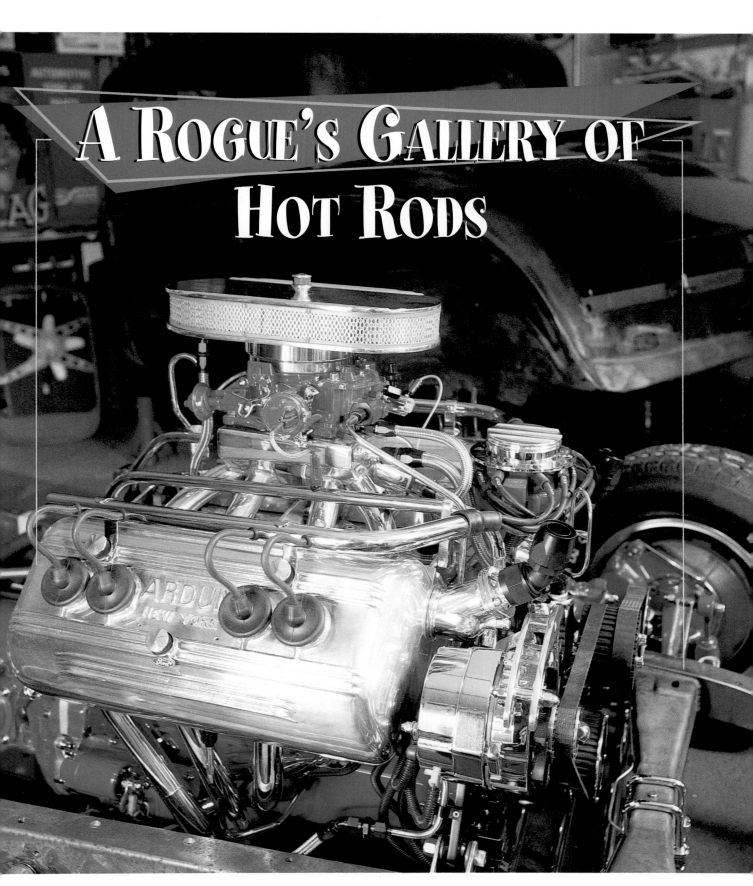

A Rogue's Gallery of Hot Rods

ot rods come in all shapes, sizes and costs, and their owners are even more diverse in their tastes, abilities, check-books, and personalities. We've selected a group of cars and owners that are as different as can be—from modern to traditional, expensive to low-buck—but we haven't even scratched the surface. What we hope to do is show you some cars that can inspire you, and that you can get ideas from. There really isn't anything new in hot rodding . . . but by taking and combining the ideas you like, you can make that hot rod project uniquely yours. Good luck.

A Deuce of a Different Kind Gary Echols' 1932 Chevrolet Sedan

Reprinted with Permission of STREET ROD BUILDER magazine, a Buckaroo Communications publication.

Some guys just have a vision. Gary Echols has built a string of Chevrolet street rods over the years. When he came upon a very nice 1932 Chevrolet sedan he had a vision for the car. You see, Echols couldn't remember ever seeing a '32 Chevy sedan done in traditional hot rod style, so he set about filling the void.

At the risk of offending the bow tie bunch it would be safe to say that Echols built his Chevrolet like a Ford. Knowing full well that stance is everything in a hot rod, he employed a Ford style four-bar front suspension and dropped axle to help get the old Chevy close to the ground.

Power comes in a traditional package too. A "W" head 348 Chevy

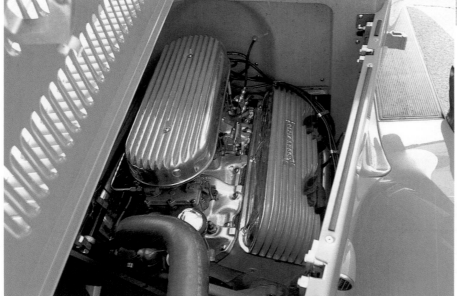

engine has been filled with all the good stuff. On the outside Offenhauser valve covers combine with an O'Brien Truckers air breather to completely cover the engine with finned aluminum.

The body was left basically stock, and Echols simply concentrated on making everything fit perfectly. Once again modifications that were common on Ford street rods were employed. A dropped headlight bar lowers the lights, providing a lower look to the front of the car. Likewise, rather than simply remove the cowl lights, they were lowered to continue the theme on the car. Rear lighting received a similar treatment; the stock taillights

were lowered and sunken into the corners of the rear pan. A louvered hood is balanced by a louvered rear gas tank cover, and that might be the key word to describe this car, balance.

The car has a theme and stays with it from front to back, top to bottom, inside and out. More of this balancing act comes with the black top insert and the rubber running boards. Inside the car a black and white interior by Jerry Hobgood, is balanced by a white steering wheel and a black dashboard.

Gary Echols combined attention to detail and balance with an unerring commitment to the traditional theme to create a timeless hot rod. This car is almost entirely homebuilt, a true showcase of what can be accomplished in a home shop. Chevrolet builders, this one is worth studying.

A Thinking Man's Delivery Dick Birdsall's 1934 Willys Sedan Delivery

Dick Birdsall took the old adage "Measure twice, cut once" to all new heights. Starting with a rare steel Willys sedan delivery, Birdsall set about building the best Willys he could think of, and trust us, he did a lot of thinking.

Employing the considerable skills of Neil Armstrong a completely tubular chassis was constructed for the Willys. Everything on the chassis is tubular, from the space frame to the four-bar brackets and shock mounts, to the fender braces. Once again we see a theme emerging and being followed throughout the car. Every bracket was conceived and formed to not only perform, but too look good while doing the job. This theme is continued throughout the car, and many hours were spent thinking and forming pieces that were aesthetically pleasing and functional. Never was the question poised, "What is the easiest way to do this?" Rather, the constant question was, "What is the best way to do this?"

While the truck appears quite stock many modifications are hidden on the car. A full roll bar is built inside the body panels and covered by upholstery. A custom rear pan and owner formed taillight brackets look stock,

but are pure fabrication. Shawn Seaman covered the perfectly straight body with Competition Yellow paint from House of Kolor.

Inside the rod, Miata seats are modified to fit the confines of an early interior. Carbon fiber dash and console inserts provide a contemporary look to the interior.

Power for the street rod comes from a 383-stroker motor topped with Delorto carburetors. The engine is detailed to the limit, and once again bracketry is incredible, and the concept is clean.

If there is one thing that can be learned from viewing Dick Birdsall's 1934 Willys it would be this: Think before acting and if you get a better idea don't be afraid to scrap those first brackets in favor of a better design. This hot rod is a combination of homebuilt and pro-built chassis. Once again, the key to a great hot rod is making a plan and sticking with it.

Wildly Subtle Wes King's 1936 Ford Roadster

Wes King likes cars with a sense of style, and performance. When he decided to build a 1936 Ford roadster he purchased an older restoration car and took it directly to Mike Adams in West Palm Beach, Florida (Palm Beach Rod Shop).

Mike and his crew set about building a completely tubular chassis with complete C-5 Corvette front and rear suspension. A crate motor is topped with three deuces and power is hooked to the independent rear through a 700-R tranny. Of course due to the perfect hot rod stance none of this can be seen unless you are in the full prone position looking up.

Covering all this modern suspension and power is an all steel 1936 Ford roadster that has been massaged to perfection. While the car appears stock things like a custom four piece hood with custom louvered removable

150

sides, tunneled taillights and custom panels between the bumpers and body are but a few of the highlights of this great car.

Rolling on steel wheels and white walls the car is so simple in appearance it often times goes unnoticed by the unknowing. Those real hot rodders are drawn to the car and upon close examination discover more and more great details.

Inside the car tan leather interior blends nicely with a 1940 Ford dash and steering wheel. A stereo is hidden behind the stock speaker grille in the forty dash, and things like drilled pedal arms add hot rod flavor. Wes King's car is a pro-built wonder that illustrates exactly where the state-of-the-art hot rod builder can take a car today.

Two Timer Mark Norman's 1940 Ford coupe

Mark Norman is a hot rodder with a single marque as his passion. For him the 1940 Ford has been the object of his considerable street rodding talents. The bright orange coupe shown on these pages illustrates a second effort on the same car. Mark originally converted the car to a street rod some fifteen years ago. In 1998 he decided it was time for a makeover for the coupe.

He purchased a complete chassis from The Forty Fort in Arvada, Colorado. The old chassis was rolled out from under the coupe (an oversimplification if there ever was one) and the new chassis, complete with fresh engine, trans and rear gear was rolled under. Of course before the this mating of body and chassis could take place the black body was stripped to bare metal and painted Hot Licks Orange by Joe Milazzo at The Auto Shoppe, in Jupiter, Florida. Mark detailed the new chassis and painted it prior to installing all the Mustang II suspension components up front along

with the rear suspension and eight-inch Ford third member (pirated from a 1970 Maverick).

Cream steelies (wheels) complete the look and carry early Ford hubcaps and beauty rings. Mark chose to keep all the stock trim, bumpers and running boards in place believing (like many rodders) that a 1940 Ford Coupe body is difficult to improve upon. Modern Chevrolet running gear, independent front suspension, power disc brakes, AC, and power steering make this coupe a delight to drive. Once again, a great example of a homebuilder putting together a top notch street rod.

A Radical Modern Sedan Roger Rickey's 1948 Chevy Sedan

We're including this sedan as a good example of what can be done with a relatively mundane car to make it outstanding. In its stock form, the '48 Chevy two-door sedan is a common, even frumpy old car. Just the normal hot rodding tricks—lowering, wheels, and paint—will change its personality considerably. Roger Rickey, on the other hand, went all the way over the top and created an outstanding hot rod.

Roger started with a plain vanilla two-door sedan. The chassis is relatively simple; the stock rails received a new tranny crossmember, a Mustang II front crossmember and IFS, and parallel leaf springs in the rear. Power comes from a well-dressed (and very reliable) small-block Chevy and Turbo 350 automatic tranny. Good, common-sense hot rod stuff.

When it came to the body, Roger pulled out the stops. The body is chopped 5-1/2 inches in front, and slightly less in back. The B-pillar was slanted forward, the windshield was V-butted, and the whole works was smoothed off. Roger also designed and built the custom front end, then painted it all school bus yellow for just a little more visual impact.

The interior is also outstanding, with a custom console (pictures of this console and some chassis details are scattered through this book), Buick Riviera seats, a molded headliner, and a custom-made back seat, all covered in tan vinyl

154

and cloth. It's comfortable because it needs to be . . . Roger spends a lot of time in it, putting on more than 5,000 miles per summer going to events from coast-to-coast.

While it may look radical, and while Roger builds cars for a living, most of what you see here can be accomplished by a dedicated hot rodder. The chassis is simple and reliable, the body modifications are radical but within reach of a careful builder, and the interior makes good use of OEM, aftermarket, and handmade parts. Look carefully . . . you'll find something on this car that you can use.

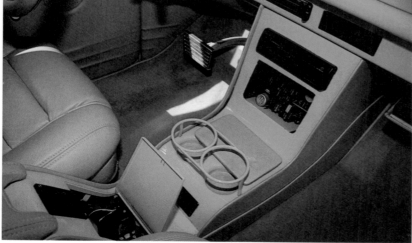

Two Brothers, Two Deuces

Randy Gribble's '32 Ford Roadster, Kevin Gribble's '32 Ford Roadster

For many, the ultimate hot rod is the '32 Ford roadster. Some prefer steel, some don't mind 'glass, but to us it doesn't much matter. The shape is the same, and it's always a good platform for whatever the owner wants to do.

Randy Gribble owns a hot rod shop in Watertown, South Dakota, and builds some great cars, nostalgia and otherwise. His personal ride (or at least one of them) for several years was the black Deuce roadster pictured here. It was (I say was because the car has since been rebuilt and changed by Randy) the ultimate nostalgia rod, with a flathead, '39 Ford tranny, F-100 steering, and a Columbia two-speed rearend. The black 16-inch

steelies and 'caps are from a '37 Lincoln, and the simple interior has red pleats and a Bell 4-spoke wheel. All very nostalgic . . . and it's based on a Wescott's fiberglass body. We like that.

Randy's brother Kevin also has the hot rod bug. His roadster is a bit more modern but still maintains many traditional hot rodding cues. Starting with a repro frame, he added a 'glass roadster body and the car's focal point, a '58 Chrysler 392 Hemi. It's fed by a Weiand intake with four Strombergs, and is hooked to a Turbo 350 tranny and a Halibrand quick-change rearend. Dark red metallic paint, a Duvall-style windshield, and a white tuck-and-roll interior finish it off.

Now, many would look at these cars, with their open cockpits and vintage power-plants and drivelines, and think that they're around-town, fair-weather garage queens. Wrong, wrong, wrong. Both cars get driven heavily, and both have at least one trouble-free trip to the L.A. Roadster Show (via Route 66 no less) under their fan belts. Build 'em and drive 'em . . . it's not just a catchy slogan in South Dakota!

Father and Son Traditional Rides

Leroy Smith's 1929 Model A sedan Mike Smith's 1923 Model T roadster

This pair is a perfect example of the basic side of hot rodding: nothing fancy, nothing trick, and in the case of the A sedan . . . nothing finished. Leroy is Mike's father, and together they built a pair of traditional hot rods that were at the beginning of today's "retro" hot rod craze.

Leroy's sedan started with a $50 Model A frame. To that, he added a a '37 Ford rearend with split wishbones, '40 Ford lever shocks, and a Model A buggy spring. Up front is a Super Bell dropped I-beam with another pair of split 'bones and '40 Ford brakes. Power comes from a '51 Ford flathead fitted with Jahns pistons, a Winfield cam, and stock heads, backed by a '39 Ford tranny converted to open drive. The body is a very stock '29 Tudor body in light-gray primer. No modifications. None. Inside is equally simple, with a '36 Ford banjo steering wheel and column, '56 MG bucket seats, and Stewart-Warner gauges. Very simple, and very cheap.

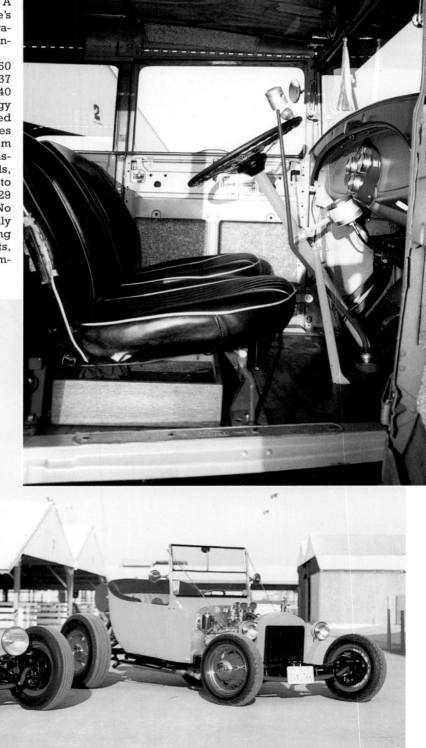

158

Son Mike's roadster may have more paint, but under that bright yellow facade it's even simpler than dad's sedan. Mike and Leroy built the rectangular-tube frame themselves, with a 96-inch wheelbase. The rearend is a Mustang 8-inch mounted with ladder bars and a Model A spring. Up front is a stock '34 Ford axle with split 'bones, friction shocks, and '40 Ford brakes. The '52 Ford flathead has a Winfield cam, Offy heads, and an Offy intake with three Strombergs. Another '39 Ford top-loader and 16-inch Kelsey-Hayes wires finish it off. The interior features '52 Ford gauges and a very basic bench seat.

Both of these cars were built on the cheap, often with cast-off parts from other hot rods that were being updated. But dollar for dollar, these cars get more attention and have more fun than any other hot rod we can think of.

13

Here comes the worst part of the job: remounting the sheet metal. To get that job done, we have to build a new radiator support in the exact same location (relative to the body) as it was before. Before cutting off the old suspension, we took the measurements indicated on the photo and recorded them. Now, we duplicate those measurements and hang a plumb bob (arrow) to mark the exact location of the new mount. When the plumb bob is in the right place, clamp its crossbar into place and build a stout mount that matches its location. If you want to play it safe, slot the hole and make it a little low. You can always install shims.

(continued from page 144)

the same penetration that the arc welder provides. One caution: Any structural welding on frames or suspensions should be performed by a certified welder. If you aren't one, find one to do this part of the job.

One more check of the measurements, and we started welding everything solid. The only problem areas were a few small gaps that needed to be filled on the inside bottom edges. For these, we fabricated patch pieces from the cut-up subframe material and welded them in. The end results are very strong.

When everything was welded solid, we set the car back on wheels and remeasured everything just to be sure. It was in right. Next step was to relocate that front sheet metal mount. To do this, we took a stick of straight 1 x 1-inch oak, hung a plumb bob from it, and laid it across the new front frame rails. We then started measuring from the holes in the frame that we'd marked earlier, and moved the plumb bob until it was hanging exactly where the old sheet metal

mount used to be. We then clamped the stick to the frame (and scribed its location just to be sure), fabricated a new mount from channel stock, and welded it to the frame.

Author's Note: I have a small confession to make. The order of events depicted in this how-to is the order that things should be done in, not necessarily the order in which we did them. With the information we had from Mr. Shaw and our own experience, we got a little cocky and cut the Olds frame first, then started hacking into the subframe. Luckily we knew what we were doing, and everything turned out fine. But after reviewing the photos and adding some more thought, we reordered the pictures in the order that they should be in. In addition, keep in mind that this story shows how we did a particular installation in a 1947 Olds—how you do yours is up to you. Just remember that while much of this information applies to subframing in general, every installation will differ. In other words, use your head, and if you don't have the qualifications to do the job right, get help from someone who does.—SH

Hot Rod Suspension Basics

EARLY FORD FRONT SUSPENSION 163

REAR SUSPENSION 174

INDEPENDENT REAR SUSPENSION 179

IN THE SHOP:

INSTALLING AN AFTERMARKET INDEPENDENT FRONT SUSPENSION 182

SWAPPING POWER STEERING 186

NEW REAR SPRINGS FOR FAT FORDS 190

CHOOSING THE RIGHT WHEELS 194

Once you have a proper frame for your hot rod project, you must add suspension. The frame must be rigid enough to hold the body without permitting distortion, and strong enough to provide attachment points for suspension, not to mention handling the torque of a modern V-8 engine.

Before we attach the suspension to the frame, let's define the job the suspension must perform. Simply put, the job of the suspension is to maintain tire contact with the road. Without springs the car would bounce down the road on its pneumatic tires, transmitting every shock up through the frame and making for a very rough ride. It would be virtually impossible to maintain control of the vehicle with solid mounted front and rear axles. If you don't believe us, try taking a nonsuspended, pneumatic-tired fork truck for a cruise at 75 miles per hour.

Through the use of springs to provide a controlled bounce, and shock absorbers to dampen the spring action, we are able to keep the tires in contact with the pavement in almost any normal condition. The job of the front suspension is compounded by the need to steer the car. Of course, many modern cars now include four-wheel steering, but to date we have not seen this modern marvel installed under a street rod. It will no doubt come one day, but in the interest of practical street rod building, we will assume that most hot rods have front-wheel steering only, and limit our discussion to that form.

EARLY FORD FRONT SUSPENSION

For years a hot rod's suspension was largely dictated by what was originally found under the car. Early Fords from 1923 to 1948 ran basically the same suspension. It seems that Henry Ford found something that worked, and stayed with it, applying the "If it ain't broke, don't fix it" theory almost to a point of fault. The system worked with one spring mounted transversely on each end of the chassis. That means the spring is clamped to a cross-member, with one eye on each end, near the frame rails. This spring is then attached to the axle and allowed to swing with a spring shackle on each end of the spring. By clamping the spring in the center, the single spring is actually converted to two quarter-elliptic springs. When either front wheel hits a bump, it pushes up against the spring, which in turn exerts a downward pressure to keep the wheel in contact with the road. The force by which the wheel is pushed downward toward the pavement varies with the spring rate. The spring rate varies by the number and thickness of the leafs in the transverse spring. The system is simple, functional, and economical for both the original automaker and today's hot rodder.

Hot rod front suspensions can be simple, like the one on Steve Grimes' track roadster. The tubular front axle is supported by two quarter-elliptic springs and two hairpin radius rods. Friction shocks work off links parallel to the spring leaves, and drag link steering completes the pictures. Elegant, no?

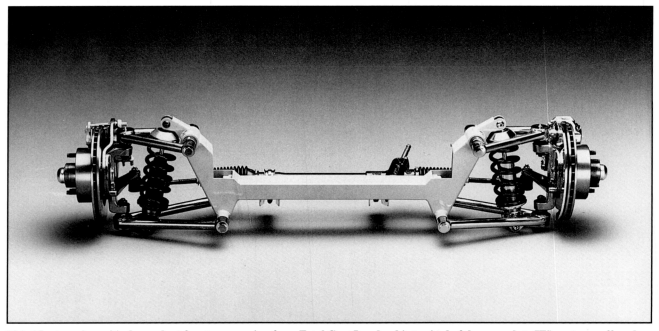

This Mustang-based independent front suspension from Total Cost Involved is typical of the complete IFS systems offered on the market today by many manufacturers. The cross-members are set up for specific chassis, while the tubular A-arms, coil-overs, and Mustang II spindles are standard. Mustang II suspensions are available in several configurations and cost levels.

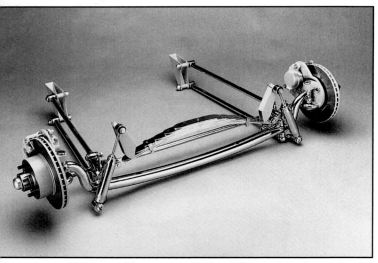

For something more traditional, try this dropped tube axle and four-link setup, also from Total Cost Involved. This suspension uses a conventional transverse leaf spring and vented discs for improved stopping power.

Locating the Early Ford Front Axle

The spring keeps the wheels on the ground, but the axle must also be prevented from moving fore-and-aft or side-to-side under the frame. These forces are handled by tubular steel struts that attach to the axle ends; the struts angle back toward the center of the chassis, where they're joined with a forged yoke

that includes a heavy cast spherical ball. This ball was located in a pocket attached to the chassis cross-member. The pocket permitted the entire assembly to pivot up and down with the movement of the axle. The triangular twin-tube system is often referred to as the "wishbone" by hot rodders, due to its familiar shape. This system cleared the stock engine's oil pan, but it often must be modified to make room for modern V-8 engines. The options are to "split the wishbones" or employ a four-bar locating system.

Splitting the wishbones involves eliminating the central pivot ball by cutting the two arms free from the pivot. Next, the fronts of the wishbones close to the axle are heated red-hot and carefully bent outwards, so the ends are located under each frame rail, or close to that point. Threaded bungs are welded into the ends of the 'bones, and spherical rod ends are installed; these rod ends bolt to brackets welded on the chassis. Wishbone splitting kits are commercially available, and we recommend using such a kit. It is easier and cheaper than fabricating your own solution to the wishbone splitting problem. Generally speaking, the closer the wishbone ends are to the center of the chassis, the better the car will ride and handle.

In its original configuration, the entire axle and wishbone assembly pivoted as one unit, with no adverse effects. However, when the wishbones are split (or replaced by hairpin radius rods), a twisting force is placed on the axle when the suspension moves. This is because each end of the axle is now traveling in

There's a secret behind this dropped I-beam axle—it's a torsion-bar suspension engineered by Lee Osborne. The end of the torsion bar is barely visible; it runs longitudinally inside the frame rail. The torsion lever runs outboard to a slot between the wishbone and the axle. Disc brakes, a Panhard bar, and cross-steering complete the picture.

its own arc, and that induces a caster change. If the left wheel moves downward while the right moves up, it forces the axle to twist. Luckily, forged I-beam axles are resilient and can absorb this twisting force without breaking or fatiguing. However, tubular axles can't twist, and will break if used with split wishbones or hairpin radius rods.

Locating the axle with a modern four-bar arrangement is much more common on today's hot rods. Basically two pairs of parallel tubular rods locate the axle front to rear. Commercially available brackets (called batwings) mount the four bars to the axle and then to the frame rail. By adjusting the upper and lower bar on each side of the axle the desired amount of caster (see definitions) can be dialed into the front suspension. Four-bars have another advantage in that when a wheel moves up or down, there is no caster change. The axle is located on one end of a parallelogram in this system; when the axle moves through the suspension travel, the end of

the parallelogram swings through an arc, but its angle doesn't change. Consequently, a four-bar doesn't induce axle twist, and they are recommended for use with tubular axles.

Four-bars are available in painted, chrome, or stainless steel with urethane rod end bushings. This system is very clean, simple, and functional.

Hairpin radius rods perform the same function as a set of split wishbones. While the radius rod attaches with two points on the axle, a single mounting point is used at the chassis. These style rods were commonly used on all hot rods up until the late 1970s when the four-bar arrangement came into vogue. While the manufacturers of the four-bar bracket sets touted them for having less binding and caster change on bumps, we suspect the largest attraction to the four-bar was the simplicity to manufacture four bars versus the more complex hairpin radius rod. Either system will provide you with thousands of miles of trouble-free motoring if installed correctly.

The ultimate in traditional front suspensions: a drilled and dropped Ford I-beam, reversed-eye spring, split wishbones, and 1940 Ford brakes with Buick finned drums. This setup is on Kevin Gribble's 1932 Ford roadster.

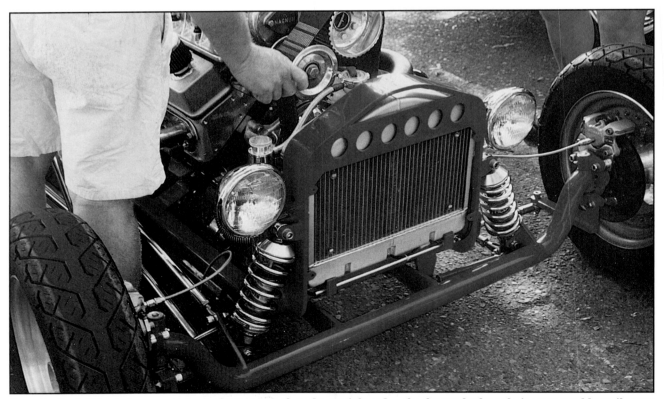

Greg Gruber's T-bucket uses a more modern approach to the straight axle—the dropped tube axle is supported by coil-overs and a four-link, but check out the steering. There's a rack-and-pinion mounted to the rear of the axle. This is something that isn't normally recommended; the trick is to have a steering shaft and U-joints that are free to pivot in the same arc as the four-link.

Shock Absorbers

While springs keep the wheels in contact with the ground, and the radius rods keep the axle under the car, as a car's speed increases, the spring action also increases. As speed increases, the wheels contact more bumps, the springs move more, and the wheels begin to move up and down in an uncontrollable fashion. The only way to maintain control is to dampen the spring action with shock absorbers. The job of the shock absorber is really better defined as *spring dampener*. It absorbs the energy in the spring and thus controls spring rebound. Once again, this dampening rate can be controlled by the stiffness of the shock absorber.

On the early Ford suspensions, the shock absorbers were lever action friction shocks or Houdaille hydraulic lever shocks. The early Model T utilized a series of leather and metal discs to dampen the spring action. A lever attached to the axle, and friction between the leather and metal discs dampened the spring rebound. This form of shock absorber was simple and worked reasonably well for the speed of a Model T. As speeds increased, a more reliable form of spring control was required. This control came in the form of hydraulic lever action shock absorbers.

A more conventional approach to steering a hot rod is the Vega cross-steer box, mounted inside the frame rail on this Pete & Jake's 1932 chassis. The Vega box is fine for cars up to 1935; larger cars should use the somewhat beefier Saginaw 605 steering box, which mounts similarly.

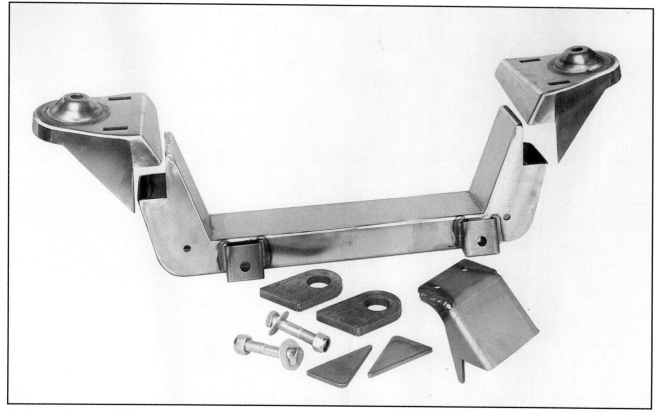

Feeling independent? Mustang II cross-member kits are available for just about any car you can think of, from Model As to late-model Chevy pickups. This is a basic Heidt's cross-member kit. You can add stock Mustang II A-arms, springs, and components, or upgrade to tubular A-arms and coil-overs—whatever your heart desires and budget allows.

Some manufacturers recommend that you don't weld to a Chevy top-hat-style frame—the thin-gauge metal of the rail can fatigue and crack. To remedy that, Chassis Engineering offers this bolt-on Mustang independent front suspension kit that mounts using the stock suspension mounting holes. This example uses stock Mustang II A-arms.

Once again the lever attached to the axle, but now instead of a series of leather discs slowing the spring action, hydraulic oil was forced through orifices in the shock body to provide resistance. The stiffness of these lever action shocks could be altered by changing the oil viscosity inside the shock. Thicker oil provided a stiffer shock, while thinner oil provided a softer shock. These lever action hydraulic shocks were manufactured for Ford by the Houdaille Company and were used on many early Ford hot rods for years.

Once again, Ford clung to the lever action technology long after other manufacturers had changed. The hydraulic lever action shock was standard equipment on Fords until 1948. The units will work well today if they are in good condition. Many early hot rodders would chrome the shock absorbers and links, then mount them to the side of the frame rails in the stock location.

Hot rodders have long been looking for better ways to do things. When the tubular shock absorbers were first introduced, they were often referred to as "aircraft shocks." Many hot rodders worked on aircraft in World War II; when they returned home, they brought the technology with them. These shocks were also becoming standard equipment on many new cars in the late 1940s and early 1950s. The lighter and more versatile tube shocks quickly became the preferred option for Ford front suspension. Early F-100 truck front shock mounts made bolting on a set of tube shocks a very simple affair, particularly on fenderless hot rods. As the level of hot rod detail increased, chrome-plated tube shocks became standard fare on many early Ford hot rods.

By selecting the proper number of front spring leafs, and the correct pressure shocks, the early Ford front suspension will provide a good ride with reasonable handling. The last, and by no means the least important, item to deal with is ride height. Few things are as important to a successful hot rod than ride height. The traditional "rake," that down-in-the-front stance that virtually defines a hot rod, can only be accomplished by lowering the front suspension.

Getting the Ride Height Right

Lowering the Ford front suspension can be accomplished in several ways. First, the front cross-member can be changed. By installing a front cross-member that has less drop, you effectively lower the chassis. A good example of this is the Model A front cross-member in a 1932 chassis. This flatter front cross-member is good for about 1 inch of lowering.

Reversing the spring eyes is also good for approximately 1 inch of lowering. This process involves having a professional spring shop roll the eyes on each end of the spring upward, placing the spring below the shackle instead of above it. Today these springs are available as replacement items from your local rod shop or via mail order.

Often it is necessary to "C" the frame for additional spring clearance after reversing the eye and changing the front cross-member. A simple notch in the bottom of the frame rail provides clearance for suspension travel. After notching the frame rail, the notch must be filled with metal and welded solid. Often the piece removed in the notching process can simply be turned upside down to create filler for the notch. All chassis welding should be done by a qualified, certified welder.

Finally, and the most common and most dramatic, is the dropped axle. By heating and bending the ends of an original Ford axle in an "S" shape, early hot rodders raised the wheels upward on the axle ends, which in turn lowers the chassis between the tires. Unfortunately, this

procedure also stretched and distorted the axle ends. Generally speaking, the less stretching and distortion, the better the job. When using one of these old dropped axles, examine them carefully for signs of structural problems. Axles can be dropped in increments of 1/2 inch, and vary from 2- to 6-inch drops.

The good news is that brand-new dropped axles are now available from a variety of sources. These axles were designed as dropped units from the beginning. No longer are there thin axle ends, distorted axle webs, or alignment problems caused by improper bending. Instead we have brand-new forgings with perfectly contoured ends. The new axles lower the car and maintain proper suspension geometry at the same time. Dropped axles are available in tube or I-beam configuration. The I-beam is constructed just like the original Ford axle, like a small I-beam (ergo the term I-beam, see how simple hot rodding can be?). The tubular axle is constructed of (and if you guess tube stock, go to the head of the class) tube stock.

Dropped tube axles are available in two basic styles: the one-piece tube axle and the three-piece tube axle. One-piece axles are most commonly found on T-buckets. Generally, the axle tube is straight, with the ends bent up at an

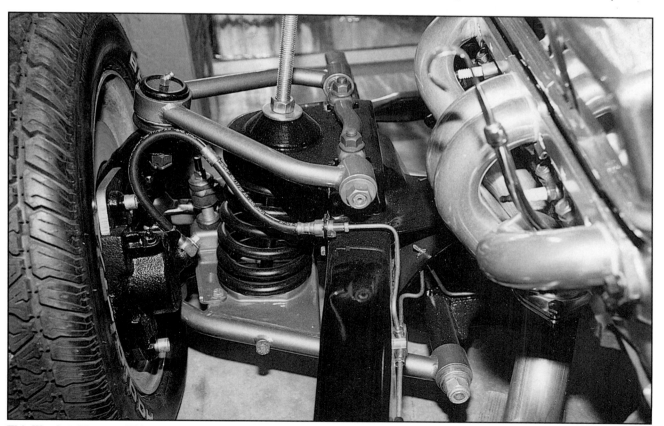

This Weedetr Mustang II front end is installed on a 1946 Ford convertible. Note that it uses tubular upper and lower A-arms; the lowers replace the stock Mustang II control arm and strut rod. This setup uses conventional coil springs with tubular shock absorbers. A threaded rod in place of the shock absorber is used to compress the suspension to ride height before the body is on.

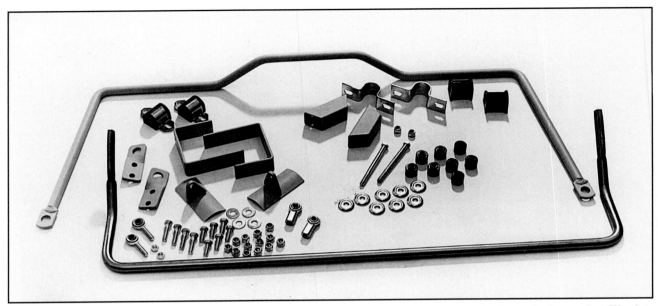

Automakers didn't start installing anti-sway bars on their cars until the late 1940s. Today, the hot rod aftermarket (Weedetr in this case) makes sway bar installation kits to fit just about any popular chassis/suspension combo; they're an excellent addition to any older car. If you install a sway bar, you can maximize the benefit by using polyurethane bushings. They're stiffer and provide more precise handling.

angle. The ends are "fish-mouthed" to accept short pieces of vertical tubing, which hold the kingpins and spindles. Spring brackets or four-bar brackets are also welded to the tube.

The three-piece tube axle employs forged ends (sometimes cast ends, but these aren't as strong) inserted in a slightly bent tube (the amount of bend in the center of the axle is often referred to as the axle "smile"). The ends are then welded and pinned to the tube. In the early 1980s some of these axles were only welded, without the pin going from front to rear in the axle end. If you are buying a three-piece axle used in a swap meet, be certain it is pinned and welded. Also, any grinding of the weld that holds the forged end to the tube center is not recommended because it compromises the structural integrity of the axle. If you want a perfectly smooth axle, we recommend either a one-piece tube axle or the standard I-beam.

It is worthy of note that to achieve the proper camber (see definitions) on a solid-axle car, the axle must be bent. New axles are manufactured with the proper, slightly positive camber. On some old dropped axles, the camber may not be true from side to side.

And finally, one other traditional modification seen on the I-beam axle is what is commonly known as the "dropped and drilled front axle." We have already covered the dropped portion of that equation, so what does the drilled portion refer to? It is the practice of drilling a series of holes in the webbing of the axle. This was done to decrease weight in the times when hot rods were also race machines. Today the practice is largely a cosmetic one, and a very

nice touch to a traditional hot rod. Having said that, be certain the drilled holes are not so large in diameter or quantity that the I-beam is weakened. Once again, when buying a dropped and drilled axle at a swap meet, examine the unit very carefully before parting with any of that hard-earned green. Today, brand-new dropped and drilled axles are available from street rod manufacturers and local rod shops. The dropped and drilled axle will forever be a mainstay of traditional hot rodding.

On all Ford axles kingpins hold the spindles to the ends of the axles. Drum or disc brakes are then adapted to these early Ford spindles; we will address that in detail in the braking section of this book.

Turning the Early Ford Wheels

Now that we have the front end of the hot rod frame rolling around, we must also control the steering. When using a solid axle, a steering box must be used to turn the wheels. Some attempts at mounting a rack-and-pinion on the back of an axle have been attempted, but this should be avoided at all costs. The difficulty arises when trying to turn the rack's steering input as it moves with the suspension. The potential for bump steer, erratic steering, and sheer terror are all present when attaching a rack-and-pinion steering unit to a one-piece axle. Just say no.

On the other hand, a steering box is a relatively simple unit to mount, thanks again to today's kits. The most popular unit today is the Vega cross-steering box. Actually, brand-new steering boxes are commercially available that

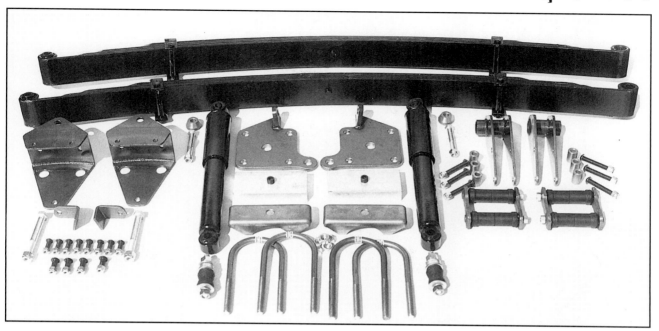

For rear suspensions, it's hard to beat a parallel leaf spring setup for simplicity. This Magnum kit includes everything necessary to install parallel leafs—from the rear end brackets and U-bolts to the frame brackets and spring eyes.

This Chevy frame has a Chassis Engineering parallel leaf spring kit installed. It includes a bolt-on sway bar kit and a crossmember for mounting tube shocks. A very simple, reliable suspension.

If you use a subframe, it makes sense to rebuild it with new ball joints, bushings, and tie-rod ends before the car is together. You may also want to replace the springs. In any case, use extreme caution and a quality internal spring compressor, like this one. Compressed coil springs contain enough energy to be lethal.

are the same configuration as the old Vega box. The steering box mounts to the inside of the driver-side frame rail. The lever on the steering box is called a pitman arm. The pitman arm connects to the drag link, which goes across to the steering arm on the spindle of the passenger-side wheel, hence the term *cross steer.* A tie rod connects the two steering arms together. When the steering box receives input from the steering wheel, the pitman arm rotates, moving the drag link. The drag link moves the steering arm, and since the tie rod has the two steering arms connected, both wheels turn in the same direction. We simply call it steering, and folks, it's a beautiful thing.

A second, less common method of achieving steering is to mount the steering box below the frame rail with the pitman arm protruding either through the driver-side frame rail, or point up alongside the outside of that rail. A simple draglink is mounted to a steering adapter on the top of the driver-side spindle. Once again steering input from the steering wheel moves the pitman arm. The pitman arm is attached to a bracket on the backside of the spindle and moves the driver-side wheel forward or back, turning it left or right. Since the tie rod connects the two lower steering arms, once again both wheels turn in the same direction—steering again. This system can be somewhat more

prone to bump steer than the cross-steering, but if proper steering geometry is maintained, this system will perform without problems. Generally speaking, unless there are some special interference problems, the cross-steer system is the preferred system.

Independent Front Suspension

It took a long time, but in the 1980s hot rodders took the plunge and embraced independent front and rear suspension. Today, one of the most popular front suspensions found under hot rods is the Mustang II independent front suspension and derivatives of that design (isn't it nice to know that the Mustang II was good for something?).

The advantage of an independent front suspension is that each wheel is able to move independent of the other. Unlike a straight axle, when the right front wheel hits a bump, the left front wheel is unaffected. This system provides smoother and more predictable handling characteristics. Simply put, the car handles better.

With most aftermarket Mustang II suspensions, a cross-member is fabricated (or more often purchased) and welded into the frame. On each end of the cross-member, upper and lower control arms are mounted. A coil spring is then mounted between a cup on the top of the frame rail and the lower control arm. A shock absorber is bolted inside the coil spring to the lower control arm and to the top of the spring pocket.

The coil spring keeps the lower control arm pushed down in contact with the road. The spring also allows the control arm to move upward when it contacts a bump or high spot in the road. The shock absorber controls, or dampens, the spring action so the control arms don't continue to bounce up and down after contacting a bump.

Other independent front suspensions that are popular in today's world of hot rods are the C-4 and C-5 Corvette, Dodge Dakota truck, and Jaguar. While there were Corvair units installed under some hot rods in the 1970s we would recommend not using, or for that matter even keeping, that suspension under a hot rod because the geometry can be difficult to work out without producing bump steer.

Custom independent front suspension from manufacturers like Kugel, Heidts, and Fatman Fabrications consists of tubular or aluminum control arms and custom cross-members designed for your car's particular chassis. These systems work very well and are cosmetically pleasing with their polished stainless steel and aluminum components, but tend to cost quite a bit more than the standard Mustang II–style front cross-member.

A Word on Subframes

Subframing a car consists of cutting the chassis off just in front of the firewall and grafting a piece of a new chassis to the old frame. If

When setting up the rear suspension, make sure the rear axle is centered in the wheel opening. In some cars, like this 1934 hi-boy, the axle should be moved back slightly to look right in the body reveal without fenders. Here, a plywood mock-up wheel is used to measure wheelbase and check the location.

done properly this modification will provide a great ride and years of trouble-free use, but care must be taken to install the subframe perfectly square to the existing chassis, and to make certain the joint has adequate strength.

Other potential problems encountered with this system are mounting of the radiator and front sheet metal. Typically new mounts and inner fender wells must be fabricated to complete the job.

Subframes can be broken down into two basic groups: front steer and rear steer. These terms relate to the position of the steering box on the subframe. Popular subframes like the 1968–1972 Nova have rear steering boxes, while others have the steering box located in front of the front cross-member, often interfering with the mounting of the front sheet metal.

Generally speaking, the subframe modification is best used under hot rods built after 1940 because they are larger and wider to accommodate the subframe. We recommend doing a subframe only if a cross-member-style front suspension cannot be employed.

The added hassle of mounting sheet metal, radiators, motor mounts, and inner fender wells usually outweighs the benefits of low cost and factory-type handling. For more information on subframes, see the frame chapter.

Front Suspension Overview

The good news is there are now kits available for virtually any old car to safely upgrade the front suspension. These kits range from economical to very expensive with exotic metals and fabrication techniques. For the average hot rodder today, buying a simple straight axle or Mustang II independent front suspension seems to fill the bill. Optional brakes and chrome and stainless components make it simple for the hot rodder to customize his suspension package.

Of course there are still those who will head out to their home shop and craft a suspension of their own liking. We applaud this effort, for it is the very core of true hot rodding. However, we must remind the reader that a precious few individuals possess the skills and know-how to do this safely and efficiently. For most of us the pre-engineered suspension, steering, and brake kits are the wise choice.

REAR SUSPENSION
Solid Axle Rear Suspensions

The rear suspension on a hot rod has one additional problem, not encountered on the front suspension. Not only must the wheels remain in contact with the road, but also these are the driven wheels. The power from the engine is transmitted to the rear axle, which turns the wheels to power the hot rod.

The most common suspension for hot rods is the solid rear axle housing. Basically, a drive shaft from the rear of the transmission connects to the ring and pinion with a differential gear set to drive the wheels. On the solid rear axle, the housing is one piece. Move the right wheel up or down and the left wheel will react. It is the same theory we dealt with on the front suspension, solid axle versus independent.

The Ford 8- and 9-Inch Rear Ends

In the rear axle–housing family the most popular unit is the 9-inch Ford, so named for the diameter of the ring gear. This unit is plentiful and strong and has a very clean housing, making it a nice-looking piece when detailed and painted under a hot rod. From the popular 1957 Ford station wagon rear housing (popular because it is narrow) to later-model housings, these rear ends have the added benefit of an easy-to-change center gear set. The "pumpkin," or gear set, can easily be changed, repaired, or adjusted as a unit once the axles have been removed.

The 9-inch has a kid brother known as the 8-inch rear end. It's not as common, not as big, and not as strong, but it is suitable for lighter-weight or mild-motored hot rods. The 8-inch housings are also typically narrower than 9-inch housings.

Ford's popular 9-inch rear end was in continuous production from the late 1950s to the late 1980s and is available in a wide range of widths. Here they are listed in order from narrowest to widest.

Donor Car	Width
1957–59 Ranchero/ station wagon	57-1/4 inch
1966–77 Bronco	58 inch
1977–81 Granada/Versailles	58-1/2 inch
1967–71 Mustang/Cougar/ Fairlane/Comet	59-1/4 inch
1971–73 Mustang family	61-1/4 inch
1957–72 Half-ton pickup	61-1/4 inch
1971–79 Ranchero/Torino	63 inch
1973–86 Pickup	65 inch
1973–86 Half-ton pickup	65-1/4 inch
1969–77 Galaxie/Lincoln	N/A. Very wide, will need to be narrowed.

The Ford 9-inch was available with a number of factory gear ratios, and the aftermarket produces an even wider variety. Differentials were available in standard, limited-slip, and Detroit Locker versions, and axles were available in two sizes: 28 and 31 splines. The 31-spline axles are much stronger, and should be used with manual transmissions or high-torque, high-power engines. These options, combined with aftermarket support, availability, and ease of maintenance, make the 9-inch Ford the hands-down favorite for hot rod rear ends.

Other Rear End Choices

Other popular solid rear axles include the Chevrolet 10- and 12-bolt rear ends. The 10- and 12-bolt nomenclature refers to the number of bolts that hold the rear access cover on the housing. The 12-bolt rear axle is the stronger and more expensive of the two. While this rear housing is generally not considered as good-looking as the Ford, a variety of custom rear covers are available that dress up these rear ends nicely. The major disadvantage to these GM rear ends is that they don't have a drop-out-style differential carrier, so changing gear ratios and repairing these rear ends is much more difficult.

Early Chevrolet, Pontiac, and Oldsmobile housings (and by early, we mean from the late 1950s to the mid-1960s) are also used under hot rods. We recommend staying away from these housings unless you are building a vintage, authentic early hot rod. While these units work fine, parts are not easy to find if you have problems on the road, and remember, these housing are now at least 40 years old! No small wonder the local parts house doesn't stock axle bearings.

Within this group of vintage housings, the Oldsmobile and Pontiac rear ends are very large and very strong units. The downside here is that parts are even more difficult to locate for these units than for the Chevrolet units of the same year. Again, if your vintage hot rod calls for an authentic mid-1950s rear axle, few things are more impressive than a chrome-plated 1957 Pontiac rear end. It's huge, but also has a very clean, smooth look.

We would be remiss if we didn't mention the early Ford rear that was used 1934–1948. While the rear is an attractive unit, and works well with flathead-powered cars, the rear gears and axles are not strong enough for late-model V-8 power. Everything from sheared axle keys to snapped axles and broken gear sets could be achieved with large tires and a modern V-8. For this reason, save that early Ford rear for a restorer or that flathead-powered roadster you plan on building someday.

Finally, we have the quick-change rear end. These axles look great, sound great (if you like a quick-change whine), and provide the added benefit of being able to change the final drive ratio by simply removing a rear cover, sliding off two gears, and switching them with a different gear set. These rear axles were originally

You don't have to keep that transverse leaf "buggy spring" setup in your old Ford; this 1946 Ford has a parallel leaf spring suspension. Note the aluminum lowering block between the spring and the rear end housing, and the bolt-on anti-sway bar.

designed for racing applications but rapidly became popular with hot rodders. Halibrand became famous for these rear axles with the finned aluminum center section for early Ford rear housings. Later Halibrand, Franklin, Frankland, Winters, CAE, and others would make their own center sections and axle housing for sprint cars and other race applications. They would find their way into hot rods too. In the 1940s and early 1950s, when hot rods were often used for both street and race duty, these rear axles allowed the owner to have a gear set for the track and another for the street.

Today the quick-change's main attractions are the great traditional looks and the "singing of a quickie rear" as the straight-cut final drive gears provide a high whine that is music to any real hot rodder's ears. It can safely be said that the Halibrand quick-change rear is the ultimate solid rear axle for hot rods.

Suspending the Solid Rear Axle

Much like the front suspension, a solid rear axle housing must be located and held in position under the chassis. This can be achieved with bars of different configurations. The rear axle must be located to prevent it from moving forward and backward under the chassis. It must also have a centering device that prevents the chassis from shifting over the rear wheel in a left to right direction.

Early Ford Suspension

Suspension for the solid rear axle is similar to the solid front axle. Under Ford hot rods the "buggy spring," a transverse-mounted leaf spring, was popular for years. This simple suspension arrangement employs a single spring mounted parallel to the axle housing. A pair of heavy U-bolts mounts the spring to a rear chassis cross-member, and hangers on the rear axle housing hold spring shackles that permit the spring to deflect when the rear wheels hit a bump. Originally, the rear axle was located fore and aft by a torque tube, which was an enclosed drive shaft that bolted solid to the rear end housing, and pivoted on an enclosed U-joint that attached to the back of the transmission. Wishbones ran from the ends of the rear-end housing to the front of the torque tube to strengthen the assembly and transmit axle torque to the torque tube. A shock absorber (either Houdaille type or tubular) was mounted on each end of the rear housing to complete the suspension.

Coil-over springs are another option, but they don't locate the axle like leaf springs do. Coil-overs require a four-bar setup with a Panhard bar (as shown here) or some sort of ladder bar system. This suspension is installed under a 1955 Chevy pickup (a top view was shown in chapter 4).

The "buggy spring" early Ford suspension only requires a fore-and-aft locating bar because the transverse spring prevents the chassis from moving in a left or right direction. The original locating device was a triangular tubular arrangement that bolted to the rear axle housing and then went toward the center of the frame X-member where a steel ball and socket provided a moveable joint, enabling the suspension to move up and down with the springs. These locators are often referred to as the rear wishbones, or radius rods.

The forward center pivot point on the early Ford rear housing is most often located on the "torque tube" a heavy-wall tube that connects the transmission to the rear axle assembly. This torque tube holds the drive shaft inside, which is known as a closed drive shaft. In most hot rod applications, an open drive shaft is utilized. When the closed drive shaft is eliminated, the "wishbone" must be split. The end ball is removed, and into each end of the two rods, a rod end is threaded into a thread insert that is welded inside the rod.

The wishbone, split or stock, locates the rear end and prevents forward and backward

movement of the housing. A more common method of locating the housing is with rear radius rods. These can be configured in several different fashions. The most simple is the four-bar arrangement, whereby two bars on each side of the housing maintain rear axle position. These bars have threaded inserts in each end of the rod. Rod ends with urethane bushings are utilized on each end of the rod. Brackets are fabricated (or purchased as a kit) and welded to the rear axle housing. Likewise, brackets are welded to the chassis for the front mounting points of these four bars. The four bars are then bolted to the axle housing and the chassis and adjusted to locate the rear axle perfectly square in the chassis. By using four bars the pinion angle can also be adjusted by threading the rod ends in or out on the top and bottom bars. By doing this the front of the rear axle can be rotated up or down to keep a proper drive shaft angle. This angle is typically 15 degrees or less.

Parallel Leaf Springs

In many early GM and Chrysler products, the rear suspension was via parallel leaf springs.

Just as the name implies, a pair of leaf springs is attached to the rear axle housing running parallel to the side rails of the chassis. A locating point (bracket) is found on the chassis in front of the axle housing, while behind the axle housing, on the other end of the spring, a shackle is mounted to the chassis. This shackle in turn connects to the spring and allows the spring to deflect upon impact with a bump on the road. Tubular shocks are generally mounted to the plate below the springs and to the rear chassis cross-member to dampen the spring action.

The spring is attached to the rear axle housing with two heavy U-bolts on each spring. The strong points of this system are good ride characteristics, simplicity, and very little maintenance. Since the two springs locate the rear housing under the center of the car, a Panhard bar is not needed. Also, the springs locate the rear axle fore and aft, eliminating the need for any radius rods, wishbones, or four-bar locators.

The height of this type rear suspension can be adjusted by placing a block between the housing and the springs or by de-arching the spring itself. Local spring shops can perform this de-arching or make custom springs for your application.

Some of the shortfalls of this system are that on many older chassis there is not sufficient room behind the rear axle to mount a parallel leaf spring. In some cases, the rear shackle is less than attractive if it is on the very end of the chassis and can be seen from the rear of the finished car. Generally speaking, parallel leaf springs work best with cars that were originally equipped with these springs and Fords 1935 and later.

Coil Springs

Coil springs have the advantage of providing soft and variable ride characteristics. They also require the most complete rear axle locating devices. Both four-bars and a Panhard rod are required since the chassis is resting on top of a coil spring that is not capable of maintaining vertical form when the weight shifts.

Coil springs are typically located on a rear bracket that incorporates a pocket to hold the spring. A corresponding pocket is formed on the chassis and the spring is located in the pocket. Tubular shocks are mounted on the rear axle up to the chassis to dampen the coil spring action. The shock absorbers should be mounted in approximately a 40-degree angle so that the

This is about as traditional as a hot rod rear suspension gets. A Halibrand quick-change rear is hung using Pete & Jake's ladder bars, a stock 1932 Ford transverse leaf spring, and tube shocks. The leaf spring locates the axle side-to-side, so no Panhard bar is required.

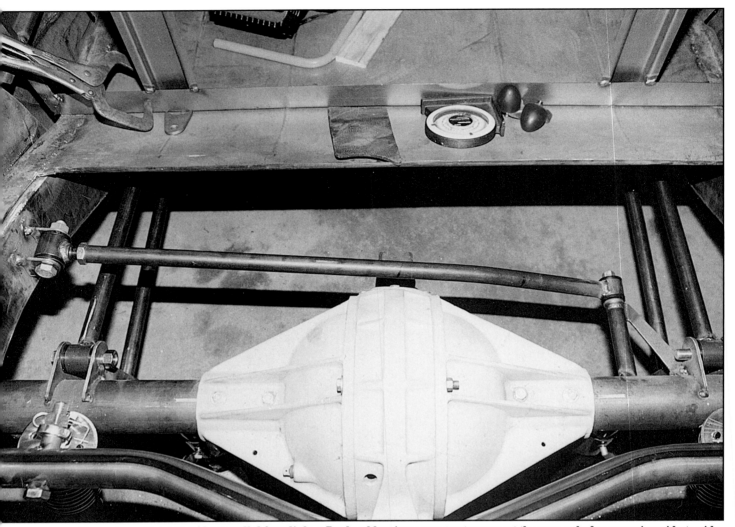

If you use coil-overs and a parallel four-link, a Panhard bar is necessary to prevent the rear axle from moving side to side. This one attaches to the frame at left with a urethane bushing, and to the rear end housing at right. The bar has a slight bend to clear the differential snout.

spring will move more than the shock absorber. If the shock absorber is mounted too vertically, the piston in the shock must move exactly the same amount as the spring, making for a too-stiff ride.

Four-bars are used to locate axle fore and aft, while a Panhard bar keeps the chassis centered over the rear axle. This Panhard rod has a rod end on each end of a heavy steel bar. One end attaches to the top of the rear axle housing and the other end attaches to the chassis. The threaded rod ends are adjusted to perfectly center the chassis over the rear axle housing. To prevent the Panhard rod from "jacking" the chassis in a hard turn, the bar should be made as long as possible. It is best to attach the Panhard rod near the backing plate on the rear axle housing and on the opposite outer frame rail.

Another way to locate the coil-sprung rear axle assembly is to triangulate the four-bars. In this system, the lower bar on each side of the

rear axle housing remains parallel to the frame rails. The upper bars are angled inward toward the center of the chassis and attach to a chassis cross-member. The two upper bars are on a sufficient enough angle to prevent the chassis from moving side to side on the coil springs. Once again threaded rod ends provide the adjustment to perfectly center the chassis over the rear axle housing and to rotate the rear axle housing up or down for the proper pinion angle.

Despite requiring fabricated spring pockets, coil springs provide a very good suspension system. Ride height can be adjusted by having custom coil springs fabricated. The ride height is initially determined by the distance between the rear axle housing and the upper spring pocket. Be certain the upper spring pocket is high in the chassis (this may require floor modifications) so that a spring of ample height will fit in between the two pockets.

Coil-over Shocks

The coil-over shock is the single most popular rear suspension system found under hot rods today. It is a complete suspension system contained in one unit. The shock absorber resides inside the spring, which is on an adjustable lower spring mount.

The coil-over is mounted like a very heavy-duty shock absorber. One mount is on the chassis cross-member, while the other is located on the outer end of each side of the rear axle housing. The brackets must be substantial since the entire weight of the rear of the car is being held up on these brackets. Likewise, the hardware that holds these coil-over shocks must be of very high quality. We recommend grade-eight bolts or better on these suspension attaching points, and the coil-over bolts should be a minimum of 5/8-inch diameter.

With coil-overs, the rear axle must be located fore and aft and side to side, either with parallel four-bars and a Panhard rod, or with a triangulated four-bar setup.

Coil-over shocks are very versatile. The spring rates can easily be changed to accommodate the desired ride quality. The ride height can be adjusted by simply moving the upper and lower attaching points. Add in the good looks of the units, and there is no small wonder that this suspension system is so popular.

Today many kits are available for all popular applications and the coil-over shocks are available painted, chrome-plated, or fabricated from aluminum. All of the units are neat, compact, and highly functional. It is easy to understand why the coil-over shock is king of the hot rod suspensions.

Solid Rear Axles in Review

The solid rear axle is the favorite of hot rodders. It is strong, simple, and easy to mount in an early chassis. The simple good looks are an added attraction. Today, rear suspension kits are available for most popular applications, including four-bars, Panhard rods, rear disc brake kits, and complete rear axle housings. A hot rodder can order an 8-3/4- or 9-inch Ford rear in virtually any wheel-to-wheel measurement required. Complete new housings are available too.

Brand-new quick-change rear axle assemblies are also available. Mounting a solid axle under your hot rod project is a good idea, one than many rodders before you have accomplished and tested for hundreds of thousands of miles. Now let's take a look at the more complex independent rear suspension.

Independent Rear Suspension

The independent rear suspension never caught on in street rod circles. Maybe it's because the cars are not designed or built for high-performance handling. What with the traditional "big and little" tire arrangement, it would be difficult indeed to build a car that truly handled well in curves.

Ride characteristics have always been the priority in a street rod and finding a suspension that provides a pleasant street ride is job one. The independent rear suspension does not necessarily provide a more comfortable ride; it simply provides a superior suspension system. Let's look at the basics of independent rear suspension.

Independent rear suspension permits each wheel to move up and down independent of all other wheels on the car, just as the name implies. The center section of an independent rear is fixed to the chassis in solid mounts. These mounts generally contain either rubber or urethane bushings to prevent transfer of noise and vibration into the chassis proper. On each side of the center section is a pair of swing axles with a universal or CV joint on each end of the unit. These swing axles on Corvette and early Jaguar XKE independent rear suspensions look like very short drive shafts, and in reality that is exactly what they are.

Each wheel is located front to back by a carrier and trailing arm that attaches to the front of the rear tires on the chassis. Since the center section is mounted in a solid fashion to the chassis, the chassis is always centered over the rear wheels, but the body and chassis can still roll left and right in extreme cornering situations. Anti-sway bars generally attach to the trailing arms on the suspension and two points on the chassis, to prevent excessive body roll. Rubber or urethane bushings are used on the anti-sway bars to permit free movement and to prevent the transfer of vibration to the chassis. Each wheel is sprung independently on these rear axles.

Jaguar XKE Independent Rear Suspension

The Jaguar XKE has long been a hot rodder's favorite. The fact that the wheels are the same 4-3/4-inch bolt circle as the ever-popular Chevrolet wheel was but one of the contributing factors. The rear assemblies are also narrow enough to fit under hot rods from T-buckets, or the wider Jaguar sedan units work well under late-1940s hot rods.

Once the suspension is removed from the factory "cage" that mounts it in a Jaguar, the center section with its inboard brakes and dual coil-over shocks is one of the better looking suspension systems ever made. Each wheel has two coil-over shocks and a single drive shaft. The outboard hub carriers are aluminum. When all of these components have been plated, polished, and powder-coated, the results are brilliant. Few things will mesmerize a hot rodder like following another hot rod with a fully plated and polished Jag rear. All those parts spinning and all that chrome is a sight to behold.

Springing and associated ride quality is handled by changing the spring rates on each coil-over shock. Generally, the XKE springs are lighter and better suited for hot rods than the heavier-sprung XJ sedans.

The inboard disc brakes on a stock Jag rear are more than adequate for the average street

On the other end of the spectrum we have this Corvette-based independent rear suspension, as built by Boyd Coddington. The center section is bolted rigid to the frame, and the suspension uprights are located by coil-overs, unequal-length longitudinal links, and a pair of transverse links. Note that the bottom of the frame rails are "C"ed to clear the half-shafts.

rod. A simple rebuild is all that should be needed for years of service. Remember to use a master cylinder that is compatible with a four-wheel disc brake arrangement.

In the seventies the Jaguar rear suspension was considered downright exotic and expensive. Today the units are more affordable than ever, but the cost to rebuild and install the unit is still much higher than a solid rear axle. Add in over a thousand dollars for chrome and polishing, and it is very easy to have several thousand dollars tied up in a Jag rear. Only the owner can decide if this expenditure is worth it. Having ridden in many cars with Jaguar suspension, we can say the handling is improved, but the ride characteristics are seldom any better than a well-engineered solid rear.

Corvette Independent Rear Suspension

The second most popular independent rear suspension for   hot rodder's is the Chevrolet Corvette suspension. Once again, the center section is mounted solid to the chassis and two independent swing axles power the rear wheels. The Corvette rear has conventional outboard mounted disc brakes (very early independents like the 1963 units were also available with drum brakes; we, however, recommend using the disc brake arrangement).

Unlike the Jaguar, suspension is provided by a transverse spring mounted behind the rear axle. The spring is center-clamped, which actually converts the single spring into a pair of quarter-elliptic springs. The early Corvettes used conventional steel springs while the later Corvettes of the 1990s used fiberglass springs.

Mounting the Corvette rear is a fabricating exercise much like the Jaguar. Once again, a pair of trailing arms must be fabricated, or the original units modified to locate the wheels and prevent them from fore-and-aft movement. Anti-sway bars limit body roll, and springing can be changed by having a custom spring built. Once again, most factory Corvette rear springs will be on the stiff side for early hot rods, but should be about right for cars 1937 and later.

The later Corvettes use an aluminum girder to locate the rear and the out shafts. Almost everything is aluminum, making for very low unsprung weight. It also provides the hot rodder with the chance to have all these components polished. The rear girder in brushed or polished finish provides a very nice structural look to any hot rod chassis.

Once again, the cost is higher than conventional straight-axle arrangements, but the handling and braking are superior. The Corvette rears look good under a hot rod, but don't quite have the exotic look of the Jaguar.

Mustang Independent Rear Suspension

The new Mustang Cobra has a fully independent rear suspension. To date, this rear assembly has not found its way under hot rods. It will no doubt happen as these parts become available in used form. Once again the big advantages are superior handling, bigger brakes, and lighter unsprung weight—all with a popular Ford bolt pattern.

Aftermarket Independent Rear Suspension

Kugel Components and Heidts both offer aftermarket rear suspensions for hot rods. These rear units come complete with a cross-member kit to fit most popular hot rod chassis. Once again cost is more than solid rear axles, but the cosmetics and improved handling can justify the cost.

Both of these units are extremely good-looking and since they come in kit form, installation is relatively simple for the home builder.

Independent Quick-Change Rear Suspension

Yes, you can have the best of both worlds, the advantage of changing final gear ratios in minutes, and the good looks and sounds of a quick-change rear. Add the great handling of an independent suspension and you have an independent rear suspension (IRS) that is second to none.

Installation kits are limited and fabricating your own suspension components may limit this application to skilled fabricators, but when installed it is a great system.

Independent Rear Suspension Overview

Generally speaking, if you were building your first hot rod, we would recommend staying with the more simple installation of a solid rear axle. If, however, you are certain that your project

Don't forget to install rubber snubbers between the frame and the rear end—most hot rods are on the low side of a practical ride height, and it could prevent a nasty shock next time you hit a pothole. This installation also has a flat pad welded to the top of the housing.

needs an independent rear suspension, be prepared to spend both more time and more money.

Today there are many kits available for the installation of an independent rear suspension. For all but the very skilled rod builder, we would strongly recommend purchasing one of these kits. In the end, the time and effort saved will make the money well spent. Try to talk to other rodders who have installed one of these kits prior to purchasing any pieces. Bear in mind that even after purchasing a kit you will often have to locate used suspension parts to complete the package.

When choosing an independent rear examine all pieces very carefully, and it may pay to Magnaflux the trailing arms to be certain there are no cracks in the metal. This is particularly important on aluminum parts. Remember, you don't know where these parts have been or how they have been treated. Often, used Corvette parts were involved in wrecks or used on racecars. Either case would warrant a complete check of the metal prior to installation. It might also be worthy of note that it is often not wise to believe everything you are told about parts purchased at swap meets. It is definitely a time for the buyer to beware.

Having said all that, there are few things that will make your chassis look and handle like a new car more than a fully independent suspension system.

IN THE SHOP:

INSTALLING AN AFTERMARKET INDEPENDENT FRONT SUSPENSION

Independent suspension used to be a rarity under early street rods; a few enterprising rodders as far back as the late 1940s had independent setups under their lakes roadsters (if we remember correctly, A. K. Miller had one of the better-known independent Hi-boys). Then, in the late 1960s and 1970s a few Corvair and Jag front ends began showing up. In the 1980s, however, rodders discov-

ered the Pinto/Mustang II suspension, and several manufacturers began making clean kits to adapt this suspension to all kinds of street rods.

But, the stock Mustang II A-arms and stuff weren't the prettiest thing when installed on a hi-boy. Now, manufacturers like Heidt's Hot Rod Shop, Kugel's, and others are building their own independent suspensions that are

1

The cross-member was still 2 inches wider than the frame, so Tom cut some pieces of 1/8-inch plate to fill the gap and connect the frame to the cross-member. Make certain you weld the outside edge of the frame to the cross-member before welding these filler pieces in.

2

The finished cross-member looks like this when installed. The job so far was easy, and it would be even simpler on a stock or stock-style repro frame.

good-looking enough to slip under any car, regardless of the suspension exposure.

We recently followed the installation of a Heidt's Superide, a complete suspension kit that includes a cross-member, spindles, tubular A-arms, Aldan coil-over shocks, a new (not rebuilt) TRW rack-and-pinion, 11-inch vented rotors (Ford or Chevy bolt pattern), bearings, polished aluminum brake calipers, and instructions and stainless hardware. It's so complete, and so well done, that if this had been a regular stock Deuce or exact repro frame, this would have been the shortest suspension how-to ever. All you do is locate your axle centerline, line up the cross-member, weld it in, and bolt on the suspension stuff. If this kit arrived in your mailbox at noon, you could be rolling out the driveway by suppertime.

But this wasn't a standard Deuce frame, and that made the installation a little more interesting. The frame consists of a pair of Just-A-Hobby rails with tubular cross-members. The rails have been pie-cut at the firewall, pinched 5 inches in the front (so the rails will end behind the grille shell), and bobbed and "C"ed at the rear. When done, it'll roll around underneath a fiberglass Vicky phaeton body, sans fenders.

However, the Superide cross-member was built with a stock-specification Deuce frame in mind. The builders thought about narrowing the cross-member and rack the full 5 inches, but that would've been too much. So, they settled on narrowing it 3 inches and making up the difference between the cross-member and frame. (Heidt's now has a cross-member for pinched-frame Deuces. However, the cross-member and rack won't be narrowed—the area between the current cross-member and the frame is simply "filled in.")

Narrowing the cross-member was no big trick. We simply put it in a power hacksaw and made a couple of clean, square cuts 3 inches apart. After beveling the cut edges to ensure good weld penetration, the two cross-member halves were clamped together with a couple pieces of straight rectangular tubing and heli-arced back together. We then located the axle centerline on the frame, and using the diagrams supplied with the instructions, lined the cross-member up on the frame and tacked it in place.

Here's where the frame modifications made this installation a little different. Because the frame was pie-cut at the firewall, the rails were "kicked up" in the front. This would result in too much positive caster if the cross-member was simply welded flat to the frame. To remedy this, we tipped the cross-member down in front

3 Here's where it gets tricky. The rack also has to be shortened 3 inches to fit the narrowed cross-member and keep the geometry correct. Luckily, this K-car rack is probably easier to narrow than some other designs.

4 Start by disassembling the unit. That's the rack in the middle, and Tom is marking the steel housing tube for the 3-inch cut.

about 1 degree, then welded it solid to the frame. The end result is that the suspension will have about 1 degree of positive camber built in, as Heidt's intended.

OK, the frame's been narrowed 5 inches, and the cross-member 3 inches. That leaves a 1-inch gap between the frame and cross-member on each side. To remedy this, the top of the cross-member was welded to the outside edge of the bottom of each frame rail, then pieces of 1/8-inch plate were cut to fill the gaps between the frame and cross-member. A little grinding and some bodywork, and the thing will look like it grew there.

The next, and probably toughest, step was to narrow the rack-and-pinion, which is a new TRW rack for a Chrysler K-car. The unit consists of an aluminum pinion housing with a steel tube pressed in to house the rack. A nylon bushing on each end supports the rack in the tube.

We started this phase of the job by completely disassembling the rack-and-pinion (one note: all the fasteners are metric on this thing). We then cut 3 inches out of the middle of the housing with a hacksaw, using a stainless hose clamp to guide the blade and ensure a nice straight cut. A good tubing cutter would also do the job well. We then clamped the two halves into a piece of angle iron and tacked them back together with a TIG welder. Work around the tube in short beads to keep it from warping—if this thing isn't perfectly straight, the nylon bushings will wear out prematurely. Also, try to get the weld right in the middle of the housing. This keeps the heat away from the aluminum housing and the nylon bushing when you're welding.

With the housing narrowed, it was time to shorten the rack itself, a job that had to be farmed out to our friendly neighborhood machine shop. The rack consists of a steel shaft with teeth that engage the pinion; each end has a threaded hole that accepts a ball joint/tie-rod end assembly. We removed these tie-rod ends, and the machinist chucked the rack up in a lathe, cut 3 inches off, then center-bored and tapped a

5

Clamp the two housing pieces together in a piece of angle iron to keep them straight, then tack-weld them together in several locations. Work around the tube in short beads to prevent warping—this tube has to stay straight! By keeping the weld in the middle of the tube, you avoid damaging the nylon bushing and the aluminum housing.

new hole in the end. Note: The rack takes a somewhat uncommon metric thread—14-1.5. Before you go to the machine shop, check to see if they have a tap this size, because you might have to go out and buy one like we did. Ours cost about $15. One nice thing about doing it this way is that the shortened rack is just as strong as it was before.

We then cleaned all the shavings and chips from the tube and rack and reassembled the rack-and-pinion using plenty of fresh grease. (Use Loctite when reinstalling the tie-rod ends to the rack.) At this point, it was time to install the rack and put together the rest of the suspension as per the instructions. (All of the hardware is stainless steel, so make sure you use an antisieze compound when assembling them. Failure to do so could result in galling and frozen nuts—an annoying and expensive problem that, contrary to the way it sounds, is not peculiar to Minnesota.)

Here's where two things really impressed us about the Superide kit: First, the instructions are very good, clearly illustrated, and easily understood. Second, everything fits together easily, with no "persuasion" necessary. It's obvious that this is a very well-engineered, high-quality kit. Even with the modifications we did, the installation took just one working day. A regular installation on a stock-spec Deuce frame should be considerably faster.

6

Clean and reassemble the rack-and-pinion, and bolt the rest of the suspension to the cross-member according to the instructions. It won't be long now and you'll be rolling!

IN THE SHOP:

SWAPPING POWER STEERING

I wanted to add power steering to my 1955 Pontiac project. (If I'd had the good sense to own a Chevy or a Ford, I could've bought the necessary adaptors from any number of manufacturers, but nothing exists for the Pontiac.) To start the job, I bought a salvage-yard Saginaw 605 power steering box and steering arm.

Granted, not everyone will be able to follow these instructions exactly (there aren't that many 1955 Pontiac guys out there), but the information presented shows the thought processes and techniques involved in swapping a steering box into any kind of "Brand X" car.

The first step of the operation was to remove the stock box. First we cut through the steering column mast and shaft (Portaband or Sawzall will make quick work of this).

The next chore was removing the pitman arm from the connector link. This link is of tubular design, and to free the pitman arm from the link you must first remove the cotter pin from the driver-side end. Then, using a very large screwdriver blade socket, remove the end plug (left is loose, right is tight). A squirt of good penetrating oil will help here, and the use of an air impact wrench will really

1

The stock box worked OK, but is 40 years old, and we wanted power steering—time for this unit to leave.

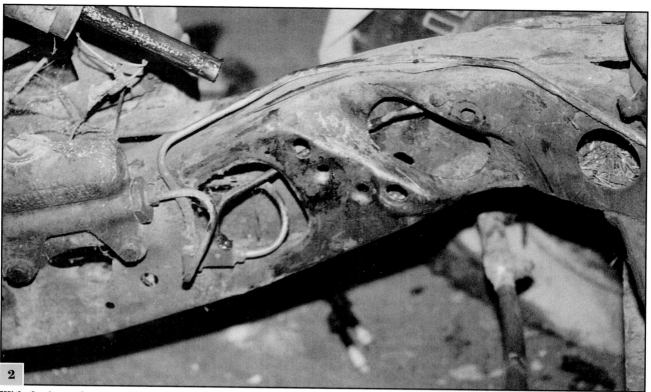

2

With the inner frame guides removed, we are ready to mount the 605 (see text). The two middle holes are from the rivets; the other three are stock box mounting holes.

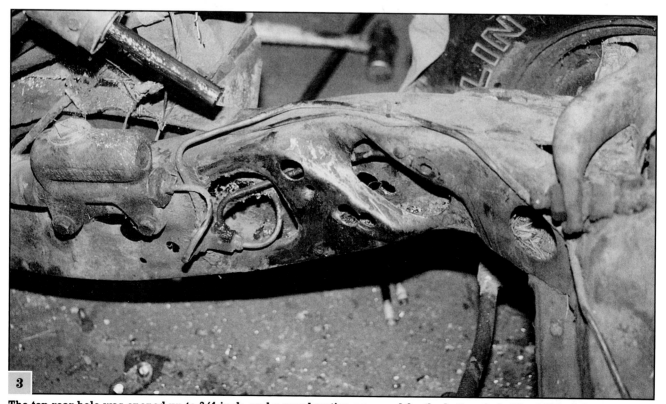

3

The top rear hole was opened up to 3/4 inch, and a new location was used for the bottom hole. The 3/4-inch hole permits heavy-wall tubing sleeves to be inserted into the frame.

4

This is the outside of the frame rail: 3/4-inch holes ready for sleeves. Stock brake lines must be moved; we will replace these later anyway.

5

Two sleeves formed from heavy-wall tubing slide into the frame rail. A large washer will cover the rivet holes and be welded in place.

make it move. After the plug comes out, a pair of springs will follow. Another squirt or two of penetrating oil, firmly tap the cross-link with a hammer and the pitman arm socket should loosen. The pitman arm has a ball on the end of it that goes into a receiver in the link. You may have to smack the pitman arm a couple times to free things up. The link will lift off—be careful to keep the sheet metal shield and springs with the pitman arm. Now remove the three bolts that hold the steering box to the chassis (located on the outside of the frame rail).

With the stock steering box removed, take it to the workbench and remove the pitman arm nut. Use a puller to remove the pitman arm.

Do the same with the new 605 power steering box. You will note that the pitman arm nut is metric; a good quality adjustable wrench might do the job; otherwise you'll have to break down and buy the big metric wrenches.

Now for the good news: The stock 1955 Pontiac pitman arm spline is the same as the 605 box, so just center the steering box (lock to lock) and install the old arm on the new box.

Carry this combo back to the car and hold everything in position. More good news: Two out of three of the box holes (the top ones) line up. However, after a little checking we decided that the angle of the box was off just a little. We opted to use the top forward stock hole. A single bolt was tightened into the steering box to hold it in place, and we marked the location of the other two holes through the steering box flange.

The stock bolts pass through the frame rail sides and have a brace/guide in between the side walls of the frame to add strength and prevent collapse of the side rails. These guides are held in by two rivets and must be removed to permit drilling of the new holes. A hammer and chisel were used to remove the heads of the rivets, then the braces were removed.

We drilled two holes approximately 3/4 inch in diameter. Two pieces of heavy wall tubing were cut to size and slid into the holes to act as sleeves for the mounting bolts. Since we had to drill in the area (as a matter of fact, partially into) of the stock mounting holes, we fabricated a couple of large washers to cover all the holes (both sides) and get us up onto the frame for good welding.

We tacked the sleeves in place, mounted the box, measured, thought, discussed, and decided it was in position.

The box was removed and final welding was completed. Be certain the frame is very clean prior to welding, and as always, if you are not an excellent welder, have a pro do it for you—suspension and steering are no place to learn how to weld!

We would have used the stock steering box bolts but they were about 1/4 inch too short, so three new grade-five bolts were used to hold the box in place.

We had decided to use the stock steering column, so the next step was joining the column to the new box. The shaft of the column was very close to lining up. The steering column would have to move about 1/4 inch to the center of the car.

On the inside, the cover plate around the steering column was removed (about eight sheet metal screws). This permitted the column to move to the right. Next a stock "rag joint" was slipped onto the Saginaw 605 box. The tubing on the rag joint proved to be the proper diameter for the steering shaft from the stock column. The steering shaft and steering wheel had been slid up into the car at this point. We pushed the shaft down into the tubing, took a measurement (in our case 2-1/2 inches, but it will vary with each cut), and cut the shaft so that it bottomed out in the rag joint tubing, and the steering wheel fit the column properly on the inside. Once again the steering wheel and shaft were slid back out.

The end of the steering column was ground straight and smooth. Then a bushing was made to support the steering shaft. This bushing was tapped up into the end of the steering column jacket. Two 1/2-inch holes were drilled in the jacket and a "plug weld" performed to locate the bushing.

The shaft was slid down into the rag joint for the final time. One last check of everything—it looked good. The rag joint tubing was welded to the main steering shaft. Then two 3/8-inch holes were drilled into the side of the rag joint tubing, and into the steering shaft approximately 1/8 inch. These holes were also "plug-welded." In effect, an insurance pin is formed with these

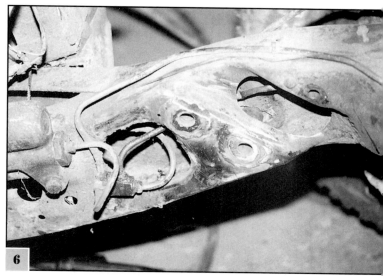

6 The sleeve-washer assemblies are welded in place; this shows the inner frame rail finished. The outer frame rail should be done in the same way.

7 The new 605 box fits in and looks factory. Stock hoses will connect to a GM power steering pump later. A late-model factory rag joint provided the proper size tubing for the steering shaft. No universals were required in the installation. Alignment was simple.

welds. This is a must. Remember, welding should be professional quality, and all parts new. This is steering we're working on folks, something you have a tough time enjoying a hot rod without!

There you have it, power steering that looks factory, uses stock parts, and leaves the geometry unchanged.

IN THE SHOP:

NEW REAR SPRINGS FOR FAT FORDS

OK, you've got the Mustang II front end installed, and the engine and tranny mounts are ready to accept your engine on that 1946 Ford frame. Out back, though, you're not sure what to do. The stock transverse leaf simply won't do the job. Coil-overs are cool, but you'll have to fabricate crossmembers, four-links, mounts on the rear end, and a Panhard bar. An independent is probably out of your budget, and is also a chore to install. That leaves parallel leaf springs, a simple, inexpensive route that works great for street rods.

Now there are two routes you can take: buy a kit or perform a do-it-yourself junkyard swap. The junkyard route means you'll have to fabricate front spring mounts and rear shackle mounts, as well as shock mounts. You'll also have to find springs that are the right capacity and size for your car.

1 This installation was done with the frame upside-down, but the kit can also be installed with the body still on the car. Start the job by marking and drilling the first mounting holes for the rear shackle brackets on the frame—the excellent instructions include drawings with measurements and explanations.

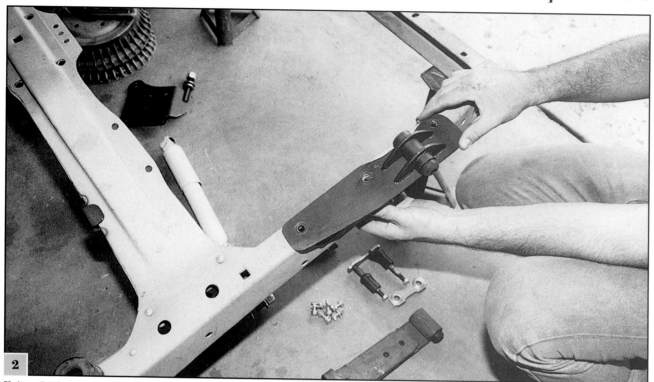

2 Using the hole you just drilled, mount the shackle bracket and use it as a template to mark and drill the other two holes. Install the supplied bolts, and these mounts are done.

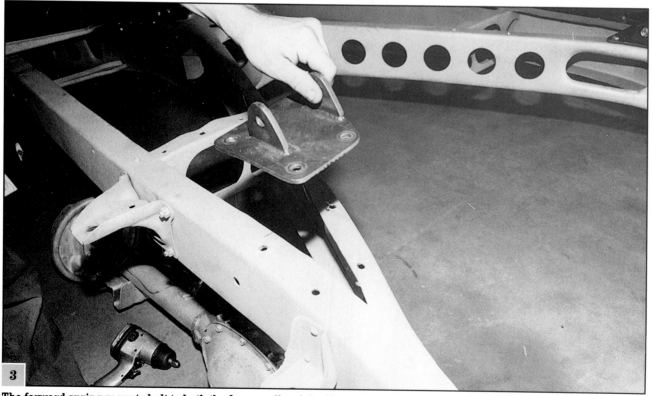

3 The forward spring mounts bolt to both the frame rail and the X-member. Follow the instructions to find the mounting location; then follow the same procedure you used for the shackle mounts.

4

You can now install the springs. It's easiest if you turn the frame right-side up; then bolt the spring to the forward bracket.

The kit approach takes care of all that, and is relatively inexpensive. For instance, this kit from Chassis Engineering includes front and rear spring brackets, shock brackets and mounting studs, regular shocks (gas shocks are an option), a pair of C. E.'s own leaf springs (designed and built specifically for this application), shackles, and all the hardware you'll need to install everything. The instructions are good, the kit is simple to install, and it works great.

Start with a straight, square frame, and remove the stock rear end, shocks, and suspension. If you can, it's easiest to turn the frame upside down to install the C. E. kit. However, if you're not going to remove the body from the frame, you can do the job from underneath. Just make sure it's securely supported on a stout set of jackstands.

In addition to the kit, you'll need a rear end from one of the following cars: 1968–1975 Nova, 1967–1969 Camaro/Firebird, 1957–1959 Ford 9-inch, or any Monarch/Granada. The GM rear ends work best in this application, being about 60 inches wide (measured from wheel mounting surfaces). The Ford rear ends are narrower and will require large tires to fill the wheel opening and offset rims to clear the frame.

This installation used a Nova rear end with the stock Nova spring perches and rubber cushions.

The new spring mounts are located using the mounting holes for the stock friction shocks; these holes are easy to spot because they're square. Take the rear spring mount first, and line up the front hole with the back shock mount hole. Install a single bolt, then clamp the mount in place and use the new mount as a guide to drill the remaining holes in the frame. Install the supplied bolts and nuts, and this end is finished.

Next, hook a tape measure in the forward shock mounting hole and make a mark on the frame 37-5/8 inches ahead of it. Go in 1 inch from the outside of the frame and make another mark. This is the location of the outside front mounting hole for the front spring bracket. Drill a hole and use a single bolt to attach the bracket. Again, clamp it in place and use the bracket as a guide to drill the remaining holes. (The instructions also include a diagram showing how to locate the brackets.) Put in the other three bolts, and repeat these steps with the brackets on the other side of the frame.

If you're working with a bare frame, turn it right-side up and bolt the front end of the springs to the front brackets. Chassis Engineering recommends that you now slip the rear end on to the springs; then install the shackles at the rear of the springs. (We installed the springs first, then slipped the rear end in between the frame and springs. It would've been easier to follow the instructions!)

With the springs attached to the frame and the rear end in place, install the U-bolts over the rear end and the shock mount plates on the bottom of the rear end; then bolt it all together. The shock plates can be switched side to side and installed two ways, with the bend up for normal ride height, or with the bend down for lowered cars. Install the plates with the shock mount tabs at the rear and pointed to the middle of the car.

The upper shock mounts can be either welded or bolted to the front side of the rear crossmember. They attach to the frame 9-1/2 inches in from the inside of the frame rails. Note that they have two holes each, so you can adjust the shocks for height.

With the shock mounts in, install the shocks and stand back to admire your work. Once the car's on the road, remember that the springs will settle about an inch after 500 miles or so. At that time, you'll want to check to make sure you still have enough shock travel and adjust the shock mounts accordingly.

5

This installation uses a Nova rear end with the stock spring mounting pads and rubber cushions (it's a good idea to get new cushions from your Chevy dealer—the old ones are usually shot). Install the U-bolts and the shock mount plate under the rear end. Note that the shock mount tab is inside and to the rear of the car.

6

You can now install the shocks, using the shock studs and bolts supplied with the kit. Normal shocks are standard with the kit, and gas shocks are available for a slight additional cost.

IN THE SHOP:

CHOOSING THE RIGHT WHEELS

1

Traditional hot rods do well with plain steelies, hubcaps, and beauty rings. These hubcaps are reproductions of the classic single-bar flipper caps popular in the early 1950s.

There can be no single piece any more important in the construction of a quality hot rod than the wheel. Let's face it, hot rods that don't roll just aren't much fun! Combine that with the styling impact of wheels, and you have a very important piece of the puzzle when building any hot rod.

From the early days of the automobile, changing wheels for special applications was common. Upgrading from the wood-spoke wheel, to the wire wheel, to the solid steel wheel was a natural transition for hot rodders in the 1920s and 1930s (although the term *hot rod* had not yet been coined).

Today, the hot rodder's choice of wheels is mind-boggling. From megabuck billet wheels to the common steel wheel and hubcap, the choices seem endless. As in all other decisions in hot rod building, the trick is to find a wheel that will continue the overall theme of the car. A very traditional hot rod might be best served with steel wheels and hubcaps, particularly if whitewalls are a part of the plan.

On the other hand, if that super smooth hot rod is pure contemporary design, the new billet wheels in 16, 17, or 18 inches might be in order. Actually, we are now seeing rims as large as 20 inches on the rear of some modern hot rods.

Selecting the wheels is a personal thing, but here are some things to keep in mind. Center the wheels in their openings. Nothing looks worse on a car than wheels that are not centered in the fender opening. Bear in mind that when you change the size of the wheels and tires, the visual effect can actually make the wheel appear to be off center of the fender opening. It is best to fit the finished wheels and tires early in a project, and then roll the car outside where it can be viewed from a reasonable distance. More than one hot rodder has built a car in the winter, inside a small one-car garage, only to find that the wheels are not centered in the visual center of the fender openings. All the measurements in the world will not compensate for finding the proper visual center of a decreasing radius fender opening.

New wheels and new sizes bring along new tires. Since most hot rods are based on a 1948

2

For a traditional look that's also competition oriented, it's tough to beat Moon discs. This modern variation from Mooneyes USA has a peaked center—looks good on hot rod or customs.

3

If it's a 1960s look you want, Radir is now reproducing some of its classic five-spoke mag wheels from the Beach Boys decade.

4

Tire makers are getting into the nostalgia act, too. Mickey Thompson is repopping the classic Cheater Slick in regular and wide-white variations. Pop a pair of these on a pair of chrome reverse steelies, and you're set to go to the drags.

5

Our personal favorite is the timeless American Racing Torq-Thrust. The originals had straight spokes and came in either aluminum or magnesium. Today, American still makes the D-spoke Torq-Thrust (a cast, one-piece wheel with slightly curved spokes) and the new fully polished Torq-Thrust II, a two-piece wheel.

or earlier body, we feel that most hot rods look best with tires that have a reasonable amount of sidewall. For the most part, 40- and 45-series tires tend to have a very small sidewall. This small sidewall (often referred to as "V-belts" or rubber band tires) tends to make the wheel look overly large and also provides a very stiff ride. Most hot rods tend to look best with a 55 or larger sidewall.

Beyond these few tips, we simply recommend that you take your time and check all the different wheels available. Carefully measure the required back spacing on the wheel (the

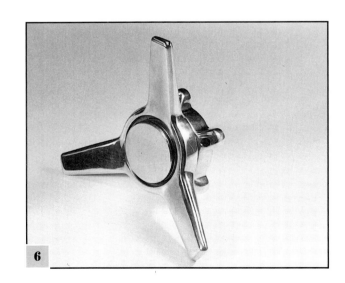

6

RIGHT
The finishing touch for a set of five-spokes is an aluminum knock-off, like this one from Sun Specs. Gives a nice, racy 1960s feel to the car.

7

For a modern look, it's tough to beat a large-diameter billet wheel in a classic 5-spoke pattern. Just remember that it is possible to have wheels that are too large in diameter...they still have to be in proportion with the car. And finally, 5 spokes is the correct number. No less, no more.

measurement from the inside of the rim to the face of the mounting flange) to correctly center the wheel in the wheelwell. Avoid bolt-on wheel adapters at all costs. It is always better to have the wheel manufacturer provide you with wheels with the proper bolt pattern and offset.

Accessories such as decorative "knock- offs," beauty bands, hubcaps, and engraved centers are great ways to further personalize your car. Today, knock-offs are for the most part decorative items that bolt on and cover the lug nuts, with the "knock-off" spinner holding on a custom cover that covers the lug nuts to provide the illusion of a true knock-off wheel. Should true knock-off wheels be used on the street, bear in

mind that the spinners need to be tightened periodically. We would recommend conventional lug nuts for street rods whenever possible.

Pick your wheels and tires wisely and you will have four pieces that enhance the look and handling of your car, and make a styling statement all at once. The wheel and tire combination is such a strong styling portion of the car that many hot rodders will have two or more combinations for the same car. For example, a set of Halibrands and black walls for that hot rod look, or a set of wide whites on red steel wheels for that traditional look. A simple wheel and tire swap changes the very essence of the car. Wheels and tires—choose them with care.

Chapter 6

Hot Rod Brakes

FRONT BRAKES **199**

REAR BRAKES **203**

MASTER CYLINDER **204**

POWER BOOSTERS **204**

RESIDUAL PRESSURE VALVES **205**

PROPORTIONING VALVES **206**

HOLD OFF/METERING VALVES **206**

COMBINATION VALVES **206**

EMERGENCY BRAKES **206**

ANTI-LOCK BRAKES **206**

PLUMBING **207**

BRAKE FLUID **208**

GETTING IT TO WORK TOGETHER **208**

IN THE SHOP:

INSTALLING BIG BRAKES ON A MUSTANG II FRONT END **209**

PLUMBING A HOT ROD CHASSIS **212**

Once you get your hot rod to go, you face an even more important problem—getting it to stop. Early hot rodders were quick to realize this, and one of the most common modifications was installing 1940 to 1948 Ford hydraulic brakes to replace the mechanically actuated brakes that were stock on Fords from 1928 to 1939. For nostalgia rods, this is still a viable conversion, and the kit to do it is still available from Speedway Motors and other sources.

But most of us want better braking than 1940 Ford brakes can provide, and today we have a lot of options, from Bendix-style self-energizing drums to NASCAR-style four-wheel discs. It's easiest to learn about brakes by discussing the individual components and what they do.

FRONT BRAKES
Drums
We'll start by discussing those classic 1940 to 1948 Ford juice brakes that were the foundation of hot rod stopping power back in the day. Compared to the mechanical brakes that they replaced, these brakes were pretty good, but there were better alternatives even back then. For starters, the Ford brakes have a fixed-shoe design, and the only thing that applies the shoes to the drums is the hydraulic pressure and your foot. Further, these brakes aren't self-adjusting. They have to be manually adjusted at regular intervals; this is done by turning a pair of large bolts attached to eccentrics on the backing plate. As the eccentric rotates, it rides against the bottom edges of the shoes and pushes them out toward the drum. These brakes are probably still OK for vintage stockers, and perhaps for traditional pre-1935 Ford hot rods, where discs wouldn't be appropriate to the look. But like any drum brake, they don't dissipate heat well and tend to fade under hard braking. You also have to learn how to adjust them properly (old Ford service manuals will be the best source for this information) and maintain them religiously.

The next step up is the Bendix-designed self-energizing brake, the kind of drum brake that most of us are familiar with. In this design, the bottoms of the brake shoes are not fixed to the brake drums. Instead, they are attached to and work against each other via linkage and springs. The advantage to this arrangement is that as the bottom of the primary shoe contacts the drum, it presses against the secondary shoe. This increased mechanical advantage makes these brakes much more efficient. While Ford cars didn't get Bendix drums until the 1950s, they did show up on Lincolns in 1939, and on Ford F-1 trucks in 1948. Both of these brakes are easy swaps onto early Ford spindles, and give good stopping performance for traditional hot rods.

The Bendix brake design is still in widespread use for the rear brakes of many cars today. There are also conversion kits and modified spindles available that allow Ford Econoline van brakes,

1949–1954 Chevy brakes, and some Chevy van brakes to be used with early Ford suspensions.

We'd be remiss if we didn't mention a classic early-Ford brake upgrade, the finned Buick brake drums. These drums were available on late-1950s and early-1960s Buicks, and consisted of an iron hub riveted to an aluminum drum that had a cast-iron lining. The aluminum drums are finned; both the material and the design help these drums dissipate heat much better than standard cast-iron drums. They also look great in the process, and it just so happens that these 12-inch-diameter drums are easily adapted to the 12-inch 1940–1948 Ford brakes.

The ultimate hot rod brake is probably the ultra-rare Kinmont disc. Designed in the 1940s and used on some Indy cars and test vehicles, the company went out of business before the design caught on. Bell Auto Parts bought the inventory and the brakes became the high-end brake for discriminating hot rodders and racers. They work well (the backing plate is stationary, and the disc is like a clutch that's sandwiched between the backing plate and a pressure plate), but are extremely rare and expensive.

This is as close to a Kinmont as most of us will ever get—it's actually a 1940 Ford drum brake with finned Buick brake drums, and a finned backing plate cover. Looks good, and the added fins do help cool the otherwise heat-retaining drums.

Moving one more step toward modern, we have this older Super Bell disc brake conversion mounted to early Ford spindles. The single-piston calipers mount to a finned plate that also covers the disc. Note the slot in the front to allow cooling air to reach the rotor.

To do this job, it's necessary to get some 1948 Ford hubs and machine them and the Buick drums so they fit together. You also have to machine the inner lip of the Buick drum so it clears the Ford backing plate. The only downside to using these drums now is that they're 40 years old, and it's difficult to find a pair that aren't worn beyond specs (the maximum I.D. is

12.10 inches, by the way). In addition, if these drums sit in a damp environment (like on a car in a junkyard), corrosion develops between the aluminum and the cast-iron liner, distorting the drums and causing uneven braking. Turning the drums might solve the problem for a while, but the heating/cooling cycles quickly cause the problem to come back.

Drum brakes are adequate for the front ends of most hot rods, but we're limited to some pretty old hardware at this point. Drum brakes are also more work to maintain, and under hard use, they tend to "fade" as they heat up. There is a new disc brake on the market that offers the appearance of a finned Buick drum with the performance of a disc brake, though. And that leads us into the next option—disc brakes.

Discs

Disc brakes consist of a metal disc that's attached to a wheel's hub, and a caliper that contains hydraulic pistons. When you step on the brakes, the pistons push brake pads into contact with both sides of the rotor. This clamping force makes a very effective brake with many advantages over drum brakes. Disc brakes are lighter, and they have fewer parts, which means they're simpler and cheaper to make and maintain. They also offer great stopping power, and the exposed disc dissipates heat much faster than any enclosed drum brake. They're far and away better than drums, and unless you absolutely have to have that traditional drum-brake look on the front of your hot rod, you should use disc brakes. It's just that simple.

There are still some choices to make in the disc brake world though. There are a couple of different types of calipers, and some choices in rotors as well. Let's talk rotors first.

The simplest disc brake rotors are solid discs of cast-iron with a machined finish on both sides. Solid rotors are OK for lightweight cars like T-buckets and fenderless hi-boys, but they can't dissipate heat fast enough on heavier cars, like late 1930s and 1940s coupes and sedans. Most solid disc brakes are aftermarket items, and some are cross-drilled to give them a racier look and slightly better heat dissipation. But cross-drilling also reduces the friction area, and if done improperly can cause the rotors to crack. Best to leave drilled rotors for racers.

Vented rotors are thicker and somewhat heavier, and have internal air passages that increase the surface area of the rotor to dissipate heat. Sometimes the vanes inside the rotor are even curved to help "fan" more air through them. Because there's more material, vented rotors can take on more heat, and the ventilation helps get rid of it faster. Almost all modern OEM brake rotors are vented. In racing applications, some vented rotors are cross-drilled as well. If vented rotors are an option for any hot rod, we'd choose them over solid rotors in almost all cases.

Calipers are the other half of the disc brake equation, and there are two basic types: floating

Finally, we have full-on modern disc brakes with this Wilwood dual-piston caliper and vented rotor mounted to the front of Kurt Senescall's T coupe. This will give great, fade-free stopping power on the strip or street. The only drawback to a setup like this is that the parts aren't OEM, and could be difficult to find out in the sticks.

Then we have something that performs modern, but looks old. So-Cal Speed Shop sells this brake, which appears to be an early Ford backing plate with a finned Buick drum. However, it's all new—there's actually a Wilwood caliper and a disc brake inside there, and the face of the drum is ventilated for cooling. Modern performance, timeless style.

and nonfloating. There are also variations in the number of pistons. Even single-piston calipers require a larger volume of fluid than any drum brake cylinder, and that's something to remember later when we talk about master cylinders. Let's talk nonfloating calipers first.

Nonfloating calipers are mounted solidly to the caliper bracket, and therefore must be precisely centered on the rotor or the caliper will try to deflect the rotor to one side when the brakes are applied. To align the calipers, the manufacturers offer shim kits that you use to adjust the caliper position on the caliper mount. To press on both sides of the rotor, a nonfloating caliper has to have one or more pistons on each side. Two-piston calipers have one piston per side, four-piston calipers have two pistons per side. Most nonfloating calipers are aftermarket units.

Floating calipers are the more common style, and are what most factory applications use. Floating calipers are simpler in design, as they only have pistons (one or two) on one side of the rotor. As the brakes are applied, this piston pushes one pad against the rotor. The caliper

is mounted so that it can slide back and forth on its mounting pins. When the piston-side pad makes contact with the rotor, the entire caliper slides over until the other pad contacts the rotor as well. This self-centering design has several advantages. First, it's half the pistons, half the parts. Second, because there's no piston on the wheel side of the rotor, there's a little more brake-to-rim clearance.

Because the floating caliper has to move on its mounting pins, it's imperative that the pins and other hardware be in good condition. If the seals and bushings on the pins go bad, the pin can get rusted and inhibit caliper movement, reducing braking efficiency. When you install or maintain your hot rod's brakes, make sure the mounting pins, bushings, and seals are all in good condition. If any of the pieces are bad, replacement brake hardware kits are cheap at the local parts store.

What front brakes you choose depends largely on the weight of your car. Keep in mind that because of weight distribution and forward weight transfer under braking, your hot rod's front brakes do most of the stopping. The larger

If you want rear discs, this kit from ECI might do the job. It adapts Cadillac Seville calipers and 1979 Trans Am rotors to an 8- or 9-inch Ford or a GM 10-bolt or 12-bolt rear end. The big advantage of these calipers is that they have a built-in mechanical emergency brake. OEM parts are also easy to service, almost anywhere.

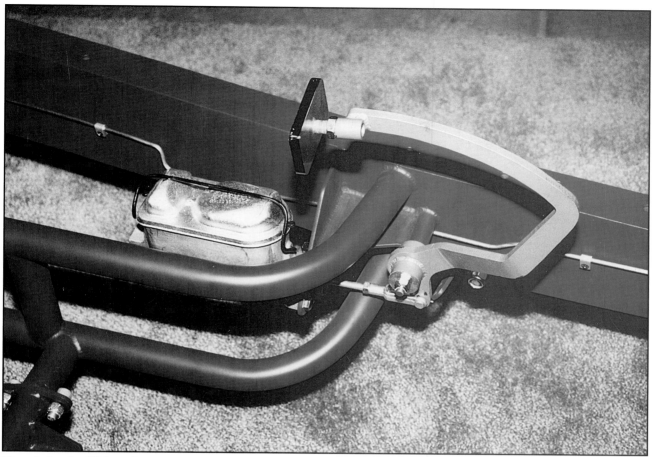

Many hot rods still have frame-mounted pedals, which puts the master cylinder under the floor, like the one on this Pete & Jake's chassis. It's compact, but with a master cylinder mounted this low, you must have check valves in the brake lines to prevent fluid from flowing out of the brakes and back to the master cylinder.

the car, the more stopping power it needs. Small, light cars can get away with vintage drum brakes or solid-rotor discs, but any larger, fendered hot rods will need more modern self-energizing drums at least 11 inches in diameter, or a good-quality vented-rotor disc brake kit.

Finally, remember that you're building this hot rod to drive—at least we hope that's the point. That means that somewhere, sometime, you're going to have to do some brake maintenance or repair, and that might occur at home, or it might happen in Flatbump, Idaho. The Flatbump NAPA store isn't going to carry 1940 Ford brake cylinders, and it probably won't carry bearings and seals for fancy aftermarket disc brake/hub kits, or pads, or billet calipers for that matter. Choose your brake components accordingly. For front drums, that probably means something modern enough to have easy parts availability, and for discs, it means a brake kit that uses OEM hubs, rotors, and calipers.

REAR BRAKES

Rear brake choices are essentially the same as front brake choices—vintage drums, modern drums, or modern discs—and they work the same and have the same components as their front counterparts. Because the rear brakes have to do less work, however, the selection process is a little different. Most of the rear ends that hot rodders install under their cars have drum brakes, and drum brakes are perfectly adequate for your car's rear braking needs. That's why most of the cars manufactured since the 1980s have a front disc/rear drum brake combination.

If you intend to use rear drum brakes, take the same care that you use with the front. Make sure the backing plates are straight, and use new or rebuilt wheel cylinders, brake shoes, and hardware. Resurface the drums and make sure they haven't been turned beyond their maximum diameter. Make sure the axle seals don't leak (axle grease destroys braking efficiency and brake shoes) and you're good to go.

If you want to go the extra mile and install disc brakes on the rear to match the front discs (don't even think about rear discs and front drums—that'd be just plain stupid), you have a couple of options. First, you can look for an

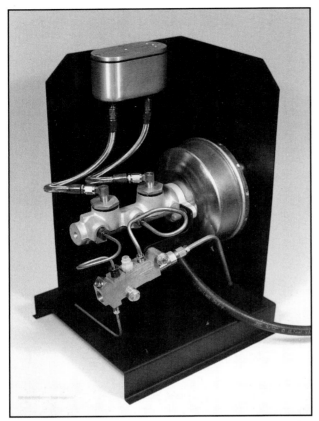

The other problem with a frame-mounted master cylinder is that it's tough to access it when it's time to add fluid. This Master Power master cylinder has a small-diameter booster for maximum clearance, and a remote reservoir for easy access. Note also the OEM-style combination valve.

OEM rear end that has disc brakes installed. Lincoln Versailles and some Ford Granada rear ends had factory discs, but these rear ends are expensive and often need to be narrowed for most hot rod applications. Your best bet is to look to the disc brake kits manufactured by the hot rod aftermarket. ECI, Master Power, Wilwood, and others make quality brackets and kits that'll adapt OEM disc brake components to most popular Ford and GM rear ends. Just remember that replacing a disc/drum system with a disc/disc system will require a different master cylinder and some other components, which we will discuss shortly.

MASTER CYLINDER

At its most basic, a master cylinder consists of a piston in a cylinder that's fed fluid by a reservoir. When you push the brake pedal, the piston pushes fluid out into the brake system to actuate the brakes. Sounds simple, but it's still very important that the master cylinder work with the rest of the components in the system. What master cylinder is best for your car depends on the volume of each wheel cylinder or caliper, and on the diameter of those cylinders or calipers.

The simplest master cylinders are the old "fruit-jar" single-reservoir units. They had one fluid reservoir and one piston to actuate all four brakes. The downside to this is that if a leak occurred anywhere in the brake system, the entire system lost pressure and you had no brakes. Besides this major safety issue, a single-reservoir master cylinder only works well when the front and rear brakes have the same needs for fluid pressure and volume.

Dual-reservoir master cylinders became the norm in the 1960s, and as the name indicates, there are two fluid reservoirs, one for the front brakes and one for the rear, and each reservoir has its own piston. The big advantage here is that your car now has two essentially independent braking systems. If one end should spring a leak, you'll still have brakes on the other end. A dual master cylinder is also necessary for disc/drum brake systems, because the front disc brakes require more fluid volume and probably a different piston diameter.

Most street rods built today have a disc/drum system, and most rear drum brakes have nearly the same pressure and volume requirements. Therefore it makes sense to match your master cylinder to the front discs. If in doubt, check with one of the manufacturers such as MasterPower or ECI. Their tech people have lots of experience in this area and can help you choose the components that are right for your car.

POWER BOOSTERS

Brake boosters come in two styles, vacuum and hydraulic. Both do the same job: amplify the pedal pressure you exert to apply the brakes.

Vacuum boosters consist of a metal canister with a rubber diaphragm in the middle. When you apply the brake pedal, full atmospheric pressure is introduced to the pedal side of the diaphragm, while engine vacuum is allowed to pull on the other side. This pressure differential pulls the diaphragm toward the master cylinder, adding to the effort you're applying to the pedal. Vacuum boosters are commonly available in 7-, 9-, and 11-inch diameters. Which you decide to use depends on your situation. If you're trying to fit a booster under your 1932 Ford, chances are you need a small 7-inch booster for clearance. But in general, it's best to use the largest booster you can get away with.

The other, less common, booster choice is a hydraulic booster, which is usually found in diesel cars and trucks. These boosters are a good choice in applications where there's little or no vacuum (cars with big, lumpy cams often don't produce enough vacuum to make a conventional booster work), or in cases where space is very limited. For instance, we know of a 1957 Ford Thunderbird with a dual-quad 427 Ford stuffed under the hood. There was no room for a vacuum booster, but a Ford diesel truck donated a very slick hydraulic booster to the cause. The booster in this case is plumbed into the power steering pump, and it works quite well. The only downside to these boosters is the need for high-pressure lines to make them work.

RESIDUAL PRESSURE VALVES

Residual pressure valves come in two different pressure ratings, and they perform different jobs. Depending on the brake system, some residual pressure valves are built into the master cylinder, while others are separate items that are plumbed into the brake lines.

The 2-pound residual pressure valve is used with either front or rear disc brakes when the master cylinder is mounted low, under the car's floorboards. This valve maintains 2 pounds of pressure in the brake lines, simply so that gravity won't cause the brake fluid to flow down out of the calipers and into the master cylinder reservoir.

The 10-pound residual pressure valves are found in either front or rear drum brake systems. These valves perform two functions. Typically, the rubber cup seals in a drum brake wheel cylinder don't seal unless they have pressure on them. Keeping this small amount of pressure applied to the wheel cylinders, prevents the rubber cups in the cylinders from bowing backwards, which could allow air to get sucked in past them. Second, the small amount of pressure helps you overcome the pressure of the brake return springs when you step on the brakes. Disc brakes don't have return springs (or rubber cups), so they don't require the higher-pressure residual pressure valve.

In fact, a 10-pound valve will quickly ruin a set of disc brakes. They apply just enough pressure to keep the pads in constant contact with the rotors, causing them to overheat and wear at an accelerated rate. Back in the 1980s when hot rodders started using front disc brakes more often (especially in Mustang II front ends), it was fairly common to see hot rodders at the Nats replacing rotors and pads, then tearing down their drum brake master cylinders to remove the residual pressure valve from the front brake circuit. That's why it's so important to know for sure that your brake components will work together.

The only time you won't need any kind of residual pressure valve is if your car has four-wheel disc brakes and the master cylinder is mounted on the firewall. On the other hand, cars with a disc/drum combination and an under floor master cylinder will need both valves: the 10-pound valve for the rear drums, and the 2-pound valve for the front discs.

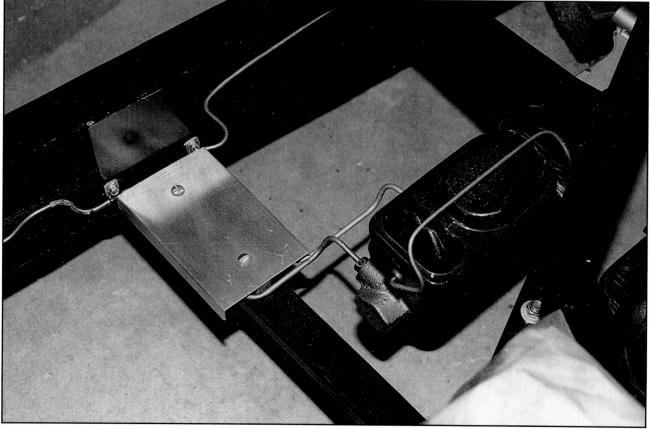

Careful routing of brake lines is paramount in the close confines of a hot rod chassis. This dual master cylinder is mounted to a 1946 Ford frame. The owner has built a small aluminum heat shield to protect the brake lines from the exhaust pipe, which will soon be installed just over the shield.

PROPORTIONING VALVES

In any braking system, it's ideal to have all four brakes working at the same rate and at the same time. As soon as a wheel (or pair of wheels) locks up and starts sliding, it loses their braking efficiency. If the front wheels lock up before the back or vice versa, you're not getting the most from your brakes, and your chances of an accident increase dramatically.

Factory braking systems on stock cars are designed so that all four brakes will lock up at the same time, so that just before lockup, all the brakes are working at maximum efficiency. Hot rodders screw up this delicate balance, however, when they take front brakes from one car, rear brakes from another, a master cylinder from a third, and install it all on a fourth vehicle with a completely different weight and weight bias. It gets even worse when you change tire diameters and widths.

To get everything working like it should, an adjustable proportioning valve is installed in the line leading to the rear brakes. For some reason, many rodders install this on the frame rail in the middle of the line. It makes more sense to install it near the master cylinder where it's easier to get at, though.

Regardless of where it's mounted, the residual pressure valve allows you to adjust the rate at which the rear brakes get line pressure. If the rear brakes are locking up too soon, you turn the valve to slow the pressure increase to them. If the front brakes are locking up first, you turn the valve to increase the pressure rate to the rear brakes, so they lock up sooner. With a few controlled panic stops on a deserted parking lot and a little fiddling, you can quickly get your hot rod's brakes working at maximum efficiency.

HOLD OFF/METERING VALVES

A hold-off valve is used in a disc/drum brake system to delay pressure to the front discs, so the rear drums have a chance to catch up. This is another way to ensure that the front and rear brakes activate at the same time. If you use a standalone hold-off valve, it must be located equidistant from the left and right front brakes, usually in the middle of the front cross-member. In OEM systems, the hold-off valve is usually incorporated into the combination valve.

COMBINATION VALVES

Combination valves are commonly found in OEM applications, usually located either right next to the master cylinder, or on the frame just below it. They perform several functions: A typical combo valve includes a hold-off valve for the front brakes (notice that there's usually a separate line coming from the valve for the left and right front brakes), a proportioning valve to balance the front and rear brakes, and a brake light switch. Keep in mind, though, that combination valves are designed for a specific vehicle, and that the included proportioning valve may not be the right rate for your hot rod. For this reason,

we recommend using a separate hold-off valve and a separate, adjustable proportioning valve so you can dial-in your hot rod's brakes.

EMERGENCY BRAKES

Emergency brakes are necessary for two reasons: to keep the vehicle in place when it's parked, and to stop the car in an emergency should the main braking system fail. For this reason, the emergency brake should be separate from the main brake system. As an example, hydraulic brake locks are key-actuated valves that maintain pressure on the brakes. Push the brake pedal down, turn the key, and the brakes stay locked. However, these systems should not be used as an emergency brake because they rely on the primary hydraulic system to work. If that system fails, so does the brake lock system.

For that reason, emergency brakes are typically mechanical. With rear drum brakes, a lever actuates cables that press the brake shoes against the drum. With factory rear discs, there's a similar mechanical action that applies the pads to the rotor, or sometimes there's a second small caliper that's mechanically actuated.

Hot rodders have also developed emergency brakes that consist of a small disc brake rotor mounted on the rear end's pinion yoke. A cable-operated caliper grabs this disc to stop the rear end. These are fine if both rear wheels are on the ground, but remember that if you're using a non-limited-slip rear end, this type of brake will allow the vehicle to roll if one wheel is raised on a jack, such as during a tire change.

ANTI-LOCK BRAKES

At this writing, true anti-lock brake systems (ABS) have not yet found their way into the hot rod world, but we're sure that will change. At its simplest, an anti-lock brake system has a sensor mounted at each brake rotor that monitors wheel speed. Each sensor is connected to a computer that monitors relative wheel speeds. If the computer senses that one wheel is locked up during braking, it opens a valve that releases pressure to that brake. The computer does this hundreds of times a second, releasing and applying pressure, to keep each wheel braking at maximum efficiency, right on the verge of lockup. This rapid pressure apply/release results in a brake pedal "pulse" that's a bit unnerving at first, but once you get used to it, you can just mash the pedal as hard as you want, and the car stops as efficiently as possible. It's a great system.

An ABS requires more complex plumbing, some sensors and wiring, and a computer-controlled valve body. It also has to be tailored to an individual car, and that's probably the biggest reason we don't see them on hot rods . . . yet.

There is another product on the market that helps reduce brake lockup, but it's not a true anti-lock brake system. It's essentially a gas-charged accumulator that mounts in the lines to the front and rear brakes. As the brake's pads (or

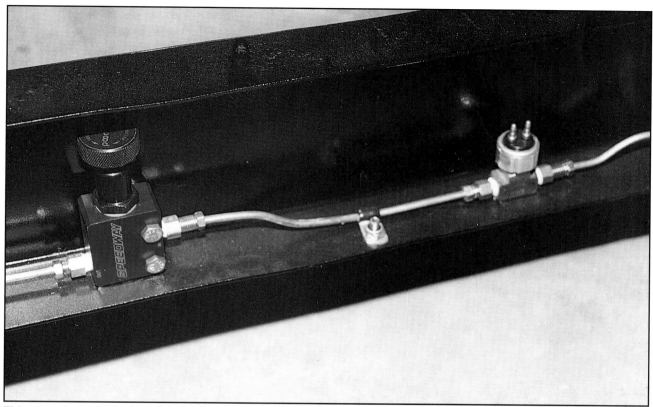

This view shows the inside of the 1946 Ford's frame rail, with the brake line held in place with conventional rubber-insulated clamps. At right is an inline brake light switch, and at left is an adjustable proportioning valve.

shoes) contact the rotors (or drums), irregularities on the surface cause the pads to send pressure pulses back down the line. The accumulator absorbs these pressure pulses, resulting in more even braking and decreased stopping distances. Think of it as a shock absorber for brakes; just as a gas-charged shock helps keep the tires in contact with the road, this gas-charged accumulator helps keep the brake pads and shoes in contact with their stopping surfaces.

PLUMBING

Of course, pushing that brake fluid around doesn't do any good unless it gets to the brakes, and that's where plumbing comes in. In automotive brake systems, we have two types of lines: hard lines and flex lines.

Hot rods typically have three or four flex lines: one for each front brake, and either one or two for the rear, depending on how the car is plumbed. Some builders like to run one flex line to the rear end, then attach hard lines to the rear end housing to take fluid to both rear brakes. Others run the hard lines to two points on the chassis, with one flex line to each rear brake. The former is a little simpler, but the latter gives a cleaner-appearing rear end in cars where that counts.

Flex lines are available in OEM black-rubber style, and the aftermarket offers some very nice Teflon-lined braided stainless lines. The braided stainless lines look nice and they're race-tough, but they sometimes require special fittings, and most aren't DOT-approved. If your state requires inspections, your car might fail if it has them. For the sake of simplicity (and cost), we prefer plain old black-rubber flex lines.

For hard lines, you also have two choices: regular steel lines with brass fittings, or stainless lines with AN fittings.

Stainless lines look great, and they never ever rust. Polish them and you have a show-worthy undercarriage. But there are disadvantages. First, stainless is hard and brittle, and bending stainless lines takes a high-quality (read: expensive) bender. Stainless also can't be double-flared, so you have to have a special 37-degree flaring tool and use 37-degree AN fittings to make your connections. Wherever stainless lines hook to OEM equipment, adapter fittings are necessary to go from the AN threads to the pipe threads on the factory parts.

Regular steel lines, on the other hand, can be bent in an inexpensive bender, they can be double-flared using a normal 45-degree double-flaring kit, and you can use inexpensive brass fittings, available at any decent auto parts store. Steel lines are also zinc coated, so they last a long time and look decent under a car that's well cared for and not driven every day.

Here's one more combination that gives good stopping power with good hot rod looks...1953-'56 Ford F-250 12 inch brakes (self-energizing), 1953-'56 Ford F-100 hubs, and Buick drums. The backing plate is flatter than the classic '40 Ford plate, but it still looks right and it works better.

When you buy tools for bending and flaring brake lines, buy good stuff. Excellent plumbing tools are available from Eastwood and Pure Choice Motorsports. If you have an industrial tool dealer near you, you should also look into the Ridgid Tool line of benders. They're expensive, but well worth it if you want to do a quality job.

You also have options when it comes to attaching the hard lines to your car. The hot rod aftermarket has very nice stainless, aluminum, and nylon line clamps available, and they're available for one line, two, or even a brake and a fuel line. They really neaten up a car's underside. If your car is one whose underside will never see the light of day, standard rubber-insulated aluminum line clamps also work well. All of these require you to drill and tap holes in a frame rail for installation.

BRAKE FLUID

There will always be some controversy among enthusiasts over which brake fluid to use—plain-Jane DOT brake fluid from the parts store, or the more expensive silicon brake fluid. Both have their advantages and disadvantages.

Regular brake fluid has the properties needed for an automotive brake system—it doesn't expand when heated, and the boiling point is high enough that it should never be a factor in normal use. However, it is hygroscopic, meaning that it absorbs water from the atmosphere—water that can corrode components and turn to steam if calipers get warm enough. That steam is compressible, leading to a spongy brake pedal. The final disadvantage to regular fluid is that it eats paint. Avoid spilling it on any painted surface.

Silicon brake fluid's only major advantages are that it doesn't eat paint and it doesn't take on water. The former makes silicon popular with people who spill brake fluid, and the latter quality makes it popular for vehicles that are stored for long periods. However, silicon expands when heated, and it also causes some rubber parts (seals, cups, and diaphragms) to swell, causing problems of its own.

The bottom line is that quality DOT brake fluid is best for regular use, and it's great for long-term use if you maintain your brake system and flush it out with fresh fluid every couple of years.

GETTING IT ALL TO WORK TOGETHER

When it comes to safety, your hot rod's brake system is the most important part of the whole car. Follow these simple rules, and your car will be a pleasure to drive and work on:

• Make sure the components work well together. Do the necessary math, get the best advice you can from other hot rodders and manufacturers.
• Use quality parts. Make sure all components are new or rebuilt. Don't cut corners ANYWHERE on your car's braking system.
• Make sure all components are solidly mounted, and all lines are safely routed well away from heat sources and moving parts.
• Test your car's brake system for leaks before it hits the road, and check it regularly once it's running.
• Whenever possible, use OEM rotors, calipers, and other parts for easy service and maintenance.

IN THE SHOP:

INSTALLING BIG BRAKES ON A MUSTANG II FRONT END

How much do you suppose a stock Mustang II or Pinto weighs? And how do you suppose that figure compares to the gross tonnage of your favorite fat-fendered flyer? Bet there's a big difference, but a lot of folks are using the same brakes on both cars. Granted, a set of stock Mustang II disc brakes is worlds better than your street rod's stock drums, but there's always room for improvement.

Several aftermarket manufacturers now offer big-brake kits that will give your Mustang-suspended rod more stopping power. This kit, from JFZ, consists of aluminum hubs; 10-1/4-inch-diameter vented rotors (compared to the stock Mustang's 9-1/4-inch diameter); a set of JFZ aluminum four-piston calipers; and all the necessary brackets, hardware, and bearings to install the setup on the stock Mustang II spindles. It's a good setup, with one drawback: If there are problems on the road, JFZ calipers and rotors will be harder to find than OEM parts. If that's a concern, find a kit that adapts OEM parts for easy (and less expensive) replacement.

Larger rotors improve stopping power for several reasons: First, the braking force is applied farther from the center of the spindle, so the brakes have a larger moment arm to work on. Second, larger rotors provide more swept area for the brakes—in other words, the pads contact more rotor face. And third, larger rotors dissipate heat faster, reducing fade. Add four-piston calipers to the package (versus the

1

The JFZ kit comes with new aluminum hubs, cast-iron vented rotors, four-piston aluminum calipers, mounting brackets, and all necessary hardware and bearings.

2

Bigger rotors mean more stopping power; the JFZ rotor is on the left and measures 10-1/4 inches in diameter. The stock Mustang II rotor is on the right and measures only 9-1/4 inches in diameter. Start the process by assembling the hubs to the carrier and rotor. Use red Loctite, pay attention to the torque specs, and install the spacers correctly according to the instructions.

Mustang's single-piston calipers), and you get a substantial increase in braking power.

The JFZ kit is very easy to install, thanks to good engineering and an excellent set of instructions. Start by removing all the stock Mustang II brakes, including the bearings and brackets. You want to start with a bare spindle.

Next, assemble the hubs, rotor carriers, and rotors. Start by installing the wheel studs in the hubs; be sure to use some antisieze compound to keep from boogering up the threads. Then bolt the rotor carrier to the hub, and the rotor to the carrier. Use red Loctite, and be sure to use the supplied spacers, or the backs of the wheel studs will contact the rotor.

With the rotor/hubs assembled, it's time to trial fit everything on the spindle. Install the hubs and bearings on the spindles (no grease and no seals this time around), and tighten the spindle nut until there's no play. Then bolt the caliper mounts to the spindles. (One note: There is a left and a right caliper mount, so don't get them mixed up.) The large side of the threaded insert goes to the outside of the car.

Next, install the calipers on the mounts (bleeders up! you'd be surprised how many rodders

3

Once the calipers are centered on the rotor, disassemble everything and reinstall the brackets with red Loctite and the correct spacers. Grease the bearings and install the rotors and calipers for the final time.

4

This adaptor lets you hook the braided stainless lines to the standard brake fittings on the chassis. Use Teflon tape on the fittings to lube and protect the threads. After the lines are in, you can bleed the brakes, inspect for leaks, and go for a careful test drive.

make that mistake!) and check to see that the caliper is centered on the rotor. The casting part-line on the caliper body should be aligned with the center of the rotor. If it isn't, use the supplied shims to shim the caliper in the center of the rotor. Be sure to use the same number of shims on each mounting bolt, or the caliper will be "cocked" on the rotor, resulting in uneven pad wear and other problems.

When the caliper looks centered, install the pads in the caliper. If they don't slide in easily, you need to fine-tune the number of shims until they do. When everything is aligned properly, blow everything apart and reassemble using red Loctite and the torque specs provided in the instructions.

Brake lines are next. If you plan to use stock-type rubber brake lines, you'll need to buy a threaded adaptor to mount the line to the 1/8-inch pipe threads in the caliper body. If you choose to use JFZ braided stainless lines, the adaptor isn't necessary. When the brake lines are in, bleed the system, starting with the bleeder farthest from the master cylinder. When the pedal feels firm, check the system for leaks and take it on a careful test drive.

And a final reminder: Make sure your master cylinder does *not* have a residual pressure valve installed on the front brake side. If it does, the pads will always engage the rotors and they'll wear out abnormally fast. Consult JFZ for more info.

IN THE SHOP:

PLUMBING A HOT ROD CHASSIS

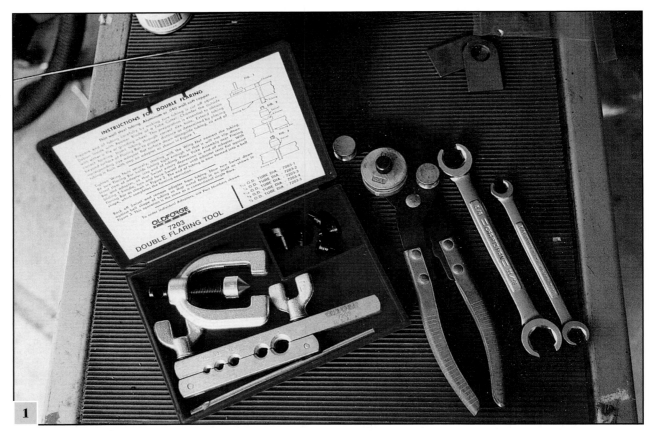

1

The basic tools you'll need are a flaring kit and a basic bender (these are from Eastwood), a tubing cutter (not shown), and a set of flare wrenches. We used the rolling cam bender from Eastwood for this installation.

The Big Olds chassis was painted, rebuilt, and ready for some plumbing. The time had come for me to run some lines. I started by calling Pure Choice Motorsports, a supplier of automotive plumbing hardware and tools. After we discussed the car and what it needed, they faxed me a chassis diagram and tech sheet to fill out, noting the location of the parts and what kind of car they were from. Pure Choice then put together a plumbing kit with all the flex lines, fittings, tabs, clamps, and instructions I needed to plumb the Big Olds' brakes. Kinda like a wiring kit for plumbing. At first the price for the kit seemed a little

steep, but then I started pricing the individual components and found that I saved a little money, and a lot of trips to the parts store, by ordering the kit.

Our kit contained three stainless braided flex lines (we only used one in back), the necessary adapters and mounting tabs for them, a couple of T-fittings, a brake light switch, a hard-line coupler, and enough line clamps to hold everything tight to the frame. Pure Choice recommended we buy the steel line locally, because it'd be cheaper; they do include stainless tubing with their stainless kits, however. The nice thing about the kit is that when it

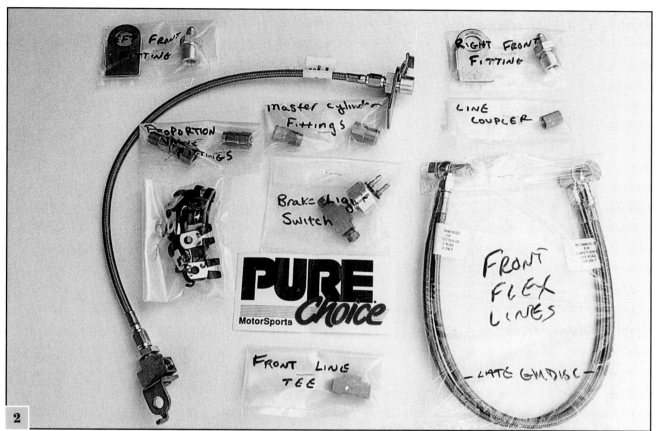

2

Here's our plumbing kit from Pure Choice; everything we needed to plumb the Big Olds except steel hard lines was in the box. It's a nice way to go that saves a lot of time, guesswork, and trips to the local parts store.

arrives, you know that everything will work with everything else in the box.

After asking numerous brake questions of Ralph Lisena at ECI (Engineered Components, Inc.; he's a very patient man, and he knows all when it comes to brakes), we also ordered a front-brake metering valve. This valve is installed at the center of the front cross-member and meters the pressure going to the front brakes so that the rear brakes will receive full pressure and activate first.

STEEL OR STAINLESS

Stainless lines look great and they'll never rust, but when it comes to building a "driver," they are (in our opinion) more trouble than they're worth. Stainless tubing is more expensive, more difficult to work with, and requires special AN fittings and top-quality (read: *expensive*) tools to bend it. And you have to get a separate 37-degree flaring tool.

Steel tubing, on the other hand, is easy to bend and relatively forgiving (some "mistake" bends can actually be straightened out). Plus, if you really screw up a piece of tube, throwing it out will not cause an economic crisis. In fact, all the steel brake line needed to plumb the Big Olds cost about $25. The tools needed are also less expensive.

3

We also ordered a metering valve from ECI; it goes on the front crossmember and meters the line pressure to the front brakes so the rear brakes activate first.

4 We started by installing all the "fixed" components, like calipers, flex lines, and the metering block. Here, the Pure Choice stainless-steel flex lines are attached to the front calipers using banjo-type fittings.

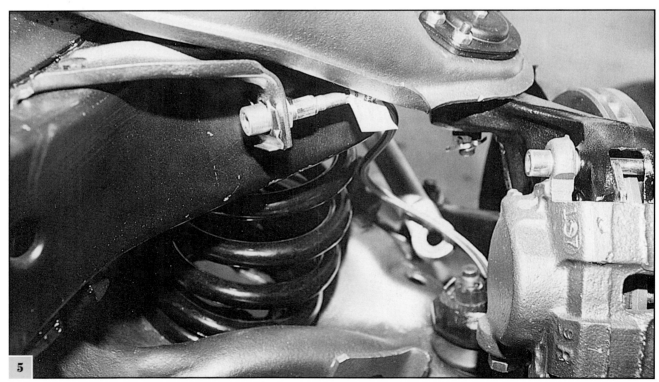

5 We then installed the calipers and hooked the flex line to the stock frame bracket using the adapter provided in the kit. Using the factory line routing on the subframe should ensure that the lines won't get pinched or rubbed.

TOOLS

When it comes to plumbing tools, you can spend as little or as much as you want, but your results will vary accordingly.

First off, don't even bother with a bender that doesn't have moving parts. That includes the inexpensive parts-store mandrel bender, and those spring benders. For steel brake lines, the basic bender is the one shown in this article, which is available from Eastwood. It has two interchangeable mandrels and can bend 3/16-, 1/4-, 5/16-, and 3/8-inch line to almost 90 degrees; with most steel tubing you can finish a 90-degree bend by hand. It's a good bender to get if you use only steel line and don't do a lot of plumbing. The only drawbacks to this bender are that it doesn't go quite to 90 degrees and it doesn't have reference marks or degree marks on it. In addition, we found that it was tough to get a satisfactory bend on the 3/8-inch fuel line with this bender.

Another good entry-level tool is the basic bender sold by Pure Choice. It's a die-cast unit with three mandrels built into one body, and it has degree marks and reference marks in place. It also bends up to 90 degrees. Pure Choice says

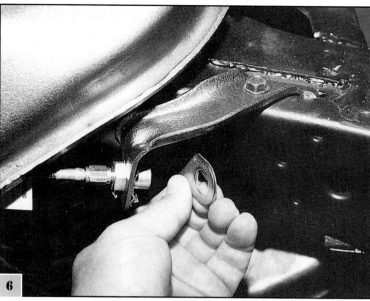

6

If you can't or don't want to use the factory line mounts, Pure Choice supplies these weld-on tabs so you can mount the lines wherever you want.

7

Next, we bent the coated steel line that went from the flex line, over the frame, and down along the front cross-member to the metering valve. Route the lines so they're away from heat sources, and potential pinch and abrasion points.

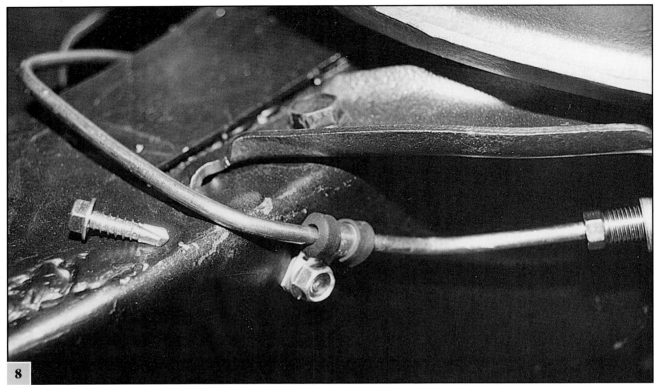

8

The kit also included these rubber-insulated line clamps. We marked their locations, drilled pilot holes, then used these self-drilling and -tapping bolts to secure them to the subframe.

9

Before the line was fastened in completely, we used a tubing cutter to cut it to length; we then de-burred the inside and outside edges of the end of the tube. Next it was time to put a new 45-degree double flare on the end of the tube.

this is an ideal bender for steel line, but doesn't recommend it for stainless because it's much more difficult to bend.

If you're going to do a lot of plumbing or if you want to do stainless, you have to spend a little more. Eastwood has a set of two rolling-cam tubing benders; the small one does 3/16- and 1/4-inch lines, the big one does 5/16- and 3/8-inch lines. Both do up to 180-degree bends with a tight radius for a nice, professional look. They also have a tab built in so you can clamp the bender in a vise for bench-top work, a very handy feature.

Finally, if you own a shop or if you want the best, Pure Choice has a set of four benders, one for each size tubing. They feature steel bodies, high-quality mandrels, degree markings, and the ability to do tight radius bends up to 180 degrees. These are top-shelf tools, and should provide a lifetime of tube bending.

BENDING AND ROUTING

We started by installing all the nontubing components. Up front, we put the flex lines on the calipers, then attached the lines to the chassis using the stock mounting points. Pure Choice also supplies weld-on tabs if you don't have or don't want to use factory mounts. We then drilled and tapped holes in the back of the front

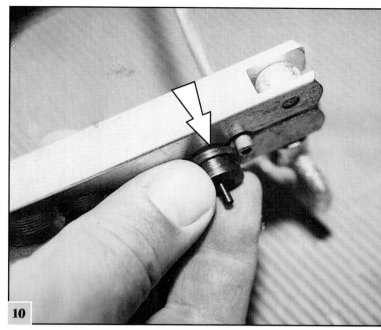

10

First, make sure the fitting is on the tube. Then, clamp the end of the tube in the flaring tool. The flaring die (arrow) has a shoulder on it that you use to gauge how much of the tube should protrude from the vise.

11

Tighten the vise; then insert the die into the tube. Put the clamping device on the vise, and tighten it until the die is flush with the vise.

cross-member and mounted the ECI metering valve (it needs to be equidistant from the front brakes to work properly).

For the rear end, Pure Choice supplied a GM-style T-block that mounts to rear cover bolts on the top of the 10-bolt rear end. In its stock

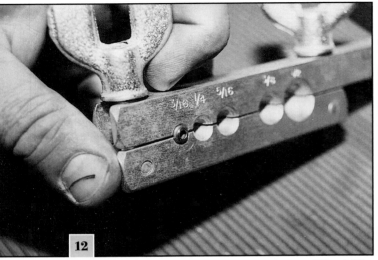

12

After the die is removed, the end of the tube will look like this, with a "bell" swaged onto the end.

configuration, this block pointed the flex line straight up. I didn't like that routing, so I straightened the mounting tab so the line would go forward. I then installed the flex line on the block and decided where to place the mounting tab on the rear cross-member before welding the tab in place.

When mounting the flex lines, make sure that they won't get pinched or abraded when the suspension moves. This is especially critical on the front end, with so many components to rub against.

With all the "hard" parts installed, it was time to bend some tubing. It helps to use reference bends; if you're not familiar with this technique, here's a brief rundown: Take a short piece of scrap tubing (8 inches or so) and put a scribe mark on it. Put the tube in the bender and align that mark with a mark on the bender. Bend the tube 90 degrees. Now, if you need to make a 90-degree bend, you simply hold that reference bend next to the tube you're going to bend, transfer the mark to the new tube, and make your bend. It allows you to position the bender correctly every time.

When you route the tubes, make sure they're well away from exhaust heat and moving components, and that they're positioned so they won't be caught or smashed flat by debris

13

Reinstall the clamp, with the pointed end centered in the tube, and tighten it down until the bell collapses on itself to form the double-flare.

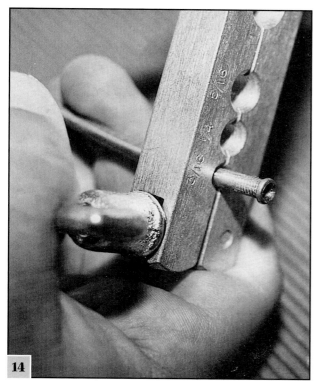

14

If you do it right, you'll end up with a double-flare that looks like this. If you're in doubt, compare it to the factory-made flares that are on the tubing when you get it.

on the road. No part of any brake line should be below the frame rail where it could get pinched. Make sure the lines are securely fastened to the frame. Pure Choice supplies rubber-insulated line clamps with their kits, or you can get some fancier aluminum clamps from a number of advertisers. Too many clamps is better than not enough.

I found that it was easiest to start at the extreme ends of the car and work my way inward when bending lines. First I ran tubes from the front flex lines to the metering block, then from the rear brakes to the T-fitting on the rear end. I then formed the line that runs from the center of the rear cross-member up the driver-side frame rail; it runs inside some partial boxing plates and is secured to them every 24 inches or so.

This car will have its master cylinder on the firewall, so the final lines from the metering block and rear brakes to the master cylinder will be done when the body's back on.

FLARING

Any time you need to shorten a line (which is just about every one), you need to put a new flare on the end. Steel lines use a 45-degree double-flare, which requires a special flaring tool to make. After you cut the line using a tubing cutter, you must de-burr the ends of the tube, inside and out. Next, you clamp the line in a special vise with a short length of tubing protruding

15

One front brake is plumbed. Next we'll do the driver side, and when the body's on we'll run the line that goes from the metering block to the firewall-mounted master cylinder.

16 We opted to use one flex line on the rear end. Pure Choice sent us a factory-style T-fitting (arrow) that mounted to the rear end cover, and a single flex line. Here, we're determining where to weld the mounting tab to the frame cross-member.

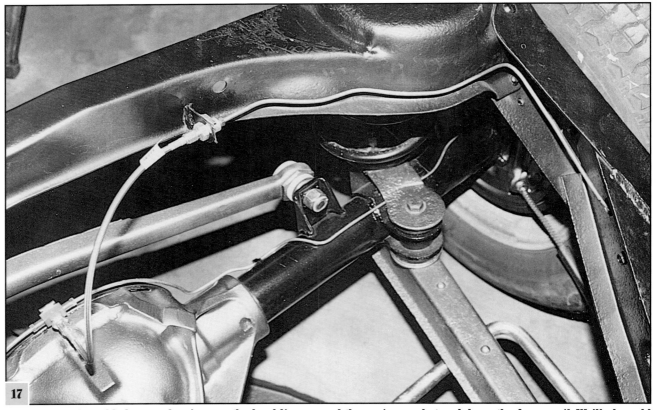

17 Here, the tab is welded on, and we've run the hard line around the spring pocket and down the frame rail. We'll also add some line clamps to keep the hard line from vibrating.

18

The lines come from **NAPA** in 6-foot lengths; this one ends about halfway up the frame rail. You can use a coupler to join two lengths, or use the junction to mount a brake light switch (shown) or a proportioning valve. Note that the line is well protected inside the frame rail, and secured to the boxing plates.

from it. You then slip a special die into the tube and use a puller-like tool to force the die down onto the tube. This produces a "bell" on the end of the line. Remove the die, and use the pointed end of the tool to force the bell inward, creating a double flare. Simple, once you get the hang of it. We used a 45-degree flaring tool kit from Eastwood; it came with excellent instructions. Pure Choice also sells flaring kits, and both companies offer 37-degree flaring tools for working with stainless line as well.

LEARN FROM OUR MISTAKES

- Before you make a flare, make sure the fitting is on the line! Luckily, I only made this mistake once on the Olds. If it happens, you can usually cut the flare off, slip the fitting on, and reflare the tube. But if you're trying to be precise and there's no "give" in the tube, you'll probably have to bend a new line.

- Before you make a bend, make sure the fitting is at the end of the line! Fittings can't slide past a bend, and you may find yourself starting over if the fitting is on the wrong side of the bend. As Burger says, "When working with hard tubing, know where your nuts are."

- If you're running one flex line to the rear end, like I did, you may find it easier to run the lines on the rear end before it's installed in the car. I had a heckuva time routing the lines around and through some of the suspension brackets, clamps, and so forth.

When the brake lines were all done and routed, I went through and tightened all the fittings, hoping for no leaks when the system gets "juiced." I finished the job by using the large Eastwood rolling-cam bender to bend up the 3/8-inch fuel line, which runs down the right frame rail, then has to bend around the rear spring cups and go under the rear cross-member. Tricky bends for such large tubing, but the Eastwood bender did it easily.

Hot Rod Engines & Drivetrains

CHEVROLET V-8s, FROM MOUSE TO RAT 223

FORD V-8s 225

MOPAR ENGINES 229

BANGERS, NAILHEADS, Y-BLOCKS, AND OTHERS 229

INDUCTION—STROMBERG 97s TO EFI 232

IGNITION 234

ENGINE—DRIVEN ACCESSORIES 235

EXHAUST 235

TRANSMISSIONS 237

INSTALLING A HOT ROD DRIVETRAIN 238

IN THE SHOP:

DESIGNING AN AUTOMATIC SHIFTER LINKAGE 240

MAKING A RETRO-TECH AIR CLEANER 243

For classic hot rod looks, you can't beat a well-dressed flathead Ford. Before the advent of the small-block Chevy, it was the engine of choice. The flathead has had its problems and its share of detractors, but today it's enjoying a renaissance of sorts. Built with care, a flathead can be just as cool and reliable as a Chevy, and they produce decent power. And with Halibrand now offering NOS blocks, they're more attractive than ever. *Hot Rod & Custom Supply*

When it comes to defining your hot rod's identity, two things are paramount: the wheel and tire package, and the engine and tranny. Wheels and tires have a huge impact on the car's first visual impression, but the engine and tranny determine whether you've got a hot rod, a street rod, or something else entirely.

Deciding what kind of engine and tranny to use is just like any other hot rod decision—it's based on your needs, wants, and abilities. Are you an accomplished mechanic? Then you're probably able to work on and maintain an odd-ball, obsolete motor like an Olds 303 or Buick Nailhead with a stickshift. In addition, you can probably deal with the complexities of six Stromberg 97s on a log intake, or setting up a modern electronic fuel injection system. If you're a mechanical klutz or newbie, stick with the simple stuff, like a Chevy small block, a Turbo 350 automatic, or a new Edelbrock Performer four-barrel, which is easy to install and works correctly right out of the box. In other words, don't try to build something that YOU can't work on.

Money will also be a prime concern. That Nailhead/stickshift/six Stromberg setup will thin your wallet much more than the more pedestrian Chevy 350/Turbo 350/four-barrel combo. Those funky old motors are neat, and we're glad they're making a comeback, but a standard rebuild on most of those motors will cost at least twice as much as a standard small-block Chevy rebuild. Parts for vintage motors are scarce and expensive, and you won't find rebuilt long-blocks in the Summit catalog or at the local parts store. You'll have to find a professional engine builder who knows or remembers how to build an old motor. So, let's take a brief look at some of the more popular options.

CHEVROLET V-8s, FROM MOUSE TO RAT

Since 1955, the Chevrolet small-block has reigned supreme among hot rodders. It was small, lightweight, inexpensive, and powerful. In fact, in 1957 it became the first production motor to have 1 horsepower per cubic inch. Factory performance parts were available immediately, and the aftermarket has had 45 years to develop every conceivable performance and dress-up item.

The small-block seems to have been designed for hot rods. First, it's short enough and narrow enough to fit in the smallest hot rod engine bay, including Model T and Model A Fords. It's always had a rear-sump oil pan, so there was never any problem clearing the steering linkage. It's available in stock sizes from 265 to 400 cubic inches, and aftermarket pistons and stroker cranks can take it even larger. That gives the small-block unprecedented versatility. Build a 383 stroker motor (a 350 with a 400 crank), and you have a reliable torque monster that's great for street use. Find a somewhat rare 1969 DZ-code 302 block, and you can build a powerful little screamer that'll run at 7,000 rpm all day long, and can survive blips to 8,000 rpm and above.

Today, the small-block is plentiful and cheap. Donor cars are everywhere, mail-order houses stock performance long-blocks ready to ship, and for a little more money, GM has several brand-new crate motors that offer the ultimate in dependable, streetable performance.

In recent years, there's been some minor backlash among hot rodders against the small-block, which has been derided as a "belly button"

motor. For a while there, it did seem that every new street rod on the block had a 350, a Turbo 350 tranny, and a 9-inch Ford rear. But there's a reason for that combo's popularity: it flat-out works, dang near every time.

The bottom line is this: If you need a simple, dependable, inexpensive powerplant, buy or build a small-block Chevy. You can build it mild or wild, and you can dress it up to look modern or nostalgic, depending on your car's theme.

Big Block Chevy

Introduced in the 1965 model year as a 396-ci engine, the Chevrolet big-block has since been available as a 402, 427, 454, and now as a 502-ci crate motor. In its first year, the big-block was available in two versions. The hotter of the two had 11:1 compression and produced 425 horses and 415 foot-pounds of torque, which definitely put this motor in the big leagues. In 1966, Chevy upped the ante by increasing the bore to produce the first 427 (the top version of this motor was still rated at 425 horses, but torque increased to 460 foot-pounds). The 454 came along in 1970, and was rated conservatively at 360 horsepower.

The big-block Chevy produces more horsepower and torque than its smaller sibling, it

The ultimate nostalgia motor has to be a flathead with the rare and expensive Ardun overhead-valve conversion. (For a color view see page 145.) This example is sitting in Bob McGinley's 1932 Ford chassis, and features numerous tricks to bring it into the new millennium. This car is on the street now, and the engine looks, sounds, and performs like nothing else.

responds well to modifications, and it is well supported with aftermarket equipment. There are disadvantages, though. A big-block is physically larger and more difficult to fit under the hoods of early hot rods. It's also heavier, and building a big-block is significantly more expensive than building a comparable small-block. Still, there's a significant "wow" factor when you open the hood to reveal a hot rod big-block, and for some guys, that's worth the extra cost and inconvenience.

FORD V-8s

Ford has more V-8 experience than any other automotive manufacturer, with continuous production of one motor or another since 1932. There are only a couple of Ford engine families that are currently popular with hot rodders though—the original Ford flathead and the Windsor family of small-blocks. Other motors, such as the Y-blocks and the Ford Engine family of big-blocks, have significant downsides, and it takes a dedicated blue-oval fanatic to build a hot rod around one.

Ford Flatheads

Henry's flathead was a milestone event in automotive manufacturing when it made its debut in 1932. It was the first low-cost V-8 engine

Does it get any prettier than an injected Nailhead? This photo was taken in 1961 of the author's 1932 Ford three-window. The Hilborn injection on this motor is mechanically operated; today a Hilborn can be converted to electronic fuel injection for vintage looks and modern performance.

The small-block Chevy can't be beat for versatility, reliability, and power. This example is right out of *American Graffiti*, with the vintage no-name valve covers and Man-A-Fre four-deuce intake.

You don't have to stick with factory fuel injection, if you choose that route. The owner of this 1938 Ford Standard built a hi-rise EFI using a variety of stock and aftermarket parts. Snorkel air duct leads to an air filter behind the grille.

in the world. After some initial teething problems, the flathead survived until 1953, when it was replaced by Ford's overhead-valve Y-block. Until the mid-1950s, the flathead was the hot rodder's engine of choice, but its dominance started to wane with the introduction of overhead-valve V-8s, and it ended with the introduction of the small-block Chevy.

In the years since 1955, the flathead nearly disappeared from the hot rod radar. They developed a reputation as crack-prone, overheating, slugs of motors that had no place in a hot rod engine bay. Luckily, a few dedicated die-hards kept the traditional flathead flame alive, and today the engine is experiencing a renaissance of interest.

Built properly and carefully, a Ford flathead can be as dependable and fun as any small-block, and nothing looks better than a well-dressed flathead in a traditional rod's engine bay. Vintage speed equipment is fairly plentiful,

and manufacturers like Edelbrock, Offenhauser, and even Navarro are still making brand-new intakes and heads for the flathead. A number of new products for flatheads are available, including electronic fuel injection setups. Modern hot rodders have adapted Ford's C-4 automatic and later-model manual trannies to the flathead as well.

The only problems associated with flatheads are the cost of building one, finding a good block (they're often cracked), and finding someone who knows how to put one together right. Oddly enough, Halibrand recently solved some of these problems when it began importing NOS flathead blocks from France. Apparently, Ford licensed the design to Simca back in the 1950s, and that company continued to build flatheads well into the 1980s. They didn't just build them, though. They continued to improve the block, reducing or eliminating the cracking, intake and exhaust flow problems, and overheating problems in the process. These improved blocks accept all standard Ford parts, and Halibrand also has NOS cranks, pistons, and rods for them. The cost of one of these new blocks is comparable to the cost of finding, fixing, and machining a vintage block, so Halibrand will probably sell as many of these as they can get.

For information on finding and building a good flathead, we recommend checking out some of the books in the source appendix.

Ford Small-Blocks

In 1962, Ford introduced a new, compact small-block V-8 that displaced 221 cubic inches. A couple years later that engine grew to 260 ci, then 289 and 302 ci . . . and it became world-famous when it became the powerplant of choice for Shelby's Cobras and the Ford Mustang. Later, the Windsor-built motor was given a taller deck and was stroked to 351 ci. Today, the 302s and 351s are good hot rod powerplants, and the engine of choice for those stubborn souls who believe that all Fords should be powered by Fords. There's plenty of aftermarket speed equipment available (but not as much as for the Chevy), and Ford Motorsports offers a full line of factory hop-up parts and even crate motors.

Ford also built slightly different 302 and 351 motors in the 1970s, named Cleveland motors for their manufacture plant. These engines had heads with canted valves and other refinements that gave them higher performance; the Boss 302 motor was a Cleveland, and the HO 351s and Cobra Jet 351s are both good high-performance variants.

Ford small-blocks have never eclipsed the Chevys in hot rodding because of higher building costs and size—the Ford small-blocks are fairly narrow, but they are longer, so fitting them into early cars requires some work. One other consideration is that most stock Ford V-8s have the oil pan sump in front, which can interfere with a hot rod's steering. For 289s and 302s, the solution is to find a Bronco oil pan with a rear sump, or one of the aftermarket rear-sump pans available from Ford Motorsports.

Don't forget the inliners for potential hot rod power—especially the vintage ones. This T-bucket is powered by an early-1950s Ford flathead six-cylinder. Funky and fun.

Street & Performance is one of the leading suppliers of late-model fuel-injection setups and engines. At right is a new Corvette LS-1 motor equipped with nitrous oxide injection, and at left is one of Chevy's new Ram Jet fuel-injected crate motors.

Small-blocks are great, but for some hot rodders they're, well, small. Don Groff chose a big-block for his project, then fed it with twin turbos to boot. Beautiful workmanship on this engine, and on the rest of the car.

The Chrysler Hemi has made a comeback recently too, due in part to the availability of new 426 crate motors from Chrysler. This example is a 1950s vintage motor, probably a 354. Nothing looks better to a Mopar fan than those huge chrome valve covers.

MOPAR ENGINES

Chrysler's most common modern hot rod motor is its small-block, produced in 318-, 340-, and 360-ci versions. These motors are slightly larger than a small-block Chevy, so they're tougher to fit into a hot rod, but if you're a Mopar fan they're a good choice. Speed equipment is available both from the aftermarket and from Mopar Direct Connection, but there isn't quite the variety that there is for a small-block Chevy, and building one is slightly more expensive.

In the last couple of years, Mopar has been making a very nice 360-ci crate motor that some hot rodders are using.

Chrysler (and Dodge and DeSoto) Hemis

In hot rodding and racing, the ultimate performance statement has almost always been the Chrysler Hemi. Chrysler's first hemi appeared in 1951 as a 331-ci motor, and its design is rumored to have been heavily influenced by the Ardun overhead-valve conversion for the flathead Ford. Dodge and De Soto had their own variants of the "baby" hemi; then, in 1956, the Chrysler hemi grew to 354 cubes, and

in 1957 it expanded further to 392 ci. The final evolution of the Chrysler hemi came in the 1960s, when the monstrous 427 Hemi came to dominate most forms of American racing and the musclecar world as well.

Today, Mopar has crate Hemis available in the original 426-ci displacements and in bigger versions up to 528 ci. Earlier hemis are popping up under hot rod hoods as well, especially the 354 and 392 engines from the later 1950s. There's a fair amount of performance equipment available both new and used, but expect to pay top dollar for most of it. In fact, cost is probably the biggest obstacle to building any Hemi—the engines, parts, and labor to build one will set you back a bunch. They're also large motors, but if you can fit it and afford it, nothing will turn heads like a Chrysler Hemi in a hot rod.

BANGERS, NAILHEADS, Y-BLOCKS, AND OTHERS

With nostalgia being such a popular trend in hot rodding, we've seen a lot of interest in vintage hot rod motors of the 1950s, including Ford four-cylinders, Buick Nailheads, Olds 303s and

Unique is the best word to describe this combination—a Model T with a Saturn four-banger. The biggest trick to this installation is to convert the engine from its transverse orientation and mounting it inline with a conventional transmission. Makes a neat hot rod motor, though.

A Hemi doesn't have to be nostalgic, though. Don Groff's next project, a 1955 Chevy pickup, is powered by this 354. Don built his own intake and adapted a GM-tuned port injection to it for modern performance and reliability.

324s, Ford Y-blocks, and even a few Studebaker motors and Chevy/GMC sixes. While they may look great and perform well, all of these engines require a high degree of commitment by the builder in terms of time, knowledge, and money. Remember, these engines are obsolete for a reason. Parts will be hard to find, they'll be costly to rebuild, and you need to be thoroughly educated in what works and what doesn't for the engine you choose.

We don't mean to scare you away from using such a motor; on the contrary, variety is the spice of hot rodding, and we'd hate to see an event with nothing but small-block Chevys under the hood. Just realize that going against the hot rod power current will require you to paddle a little harder.

Once you pick a motor, you have to build it, a subject that's several books all by itself. What you do to your hot rod motor's internals is up to you, just be certain you keep in mind the car's intended use when you build the motor. A little cam is a good thing, and a lot of cam is even better at the strip, but remember that lumpy cams can make life on the street difficult. Only build your motor as trick as it needs to be.

Once you pick an engine, you have to work on some of the other systems that work with it. The systems that affect fitting the engine and reliability the most are induction, ignition, and exhaust.

Ford builds small-blocks too; the 302s and 351s are a bit tougher to fit into older cars, but it can be done with satisfying results. This example features a B&M supercharger.

HOT ROD ENGINE STATS

Engine	CID	Length	Width	Weight	Sump
SB Chevy	265–400	26.5	19.5	535	rear
BB Chevy	396–454	30.5	22	635	rear
Chevy 6	235–250	30.5	16.5	415	rear
Ford flathead	221–255	30	26	525	rear
Ford SB	260–351	27	20	460–550	front
Ford BB	332–428	30	23	650	front
Chrysler Hemi	426	32	28.5	690	center
Olds V-8	350–455	29	21.5	620	rear
Pontiac V-8	455	29.5	23	650	rear
Buick V-8	455	29	23	600	rear
Buick Nailhead	264–322	30	22	630	rear
Cadillac	472–500	30	23.5	625	center

• length is from fan mounting face on waterpump to bellhousing mounting face on back of block
• width is measured between the outside edges of valve covers or heads, whichever is wider
• weights are approximate for a long-block with intake, less flywheel

Nostalgia motors need nostalgia parts. This is just a portion of the flathead Ford four- and eight-cylinder speed equipment in Fred Rowe's collection. Fred has definite plans to use much of it, too.

They may be a little tough to tune, but nothing says *hot rod* quite like three two-barrels under the hood. This Chevy intake sports three Rochester carbs with vintage-style air cleaners from Main Street Hot Rods.

INDUCTION—STROMBERG 97s TO EFI

How you feed your hot rod engine has a lot to do with the car's personality and reliability, and in extreme cases, it might cause fitment problems in the engine bay. We'll talk about the most modern induction systems first.

Electronic Fuel Injection

On the new end of the spectrum we have factory-made electronic fuel injection (EFI). An EFI system is quite simple—a conventional butterfly controls air flow; an electronic solenoid (or solenoids) controls fuel flow; electronic sensors monitor intake air flow, temperature, air pressure, throttle position, and the completeness of the burn; and a computer uses this information to constantly adjust the timing and duration of the fuel injector pulses. A decent EFI system will cost more than a carb and will require more effort to install correctly, what with the wiring and such. However, once it's up and running, it's extremely flexible and requires almost no maintenance.

If you want EFI for your hot rod, you have several options, both in types of EFI systems and in sources. The two main types of EFI available are throttle-body and multi-port. Throttle-body injection uses a more-or-less conventional intake manifold with a throttle-body mounted in place of the carb. One or two fuel injectors are mounted in the throttle body, and they spray timed pulses of fuel down into the manifold, just like a carb does. Multi-port systems are more sophisticated in that they have special intake manifolds, and they feature one injector for each cylinder. The injectors are placed in the intake directly over each intake

Chassis Engineering makes motor mounts to put a wide variety of engines in an even wider variety of cars. This example is a small-block Chevy mounted in a 1947 Chevy.

port in the heads. Multi-port fuel injection is more efficient and produces more power, but the extra injectors and associated plumbing make them slightly more complex and more costly.

If you want to use EFI on a hot rod, your first option is to find a donor car that has an injected engine of your choice; these days that's most likely a Ford Mustang 5.0 or a Camaro. Both Ford and Chevy have very good factory EFIs that feature multi-port injection systems. The aftermarket has come to the rescue when it comes to installing these systems in a hot rod, too. Complete aftermarket wiring harnesses are available, along with hopped-up computer chips, high-flow intake runners and intake bodies, and even complete multi-port injection manifolds for a variety of engines.

Several companies, such as Holley and Accel, also manufacture aftermarket throttle-body injection systems, which are very simple to install and use.

You can also buy an induction system that has a good nostalgic look with the modern function of EFI, thanks to outfits like BDS and IDA Automotive. They can take vintage mechanical fuel injection systems (like Hilborn and Algon stacks, or even the Hilborn hat-type injectors) and modify them to function as a modern EFI. We've even seen an IDA setup that looks for all

the world like six Strombergs on a log intake, but it is in fact a multi-port EFI system that uses two of the Strombergs to manage airflow.

If you want a crate motor, EFI, and easy installation, Chevrolet just introduced the Ram Jet 350 crate motor. For $4,500, you get a complete Chevy 350 crate motor with Vortec heads and a complete fuel injection system that bears more than a passing resemblance to an early 1960s Rochester mechanical fuel injection unit. It produces 350 horses and 400 foot-pounds of torque, and features a four-bolt main block, a roller cam, and roller rockers. The beauty of the Ram Jet, though, is its simplicity. It uses GM's MEFI-3 control module, which was originally developed for marine engines, so the fuel injection system is self-contained. There's no external computer, and no external sensors. Just hook it up to fuel and a 12-volt power supply and it's ready to go.

Carburetors

We believe in electronic fuel injection—it's reliable, efficient, and clean-burning, which is going to be every hot rodder's concern as time goes on. But for a lot of us, $4,500 is still a lot of money to pay for a crate motor, and even a bargain fuel injection setup is still out of reach, financially. In that case, there's nothing wrong

These tubular engine mounts are custom fabricated. They use a urethane bushing to minimize engine movement while still keeping vibrations from reaching the chassis. *Tim Remus*

with a good ol' carburetor. What carb or carbs you choose depends on what you're after in terms of performance and looks. Most of us will be just fine with a single four-barrel carb on our street motors (in fact, one of the most scary-fast hot rods I've ever driven had a very hot 302 Chevy DZ motor with a single Holley four-barrel), and the aftermarket is currently awash in great carb choices from Edelbrock, Holley, Barry Grant Fuel Systems, and Demon.

The next step up is multiple carbs, either two four-barrels or three two-barrels. For real-world performance and ease of maintenance, it's tough to beat two fours, and this is a combination that's been overlooked in the recent past. But if it's nostalgic good looks you want, three twos are the way to go. Vintage Stromberg 97 carbs look right for this application, but more modern Rochester two-barrels can easily be substituted for better reliability, and they're a lot easier to find at this point than Strombergs. Properly tuned and set up with progressive linkage, three twos can be a good, streetable carb setup, but they do take a little more maintenance and care.

Of course, hot rodders of old used to think that if three is good, four must be better and six is great! We'd caution against most four and six-carb intakes though. Vintage Edelbrock and Man-A-Fre four-carb intakes are still around, but

they are notoriously tough to tune for the street. Likewise, vintage six-carb intakes are still fairly easy to find for a variety of hot rod engines, but tuning and maintaining six two-barrels is just about a full-time job. Most guys who run these intakes on the street are only using the two center carbs; the outer four have block-off plates and no fuel supply.

IGNITION

Once your engine has gas, you have to light the fire, and that job falls to the ignition system. Aside from magnetos (which are not normally used on the street), there are three basic types of ignition systems found on hot rods today: points-type distributors, electronic distributors, and crank-trigger ignition.

Points-Type Ignition

Points ignition was used in just about all cars until electronic ignition came along in the 1970s. You should be able to find stock and aftermarket points distributors for just about any hot rod engine you can name, and when they're set up right, a good old-fashioned distributor will work great for hot rod use.

If you're going to use a points distributor, get it checked out by a good distributor technician. Have it spun up on a distributor machine so you can check the operation of the points and make sure the advance mechanism is working OK and that the advance curve is correct. A good distributor guy can adjust the springs and weights on the advance mechanism to dial a distributor in for your particular motor and driving style.

A points distributor that's properly set up and maintained works fine, but if you're going to run one you should be well versed in installing, setting, and maintaining it. You may also want to pack a tune-up kit (points, condenser, cap, and rotor) along with a dwell meter in your trunk. If you don't want to carry spares, we'd caution against using an older aftermarket distributor. If it breaks down on the road, parts could be difficult to find.

Electronic Ignition

In an electronic distributor, a magnetic reluctor takes the place of the distributor lobes, and the points are replaced by an amplifier. As the tips of the magnetic reluctor pass the amplifier, they cause the coil to fire a spark that the distributor then routes to the correct cylinder.

Electronic distributors are more reliable, more precise, and they usually generate a more powerful spark than a points-type ignition. The only drawback is that most of them are larger in diameter than a conventional distributor, and this causes fitment problems, especially on Chevy motors where the distributor is often right up against the firewall. Some aftermarket electronic distributors are smaller in diameter, though.

The other disadvantage to an electronic distributor is that it doesn't "look right" on a nostalgia motor. However, aftermarket electronic ignitions are available that can be installed in vintage distributors, giving the right look with modern performance.

Crank-Trigger Ignition

Until recently, crank-trigger ignition was hardware for racing only. However, newer engines such as the Chevy LS-1 use crank-trigger ignition, and those engines are turning up in a number of hot rods. A crank-trigger ignition uses the same principle as an electronic distributor, except the reluctor assembly is very large in diameter and is mounted directly to the front end of the crankshaft. As it turns, it passes an amplifier that generates the coil firing signals. Because they work directly off the crank, these systems are supposed to be more precise than conventional distributors, and they save some space. Retrofitting one to an older engine probably wouldn't be worth the effort, though.

ENGINE–DRIVEN ACCESSORIES

One of the biggest problems in stuffing a newer engine into an old engine bay is the belt-driven accessories on the front of engine—water pumps, fans, alternators/generators, and AC compressors. The problem is threefold: First, the need for pulleys and belts to drive all these things eats up precious room for the radiator. Second, components like alternators and AC

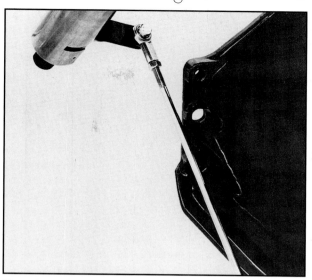

If you're going to use a column shift, linkage like this Lokar kit will make the installation simple. Keep in mind, though, that if your motor mounts are too flexible, engine torque can cause a direct connection like this to shift the tranny into neutral. Polyurethane motor mounts or a torque strap can solve this problem.

compressors often need to be moved so they don't interfere with hood panels or inner fender panels. Third, when you start mixing and matching brackets and pulleys, it's tough to keep them aligned properly so the belts run true.

Luckily, there are several solutions. The aftermarket has lots of pulleys and brackets available, usually with the space constraints of a hot rod engine bay in mind. You can also switch over to a serpentine belt system, which uses one long multispline flat belt to drive everything. The advantage is that one belt takes up less space than two or three, but the disadvantage is cost. You usually have to buy a custom serpentine system that includes all the brackets, pulleys, tensioners, and other hardware to do the job. If you can afford it, they work great, though.

Finally, you can build your own brackets. By choosing your accessories and pulleys carefully, you can custom-build brackets that will do the job. You have to have good fabrication skills and a good working knowledge of how all the belt-driven components work, but it can be done.

EXHAUST

First things first: If it's a hot rod, it has dual exhaust. The only exception to this is if you have a hopped-up vintage four-banger, then a single big pipe is appropriate. Any six- or eight-cylinder hot rod engine worth its salt should have dual exhaust. No exceptions.

Fitting dual exhausts in a hot rod can be a tough proposition, and it's something that should be considered through the entire building process, not just the end. We'll start at the front, with the exhaust manifolds or headers.

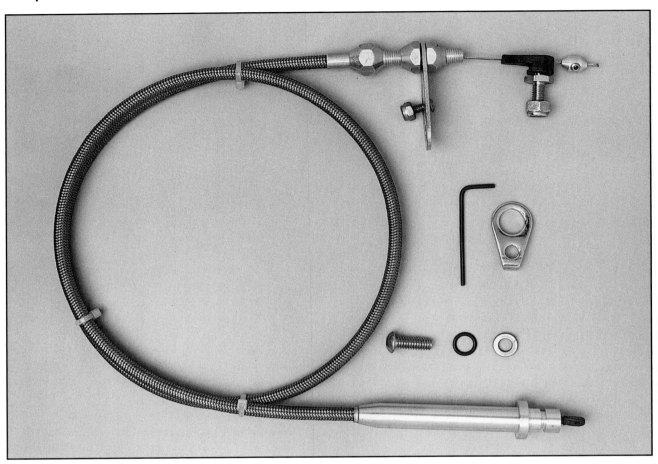

Lokar also makes cable systems for tranny kick-downs and throttle pedals. This cable connects the throttle linkage to the kick-down on a Turbo 350 automatic transmission.

And that's your first decision: manifolds or headers. There are a few OEM cast-iron exhaust manifolds that flow well, but you're almost always going to get better performance from a good set of tuned headers. For most hot rods, you should be able to find an aftermarket set of headers that will fit for most engines. For instance, several manufacturers offer block-hugger headers for small-block Chevys, and they'll fit in just inside the frame of just about any hot rod.

If you can't find headers for your motor/hot rod combination, you can build them yourself. Headers by Ed offers complete header kits, and you can buy mandrel bends and tubing in mild or stainless steel from a number of sources. Building headers takes some serious thought, though. You not only have to fit all those tubes past your motor mounts, steering, and other parts . . . you also should get each tube to be the same length from head to collector for optimum performance.

Stainless or Not?

If you have a little extra money, stainless steel headers, tubing, and mufflers are a good investment. Hot rods generally aren't used year around, and sitting in the garage for the winter months is when a steel exhaust system rusts. Your other options are aluminized pipe, which holds up pretty well, or exhaust coatings like Jet Hot. Coatings are a good option for headers and exhaust pipes; a ceramic thermal barrier coating is applied to the inside and outside of the pipes, then baked on. The coating keeps heat in the system and prevents corrosion for a long time. We know of headers and pipes that have been on hot rods for 10 years with no rust. If you can't afford or don't want stainless, a good quality header coating is worth the cost.

Tubing and Mufflers

After the headers or manifolds, you have to route the exhaust pipes through the frame to the back of the car (never have an exhaust system that ends under the car—it's a sure way to poison yourself with carbon monoxide). There are two main options here: bending pipe or fabricating. The easier option is to find a good, experienced custom exhaust shop. They can custom-bend exhaust pipes for your car in plain steel, aluminized steel, or stainless. Just make sure they know exactly what you want, and where you want the pipes routed.

The second option is to build the exhaust yourself, using mandrel bends and straight tubing sections. This takes more time, but you're guaranteed to get what you want, the bends look cleaner (without the squashed look a pipe bender can give), and you can give more attention to details like hangers. To do this you'll need to buy a stock of 180-degree mandrel bends and some straight tubing. By cutting the mandrel bends with a band saw and rejoining them, you can route tubing around just about any obstacle. The result is a true custom exhaust system that you'll be proud of.

TRANSMISSIONS

The final driveline element is the transmission, and the big decisions are whether you want an automatic or a manual, and how stout a tranny you need for your engine's power.

Automatics

Automatics are still the tranny of choice for most builders, both for simplicity and maintenance. A good automatic tranny is easier to use, and much easier to install and hook up. The only disadvantage is their size; automatics are much larger than manual trannies, and the chassis often has to be modified to accommodate them.

In the GM world, the Turbo 350 is the most popular tranny, followed closely by the Turbo 400. Both are three-speeds, but the Turbo 400 is a stronger tranny and capable of handling more power. However, it's not as efficient (more horsepower is lost as heat), and it's larger than a 350 (especially at the back end), so cross-member interference can be a problem.

In recent years, hot rodders have also been blessed with the 700-R4 and the 200-R4 automatic transmissions. Both are four-speed overdrive trannies with lock-up torque converters, and they offer a lot of advantages. First, the overdrive fourth gear means you can have a low-geared rear end for quick starts, and still have a reasonable engine rpm at highway speeds. Second, the lock-up torque converters act like a clutch at highway speeds, so these trannies are much more efficient. Of the two, the 700-R4 is the heavier unit, and it can be modified to handle lots of horsepower. The 200-R4 is much lighter duty, and is best suited for mild-motored street cars.

Ford has its choices as well, notably the C4, the C6, and the AOD (automatic overdrive). The C4 and C6 are conventional automatic three-speeds, with the C6 being the stronger and larger of the two. The AOD is the Ford equivalent of the 700-R4, and is a good choice for the same reasons.

Shifting an Automatic

Most hot rodders choose to install floor shifters for their automatic transmissions, and most of those shifters come from aftermarket suppliers like Gennie Shifter or Lokar. Installing one of

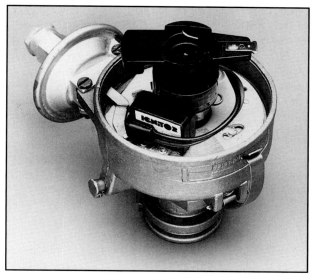

Electronic ignition is generally more powerful and more reliable than points ignition; and now, almost any points distributor can be upgraded to electronic by adding this ignition module from Pertronix. This is especially good for older nostalgia motors.

these shifters is as simple as following the instructions; the biggest trick is locating the shifter on the tranny so it clears any floor supports.

Column shifters are still found though, and the choices here are modified factory linkage or an aftermarket kit. Hookup is straightforward, but you have to use some trial and error to make sure that the shift mechanism and the transmission shifter are in synch: i.e., P means park, R is reverse, etc. The only downside to the aftermarket column shift linkages is that they go directly from the column to the transmission. If you have rubber motor mounts, the engine and tranny can move enough on acceleration to pull on the linkage and shift the tranny out of gear. This can be overcome with polyurethane motor mounts or a torque strap, or by installing an OEM-style shift linkage that uses a bell-crank-style intermediate link.

Manual Transmissions

But, everybody knows that real hot rods have three pedals. Face it, a four-speed (or three or five) is FUN to drive. It's good to row through the gears, it's good to work that clutch pedal, and it's good to shift for yourself. We're not going to go through all the manual tranny options here—there are simply too many, from the 1939 Ford top-loader three-speed to a new Richmond Gear six-speed.

However, building a hot rod with a stickshift is a little more work, mainly because of that third pedal and the linkage it requires. For the most part, hot rods with a clutch pedal are going to have their pedals mounted under the floor, not on the firewall. For nostalgia rods, you can still use a Gennie early Ford pedal assembly, with

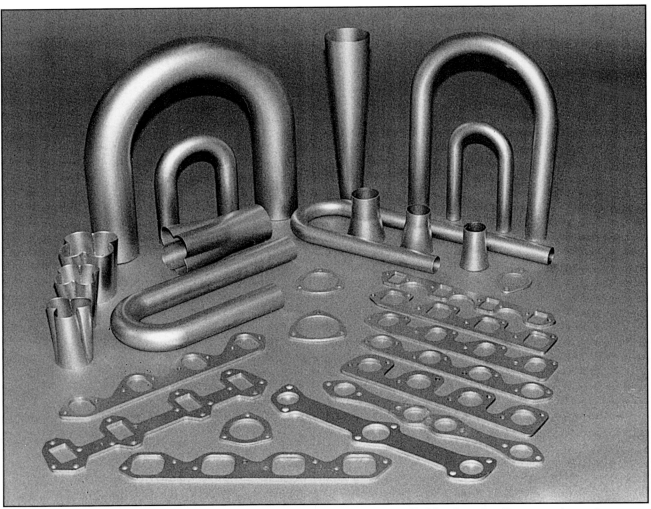

Block-hugger headers are available for most popular engines, but if you can't find headers that fit your engine and your car, a header kit from Headers by Ed might fill the bill. Ed sells header flanges for just about any engine you can think of, along with mandrel bends, collectors, flanges, and muffler blanks.

some modifications. Otherwise, you can opt for an aftermarket pedal assembly from Pete & Jake's or the Deuce Factory.

With underfloor pedals, clutch linkage is a relatively simple affair, usually consisting of a simple adjustable link running from the pedal arm to the throw-out arm. A stout return spring is also necessary.

Clutches can also be activated hydraulically in two ways. The first is to use a master cylinder connected to the clutch pedal (this is especially common when the pedals are hung from the firewall); then run a hydraulic line to a slave cylinder that actuates the throw-out arm. The pedal feel is different, but hydraulic clutches have been used in hot rods and a number of OEM applications for years. A newer hydraulic option is a hydraulic throw-out bearing, available from McLeod Industries. This specialized piece fits over the transmission output shaft, and replaces both the conventional throw-out

bearing and the throw-out arm. A clutch master is used to supply hydraulic pressure to the throw-out bearing, which expands and activates the clutch. This is a good solution for vehicles that don't have a lot of room for linkage.

INSTALLING A HOT ROD DRIVETRAIN

Before you pick an engine, you first have to make sure it's going to fit. Before you blow your project car apart, measure the width, length, and height of the engine compartment; then make those same measurements on the engine you want to use. If it fits easily, no problem. If it doesn't, relax. You can always find a way, but it may mean modifying or doing without hood sides, or moving the firewall back.

Doing an engine swap has gotten considerably easier over the years as the aftermarket has developed more engine mount kits. Today, you can install almost any popular engine in a Ford or Chevy hot rod using bolt-in engine and

Mandrel bends can also be used to custom-build a complete exhaust system, like on this 1946 Ford chassis. Note that there's a slip fit joint just ahead of the rear axle, so the system can be disassembled and removed after the car's together.

transmission mounts. If you want to do something different, you can still use some aftermarket parts to get part of the job done. Before we get to the how-tos, we'll go through the process of correctly positioning an engine in the chassis, and discuss what kind of motor mounts to use.

If you're doing a simple installation, like a small-block Chevy and a Turbo 350 tranny into a 1932 Ford (or any Ford or Chevy for that matter), do some research and buy an engine mount kit from the aftermarket. Pete & Jake's, Total Cost Involved, Chassis Engineering, and many other companies offer complete kits that are well engineered and will do the job simply.

If you have to build mounts, here's what to do: Get the car's frame sitting at ride height, and have the body (or just the firewall, if that's an option) positioned on the frame. Have the radiator and radiator mounts available as well. Bolt the engine and tranny together, and using a good, sturdy engine hoist, swing it into position between the frame rails.

Position the engine so that it's centered between the rails, and so the carb mounting surface is level front to rear and side to side. Position the engine as high as is practical so there's plenty of clearance between the oil pan

and the ground. Position it as far back as possible as well (just be sure that you'll still be able to remove the distributor and valve covers if need be). Install the headers or exhaust manifolds and check for steering shaft clearance, and make sure that things like the starter, fuel pump, and other accessories have plenty of room.

Once everything is in place, decide what kind of motor mounts you want. Stock rubber mounts are good for street cars because they offer lots of flexibility and isolate the car from engine noise and vibration. The downside is that sometimes they're too flexible for performance applications. Polyurethane mounts are generally good for hot rods. They're stiffer than stock, but they still offer a decent degree of vibration damping to the chassis. Solid motor mounts are for racing or very hot street applications only—if you don't care about vibration and noise, go right ahead.

If you have to build motor mounts and tranny mounts, make sure they're strong enough to do the job, and that they're not going to place any unintended stresses on the frame rails or other chassis members. Remember also that motor mounts need to be strong in just about every direction—up and down, side to side, and front to back. Build 'em stout.

IN THE SHOP:

DESIGNING AN AUTOMATIC SHIFTER LINKAGE

BY LANE ANDERSON

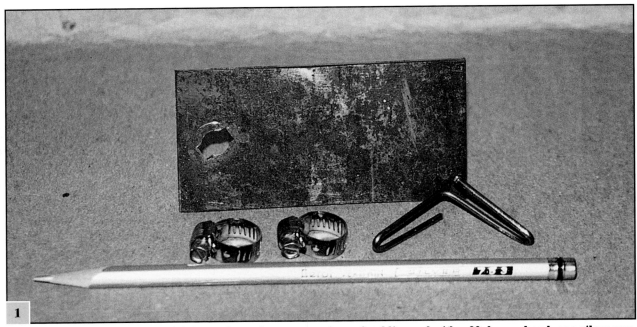

1

Here's what you'll need to do the job: two hose clamps, one piece of welding rod with a 90-degree bend, one silver pencil for marking metal (available at an art supply store), one 3/16 x 2 x 4-inch steel plate. *Lane Anderson*

2

When you mix and match automatic trannys and column shifters—as hot rodders usually do—you can't assume that everything will automatically be correct. That is, the "PRNDL" on the column might not always match up with the "PRNDL" in the tranny.

With a lot of money invested, you need to be sure that when you put the shifter into drive the transmission really is in drive. If this isn't the case, it's not only annoying, but if a tranny is operated when it's not completely in gear . . . well, few things smell more expensive than burning clutch plates in an automatic.

Drill a 3/8-inch hole, and with a couple swipes of the "Armstrong Milling Machine" (square file) the plate is ready to be bolted to the selector shaft of the transmission. *Lane Anderson*

And, when you put the shifter in park, are you sure the tranny is securely in park? Remember several years ago when one of the big three automakers had a problem with cars that "jumped" out of park, sometimes with disastrous results? The same thing can happen to your street rod if your shift linkage isn't set up right.

Well worry no more, Bunky. Just read on and we'll show you how to be sure that park is park and drive is drive. Incidentally, you can use this same technique to determine the correct linkage length and mounting location on an aftermarket column-shift linkage.

3

Attach the pencil to the shift rod with the welding rod and two clamps. *Lane Anderson*

4

Put both the tranny and shifter into Park. Position the clamp assembly so the pencil is located in the middle of the steel plate. Mark an arc on the steel plate. *Lane Anderson*

5

Put both the tranny and shifter into drive. Mark another arc on the steel plate. Where the two arcs cross will be the location of the hole for the shift linkage. *Lane Anderson*

6

Draw up any exotic-looking shift arm you desire and remove everything that doesn't look like your design. *Lane Anderson*

7

Here's your shift arm, esthetically pleasing and functionally correct. *Lane Anderson*

IN THE SHOP:

MAKING A RETRO-TECH AIR CLEANER

1

Here we go, a hunk of aluminum, a crusty old Olds air cleaner, and a little work will result in a nice-looking retro-tech air cleaner.

I've always liked those big funky Olds and Cadillac air cleaners; they're a stock piece, but they look custom with those two big forward-facing scoops. So a couple of years ago, I was wandering through a junkyard when I found a rough one. I picked it up, added it to the pile, and paid five bucks for it. Looked cool hanging on the garage wall, too.

But these air cleaners are so big they can overwhelm a normal-sized V-8 engine. When I dropped the 455 into the Big Olds, though, I knew that this air cleaner was a natural for it.

The Olds motor is big, with an intake that's practically a yard wide, and the air cleaner sits low enough to be in proportion with the motor. Originally, these cleaners were oil-bath types. To convert them to dry-element, just toss the stock bottom plate and replace it with a 12-inch-diameter OEM filter bottom and air filter (ours came from a 1970s Chevy Van with a V-8 and four-barrel) and plop the Olds top on. Works like a charm.

But once it was on the Olds motor, it still needed something different. I thought about

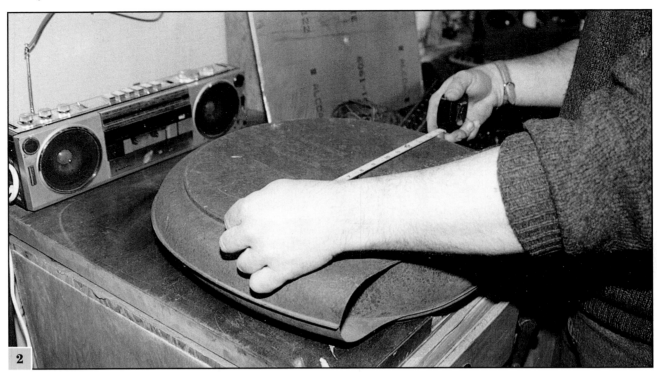

The air cleaner top isn't round, but oval. I measured the length and the diameter of the round ends, and measured the location of the mounting hole.

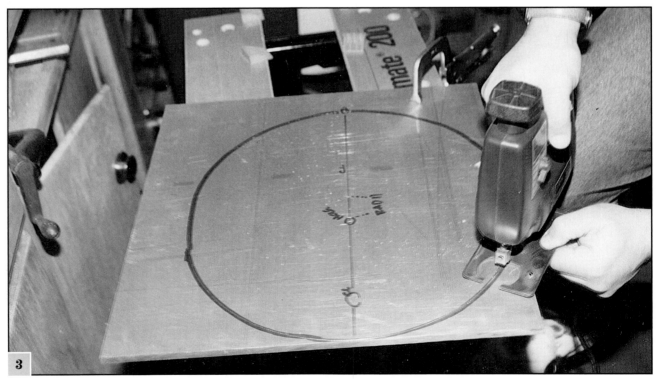

Mark the centerline on the aluminum plate, then center punch the locations of the two radii and the mounting hole on the centerline. Use a dividers to scribe the semicircles on the plate. To make the lines show up better, go over the scribe marks with a permanent marker, then carefully rescribe them (a can of DyChem—that blue stuff that you spray on aluminum—works better, but I couldn't find any; must be with the WD-40). Cutting the shape out with a jigsaw took about 20 minutes, but it worked and I only broke the blade once.

louvers in the top, and while they'd look good, they wouldn't make sense, and you'd have to block them off to make the air cleaner functional. But what about fins? The finned valve covers on the Olds look good, and it'd be neat to have a matching air cleaner.

With that in mind, I went to the local metal supply house and picked up a chunk of 3/8-inch aluminum big enough to cover the air cleaner top (in this case, about 15 x 17 inches). At $3.65 a pound, it set me back about $40.

The air cleaner top is not round. It's more of an oval shape with round ends and about 3-inch flat spaces on both sides. After measuring and laying out the shape on the aluminum, I scribed it, marked the scribe with permanent marker so I could see the line, then cut out the shape with a jigsaw and smoothed the edges with a disc sander.

Now, small aluminum-shaping operations can be done with an ordinary router with a carbide bit. Unfortunately, the only way to accurately cut fins in a job this big is on a mill, and while you probably don't have one in your shop, I'll bet you know someone who does. (A guy could also take a machining class at a votech and use that time and equipment to produce something like this.) In my case, I took it up to Barry Larson's garage, and he showed me how to set it up and turned me loose on his Bridgeport. Barry's mill is set up with a digital position indicator and a power feed, so after he showed me how to do the first center cut, I unlocked the table, moved it over 0.3750 inch (I wanted 1/8-inch fins 1/4 inch apart, so we used a 1/4-inch ball-end mill; the cuts are 0.200 inch deep), relocked it, and started the next cut. This process was repeated again and again, until three hours later I had a finned air cleaner top. Gave me a whole new appreciation for billet parts, let me tell ya.

After the cutting was done, we clamped it to a table and used some 180-grit paper to knock the burrs off, then followed that with some 320-grit. The part still looked too much like a billet piece, though, with its sharp-edged fins. So, I spent several more hours with a die grinder and file, rounding the ends of each fin. Then I polished them up, and painted the grooves black. Looks good now; in fact, it's the kind of piece that I'll probably keep when I sell the car, I like it so much.

The only thing left is to heat and shrink the three raised beads on top of the air cleaner so the aluminum will lie flat. The result is what you might call a retro-tech air cleaner.

4 Yep, me and Boyd, uh-huh. Now, we're not going to teach you how to run a Bridgeport in one caption, but we will tell you that an idiot editor with no previous machining experience can be taught to set one up and cut grooves in a slab of aluminum in very little time. If you shop around, you can find a decent, used Bridgeport (less tools) for about four grand. In other words, you won't be seeing one in my garage anytime soon.

5 To give the piece the right look, I spent several more hours with a die grinder and file, shaping the ends of each fin so it eventually looked more like a cast part. I then polished it, and painted the grooves with matte black paint.

Hot Rod Interiors

SEATING 247

STEERING COLUMN MOUNTING AND SELECTION 249

PEDAL LOCATION AND MOUNTING 251

DASHBOARD GAUGES 252

SAFETY 254

SELECTING MATERIALS 255

PATTERN 257

CARPETS 257

INTERIOR OVERVIEW 257

IN THE SHOP:

    HANGING A STEERING COLUMN 258

    ANCHORING SEATBELTS 262

    INSTALLING A FOUR-POINT HARNESS 264

    INSTALLING NEW GAUGES IN OLD DASHES 267

    RESTORING HEATERS 271

Few things in a good hot rod are as important as the interior. Even though almost every hot rodder would agree with that statement, it is amazing to us how many poorly planned and executed interiors we have seen in otherwise wonderful cars.

We're not sure if it is because it is typically the last part of the project and money and patience is often being stretched, or if it is a simple lack of thought and planning. Regardless of the reason, the results are often a disappointing cockpit in your hot rod. If the interior portion of the project is done poorly, the average rodder must live with the mistakes for at least several years and quite possibly for the life of the car. The cost of interior work today usually prevents rodders from correcting mistakes. It is for this reason that it is imperative to take your time and carefully plan the interior. Hopefully this chapter will be an aid in planning and constructing a safe, comfortable, and functional interior space in your next project.

With the body mounted on the chassis and the steering box or rack-and-pinion mounted in it's final position, you can start planning your car's interior. The firewall and floor should be complete, and the dashboard mounted in the body. Doors must be hung and fitted to the body. The glass need not be in the body, but if power windows are to be used we recommend installing them prior to mounting seats, but leave the window control switches unmounted for now.

While many people perform this process after the bodywork is complete, we recommend this fitting be done prior to final paint work. It provides the builder with more options and you are much more comfortable fitting seats and steering prior to applying the final finish on the body.

SEATING

Selecting the seats for your car is an involved process. The first decision is, stock or modified? For the resto-rod or traditional hot rod, the stock seats often work best. The seat is designed to place the driver in a relatively good position for viewing out the windshield and steering. Having said that, remember that many cars that are 60 and 70 years old were designed for a smaller generation. If you are 6 feet or taller, you will often find stock seats to be too high for good vision. Add about a 3-inch top chop and the problem compounds itself.

A common solution to this problem is to remove the stock seat frame from the floor of the car, and then mount the seat directly to the floor. This will usually result in about a 4-inch reduction in seat height.

Another pitfall of stock seating is that oftentimes the seats are nonadjustable. Mounted in solid fashion to the floor, it is a one-position-fits-all situation, which frankly doesn't work well, particularly for large-frame people.

This can be remedied by shortening the package tray behind the seat (in a coupe or road-

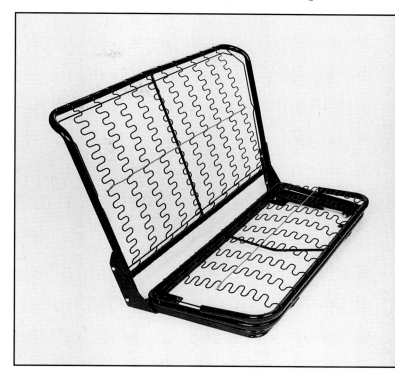

A basic hot rod is sometimes defined (by us anyway) as engine, tires, and a place to sit. That makes your hot rod's seat pretty important. One way to start is with a new steel seat frame, like this one from Glide Engineering. A good upholsterer can pad it and cover it to your tastes for a truly custom interior.

ster) and moving the seat rearward a few inches. It is amazing how much difference even 2 inches can make in seating comfort. When moving seats rearward in sedans, be mindful of the amount of legroom you are stealing from the rear occupants. We have seen many sedans and particularly Victorias where the rear seat is rendered virtually useless because the front seat has consumed all of the rear legroom. This is a decision determined by the amount of time you will be carrying rear-seated passengers.

Sedan deliveries present special problems. For starters, the doors are typically the same size as a four-door sedan front door. These short doors and associated windows can make seating difficult. If the seats are moved rearward too far, the driver is now in the cargo area and unable to see out of the windows. Second, often the cargo area is raised on sedan deliveries. This means if you plan on moving the seats rearward, the floor must be modified, something that should be planned for early on in a project.

Finally, trucks deserve some special attention when it comes to interior planning. Early truck cabs are typically quite small; after all, these vehicles were designed to haul cargo first, people second. Beyond that fact, most pickup trucks in the 1930s, 1940s, and 1950s were used for local hauling.

Want something even easier? TEA's Design offers a full line of pre-upholstered front and rear seats in several styles, and in the fabric of your choice. TEA's also offers matching fabric that you can use to finish the job.

It was only in the late 1960s and later that the pickup truck became a long-range vehicle.

Since the early cabs are small, seats are typically positioned as far rearward as possible. At times, even this does not provide the needed room. When this occurs you must determine early in the project (like the first day you bring the old truck home) if you are going to fit in this vehicle, and if so, for how long. If you're building a 1928 phone booth pickup for a local cruiser it might be fine, but if you're planning on driving 2,000 miles to the Nationals you might need another vehicle. The other solution to the lack of room in a pickup is to modify the cab by adding inches either behind the doors, ala king cabs of today, or through the doors. Once again it is amazing what a few inches will do for overall comfort.

Meanwhile, back to the seat decision. If you opted for stock seats, simply mount the seats in good position for the driver (or drivers) and move on to the steering column portion of this chapter. If more than one person is to drive the car, it is best to mount any seat on adjustable tracks.

If you have decided to go for custom seating, there are two basic choices: new custom seats or used seats from a late-model car. A second decision is bucket seats versus bench seating. The main factor in selecting custom seating is, like before, the space limitations.

Thankfully, since the 1980s, late-model passenger cars have become smaller, providing many seating options for hot rodders. Everything from Fiero to Taurus SHO seats works well in rods, not to mention many of the import cars. Bucket seats have the added advantage of providing individual adjustment for the occupants in both legroom and seat back inclination. In earlier hot rods, bucket seats fill the interior, in later cars a center console is in order, providing room for controls, wiring, and storage.

If used seats can be located with the leather in good condition they can be dyed to blend with the car, or the remainder of the interior can be dyed to match the seats. This can result in substantial savings on your interior. Even in sedans, often a used back seat can be located and

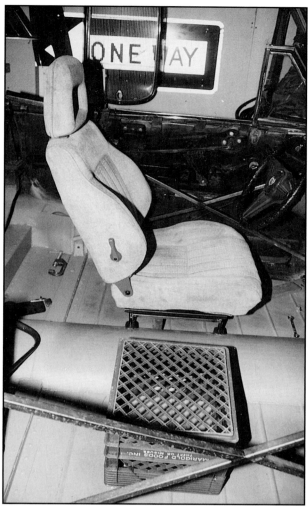

Then again, you can always pick up a nice pair of salvage-yard seats. Try to make arrangements with the yard ahead of time so you can get what you want when it comes in. Seats in a junkyard often get wet, dirty, or otherwise damaged. The other challenge is figuring out a seat mounting system to adapt them to your old car.

mounted in the rear. If the seat is a bit narrow a pair of fabricated armrests will fill the side-to-side void nicely.

After seats are selected, they must be safely mounted to the floor of the car. Obviously the floor must be structurally sound and rust free. Mount the seats with the same bolts that held the seat in the car originally, if possible. If that is not possible, mount the seats with the same diameter bolts and large washers.

Seats should be mounted to the floor of the body as a matter of safety. In the case of a serious collision, the body and the chassis can bend, fold, and crush at very different rates. It is best if the seats and the associated seatbelts are mounted to the floor. This method ensures that the seats and belts will move together should bending occur.

STEERING COLUMN MOUNTING AND SELECTION

After the seats are mounted in the car, the steering column can be installed. The column should be mounted so the driver has room to extend his arms forward but still have elbows bent comfortably. The adjustability of tilt and telescopic steering columns is a good thing for multidriver cars. We feel that the car should be planned to be comfortable in the "neutral" position of both tilt and telescopic. The adjustments should be used for a second driver, or long-drive comfort, not to make the car drivable.

Select a steering wheel that has a grip thickness that feels good in your hand. Then select the steering wheel diameter that provides ample room between your thighs and the steering wheel, while still providing ample leverage to turn the front wheels. The larger the wheel, the less effort required to turn those wheels.

To start the locating process, sit in the car and hold the steering wheel only, moving your arms up and down, forward and back to find the most comfortable position for the wheel. With the help of a friend, measure the distance from the back of the steering wheel to the floor. Next, use an old broomstick or other suitable round stock, and tape, screw, or bolt it to the steering wheel.

Now that you are back in the car with your makeshift steering column, move the steering wheel to the perfect position for the driver (feel free to make "motor sounds" at this time if you're alone in the garage). Mark the position of the broom handle on the floorboard of the car. Assuming you have the steering column, cut a hole in the floorboard that will permit the column to pass through the floor. Mount the steering wheel to the column, and climb back into the car. Slip the mast of the column down through the hole in the floorboard and slide behind the wheel.

Once again, locate the steering wheel in the perfect location. While holding it in this position, observe the required "drop" from the dashboard to the steering column. If possible, suspend the column from above by a pair of ropes, or brace it from the floor to the steering wheel to hold it in position.

There are many aftermarket steering column drops available today that are adjustable. These look great and work well. The other way to mount the column is to simply thread the ends of a piece of 3/8-inch, then bend it around the steering column in an open U-shape. You may also be able to use an exhaust clamp U-bolt if you find one that fits your steering column diameter. This large U-bolt will hold the column in place from underneath and then each threaded end will pass through the bottom flange of the dashboard. Final adjustment can be made by threading the U-bolt up or down through the dashboard to adjust the height.

With the steering column hanging in this U-bolt, slide behind the seat and check for comfort. Move the steering wheel up and down, forward and back, experimenting to find the perfect location. Sit in the seat for some time to get the feel of being behind the wheel. When you are certain that the steering wheel is exactly where you want it, you can complete the column drop and final floor mount on the steering column.

The floor mount is usually a simple flange affair that slides over the mast of the steering column and then bolts to the floorboard. Once again, these flanges are available from mail-order houses and your local rod shop. The floor flange is also a fairly easy piece to fabricate at home. A pair of set screws prevent the column from moving in or out of the floor hole.

Forming a piece of sheet metal to close the gap between the steering column and the dashboard completes the column drop. The U-bolt can be welded or simply clamped to the steering column. This completes the mounting of the column inside the body. If possible, run a second brace from the back of the column drop, forward to the firewall. This second brace triangulates the column drop, making it very solid. It also helps to stiffen the firewall if swing ped-

als are to be mounted on the firewall. It is imperative that the steering column be very solid and have no movement whatsoever when the mounting is complete.

Outside the firewall, the steering must be attached from the base of the steering column to the steering box or rack-and-pinion steering. Use NEW, quality universals that are designed specifically for automotive steering. Several aftermarket companies make steering universals and connecting kits that are well worth the money. We strongly recommend using these kits. The steel shaft and associated universal joints should be mounted in such a fashion that no binding occurs when turning the wheel from full right to full left. It should feel like one smooth, fluid motion. There is NO room for compromise in the steering system of a hot rod.

The steel shaft and universals should also incorporate either a stock "rag-joint" (a rubber disc piece) or a combination universal and vibration dampener to provide a nice, vibration-free steering wheel. We recently built a car and employed one of these combination steering universal joint and vibration dampeners. We were amazed at how much difference this piece

A focal point of any hot rod interior is the steering wheel and column. Tilt columns work well and look OK in larger cars, but often look too bulky in an early hot rod. Mullins Steering Gears offers this all-new traditional steering column, column drop, and sprint-car style four-spoke wheel.

Good gauges are vital to keep tabs on your hot rod's powerplant. These gauges from Classic Instruments have a clean, classic style and curved-glass lenses for easier viewing and good looks. The speedo is also electronic, so you can adjust it to match every hot rod's unique combination of transmission, rear end gears, and tire sizes. Your speedo will actually be accurate!

made in driver comfort. It provided a smooth, solid, vibration-free feeling to the wheel.

PEDAL LOCATION AND MOUNTING

Seating and steering are big items, but the third component that makes the difference between a comfortable and efficient drive and a tortured and cramped interior is the pedal placement. We have had the pleasure and alternately displeasure of driving many hot rods. It is amazing how many times we get into a car that has the throttle pedal mounted in a position that requires twisting your leg in two directions to apply pressure to the all-important "go pedal." We are not talking about a position that is proper for the owner but difficult for a non-owner, we are referring to pedal positions that no human could master.

Once again situate yourself behind the wheel, adjust the seat and steering wheel to the perfect driving position (which you should have achieved during fabrication). Now move your right foot to a position that is very comfortable, toward the firewall of the car where the throttle

pedal could be located. Mark that spot, and explore the engineering required to mate the pedal to the throttle linkage on the other side of the car. Cable throttle linkage has made this a very simple and versatile project.

Once it has been determined that the throttle is both comfortable and functional, mount the pedal to the firewall and double-check for comfortable location. The brake pedal should be to the left of the throttle (surely we didn't have to mention that) and the face of the pedal should be a bit higher than the throttle pedal. In an ideal installation, the driver should not have to lift his foot off the floor to move it from the throttle to the brake pedal. It should be a simple pivot operation that permits the right foot to move from throttle to brake.

If you have to lift you foot it takes longer to get onto the brake pedal, which could be critical in an emergency, and it is also tiring. Care must be taken when positioning the brake pedal. By fabricating master cylinder mounts in the proper location, the factory-length pedal should be maintained. The pedal can either hang from the firewall (if the firewall is braced properly) or come up through the floor if the master cylinder is mounted to the chassis.

The brake pedal must also be located in such a fashion that it clears the steering column mast. If the car is equipped with an automatic transmission, the pedal can be located to the left side of the steering column mast if need be, but we would recommend this only if there is not another solution because it requires left foot braking, something that many drivers are uncomfortable doing. If at all possible, keep the brake pedal to the right of the steering column and fairly close to the gas pedal.

If you are building a car with a four-, five-, or six-speed manual transmission, a clutch pedal must also be mounted. Here again, swing pedals can be mounted from the firewall if the firewall is braced properly, or up through the floor. Clutch linkages can be fabricated utilizing cables, rods, or hydraulic slave cylinders. Street rod component manufacturers make kits for both the pedals and the linkages that can be adapted to most situations.

The face of the clutch pedal should be on the same plane as the brake pedal. All pedals should have rubber pads or raised aluminum cleats to prevent your foot from sliding on the brake or clutch pedal. This is very important because wet shoe soles can slip off a metal brake pedal pad when you least expect it.

You have now completed the three most important features of your hot rod interior: seating, steering, and pedal arrangements. From here you must design a dashboard, door panels, and consoles to provide the other creature comforts that make a good hot rod a pleasure to drive.

DASHBOARD AND GAUGES

One of the most important parts of any hot rod interior is the dashboard. Esthetically it must be pleasing to the eye and combine well with the rest of the interior and the exterior of the car, and it holds those all-important gauges. Since the engine is the heart of a real hot rod, the gauges monitor the vital fluids that let the engine live.

First you must determine what type of gauges will be employed. There are basically three choices: aftermarket analog gauges, aftermarket digital gauges, or a gauge cluster from a late-model donor car. The most popular is the simple set of round analog gauges with gauge faces colored in either white or black. Second would be the digital gauges available from a variety of aftermarket manufacturers. The most difficult (although often the most rewarding) is adapting a late-model dash or gauge cluster to an early car.

Lately we have seen things like a narrowed 1959 Chevrolet dashboard mounted in early cars with stunning results. For this exercise we will assume you are going with a stock dashboard, but upgrading the gauges.

We're partial to bead-rolled aluminum panels or tuck-and-roll, but prefab door panels make upholstery a job that's within anyone's reach. This formed panel is from R.W. & Able; RodDoors also makes a variety of styles.

Seat yourself in the car again, with the steering wheel in place, and view the dash. You must have a clear view of the gauges while driving, and it should not require moving your head to see the gauges, especially the speedometer. Look for a clear opening for the gauges, on the dash.

Next cut a piece of poster board to the shape of the dash and draw circles to represent the gauges, in the exact size of the gauges. Tape the mocked-up panel in position, finding the best location for a clear view of the gauges. Once you have arrived at the best location, transfer the gauge locations to the dashboard, cut the required holes, and mount the gauges.

If you are mounting the gauges in an aluminum panel, determine what the best finish is for your application. While you might love the look of a polished aluminum or stainless steel dash, if you're building a roadster or convertible these shiny dashboard panels may produce unbearable glare when driving. Perhaps a brushed, semigloss paint or leather-covered dash would make more sense.

After mounting the gauges, the AC should be mounted. The air outlets should be positioned in such a manner that the cold air can be directed toward the occupants of the car. Automotive air conditioning relies heavily on the ability to blow cold air on and around the passengers. Likewise, the control for the heat and AC should be mounted in a location that is accessible to both the driver and passenger whenever possible. There are several companies that design and sell air conditioning for hot rods. We strongly recommend using these kits over adapting late-model used parts in your hot rod. The kit AC units are designed to cool the early car and can be ordered complete with matching AC compressor, engine brackets, controller, and dash outlets. The kits can be customized to blend nicely with your interior style, and even climate control is available for the ultimate in interior comfort.

After the climate control is mounted, the remaining dashboard and console space can be consumed with switches for headlights, interior lights, windshield wipers, and the stereo. We will not address the installation of stereos in hot rods here, as many books are available on the topic. We will, however, advise that you plan well in advance for stereo components if you plan on putting a serious sound system in a hot rod. Oftentimes space is limited and special fabrication of door panels, kick panels, and under-seat areas is required.

Control switches for accessories should be mounted in the most accessible areas possible. Hiding switches inside a console makes for a clean look, but can also become tiresome if every time you want to lower a power window you have to open a console. It is a tradeoff that is fine for some rodders; others would not like it at all. I

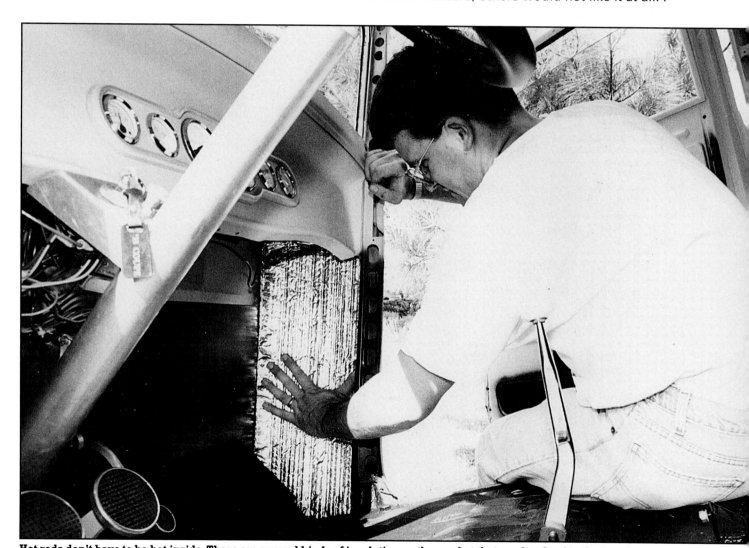

Hot rods don't have to be hot inside. There are several kinds of insulation on the market that can be glued to the interior surfaces to reduce noise and heat intrusion. This foil-backed type is economical and works well. To install, it's just a matter of cutting it to fit and gluing it in with construction adhesive. Noise and heat levels dropped dramatically in this 1933 Plymouth coupe after we lined it with insulation.

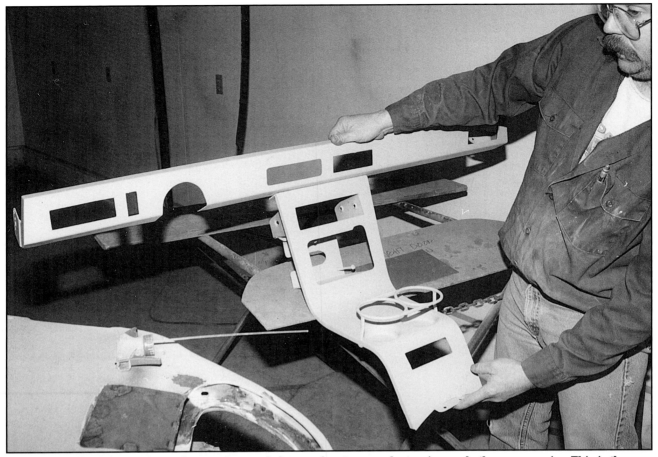

In larger cars especially, a console can give needed space for storage, electronics, and other accessories. This is the console and under-dash unit Roger Rickey built for his 1948 Chevy sedan. Note the built-in cupholders.

guess it is important to know your own personality when designing such "trick features."

SAFETY

Sadly, safety is not always a priority when building a street rod. We still know people who will not install seatbelts because they "don't look good." Well, people, here's a news flash. Street rods today spend a lot of time on interstate highways and the speed limit is often 70 miles per hour, with many cars traveling in excess of 80 miles per hour. Should you be unfortunate enough to have an accident at these speeds, you will need all the safety gear you can muster.

Lap belts are a bare minimum for each passenger. Taller bucket seats with headrests are a good thing and in a closed car a three-point belt system should be employed. Many rodders like to use four-point racing harnesses rather than three-point belts for the performance look. This is a fine idea as long as the harness is pulled snug when you are driving. This can tend to be uncomfortable for long trips, and oftentimes if you are strapped in properly you will not be able to reach the radio or AC controls.

Regardless of the belts used they should be mounted through the floorboards with very large washers or a welded pad where the belts pass through the floor. The belts should bolt to the floor several inches behind the back of the seat whenever possible. Be certain seatbelts are clear of any sharp objects on the floor or seat, and never bend any seatbelt mounting plates because this could compromise the integrity of the mounting tab. Use new belt material—belts from salvage yards could have been stressed during a past wreck, and sun and water can take a toll on the strength of the belt. Do not mount the belts to the chassis because the seat and the seatbelts should move together in case of a serious wreck.

Padded steering wheels and collapsible steering columns are also things to consider when building safety into your hot rod interior. Should your chest impact the steering wheel during an accident, padding can make the difference between bruises and serious injury.

Other safety considerations would include building in a side impact barrier in each door, and for convertibles, installing a roll bar and adding strength to the windshield area. Inside rearview mirrors, side view mirrors, and interior high-mounted third brake lights all contribute to safety in a street rod. Mirrors inside and out should be large enough to actually see the road behind you and also the lane alongside you. While tiny peep mirrors may look good cosmetically, that is of little consolation when a car you couldn't see has just sideswiped you. Hot rodders and racers alike have come a long way in building safe vehicles. Let's all make this a serious priority when building and driving hot rods.

SELECTING MATERIALS

After fitting all the components in the interior of your hot rod, it is time to deal with the cosmetics of the interior. Of course color is a totally subjective choice, but might we suggest that the interior color be somewhat neutral. Black, tan, gray, and white are colors that will go with virtually any exterior color. While that lime green vinyl with lavender piping may look great with your slime green pearl exterior paint and purple flames, just suppose you'd like to change the exterior color of the car some day? Suddenly that bright green and purple interior is a little hard to live with.

The choices of interior materials range from blankets to fine leather. The blanket look is great fun for a beater, barn car, or temporary cover. With this approach you'll always have on hand a picnic blanket and a work cloth should you have to slide under that hot rod on the side of the road. While traditional Indian designs seem to be in vogue for many rodders, don't overlook such fashion statements as *Star Wars* blankets, or wild beach towels. This form of upholstery is strictly fun, but then again, hot rods are supposed to be strictly fun!

In the 1980s tweed became popular in both synthetic and wool. It has a very contemporary look and is easily stretched over things, including multilayered door panels and even floors.

You don't have to stick with the stock dash, either. The owner of this 1948 Chevy convertible went way out there and narrowed this 1959 Chevy dash to fit. It's a natural. Check out the OEM-style power window controls on the armrests too—all the comforts of a new car.

Some of us like music to go with our exhaust note, but a modern stereo face has no place on a traditional hot rod dash. This enterprising builder hid his stereo behind the car's stock speaker grille, which is hinged and latched for access.

The material is durable, but subject to possible staining, and some material tends to "ball up" as it wears, with unsightly balls distracting from the texture of the cloth. That brings us to another point: This material is very coarse and can be uncomfortable to sit on with short pants. If you live in a warm climate and are inclined to wear shorts frequently, it would do you well to sit on a piece of this cloth before covering your seats.

Naugahyde or other brands of vinyl are yet another choice for interiors. This material is durable, available in thousands of colors, and relatively easy to work with. Once again, select your material wisely. Cheap vinyl is just that, cheap. It pays to spend a bit more on the material to have something that feels and looks more like leather. Marine-grade vinyl should be used in all open cars because it is much more resistant to the rigors of sun, rain, and wind.

Actually, marine-grade vinyl is a good idea for any hot rod. A shortcoming of vinyl is that some people don't like the fact that it is cold to sit on in the winter and hot in the summer. Perforated vinyl is available for the seating area, and can go a long way to keeping the seat cool in warm weather.

And then there is leather. Nothing feels, smells, or looks like real leather any better than . . . real leather (now that was a profound statement). Much like any other interior material, leather is available in many grades and price levels. Buying very cheap leather may lead to premature cracking, fading, or staining. It is best to work with your upholstery shop in choosing the proper hides for your car. It also pays to use a shop that is experienced in working with leather; the material is very expensive, so mistakes and miss-cuts must be held to a minimum. If you are purchasing your own hides, select them carefully. Watch for imperfections (all leather has them) from cuts in the hide itself to scars and color variation. We would recommend taking along an expert when buying leather.

PATTERN

After you have chosen the material and color of choice, you must decide on a pattern. Here, too, it is our belief that simple is forever. Few things are as timeless as the rolled and pleated interior. It matters not if you choose the narrow 2-inch pleats or the wider 4- and even 6-inch pleats—this style of upholstery will always be at home in a hot rod. You will probably never tire of the pattern, and the chance of a future buyer finding the pattern offensive is slim.

On the more complex end of the scale we find diamond tufted, diamonds and buttoned, and the multi-layered sculptured look that is popular with the more contemporary hot rodders. Let's look at each of these designs.

Diamond tufted interiors were all the rage in the 1950s and 1960s. It is an attractive treatment and can be done with stitching or the more traditional method of folding the material. Besides making for a very busy look inside the car, cleaning is difficult, as dirt tends to settle in each pocket formed by the tufted upholstery. Diamonds and buttoned has the exact same pros and cons but with the added detractor of the buttons becoming loose and gathering even-more-difficult-to-dislodge dirt.

The layered and sculpted look is one that has been with us for about a decade at this point (2001). While it can be very attractive, it can also be greatly overdone. A little restraint goes a long way to a successful interior. Sculpting around door panels and associated armrests is attractive, and a leather-inserted seat with tweed surrounds is also very pleasing to the eye. This combination provides a comfortable seating surface but still permits sculpting of the door panels, dash, console, and headliner (welcome to the age of the hard foam headliner). While the sculpted look was pioneered with the wool tweeds, today both vinyl and leather have also been employed in this style of interior with great success. Only time will tell if this is fashion or style (with the assumption that fashions change, style is forever). In 10 more years we could be saying, "remember when" or we could still be plying layer upon layer of upholstery.

CARPETS

Finishing the floor in your hot rod is an all-important part of the interior. We recommend using formed carpet sets if they are available for your car. Oftentimes the custom configuration or the interior and custom fabrication of the floor prohibits the use of precut carpet.

As with all interior materials, the use of cheap material is a false savings. Carpet takes a real beating, so it makes good sense to spend a little more and purchase good-quality carpet.

The jute underlay that goes under carpet should also be of high quality, and the use of sound deadener and insulation is recommended on all hot rod floors. The added insulation will make life easier for the AC unit, and keeping the noise out of the cockpit makes long trips a pleasure.

INTERIOR OVERVIEW

As we stated in the beginning of this chapter, few things, possibly nothing, is more important than interior design and execution when building a hot rod. If you're not comfortable and relatively safe while inside your hot rod, you will spend less time in the car. There is really no reason for an uncomfortable interior if the planning is an integral part of the car. Start early, make few compromises, and stick to your plan. The result will be many miles of comfortable motoring.

IN THE SHOP:

HANGING A STEERING COLUMN

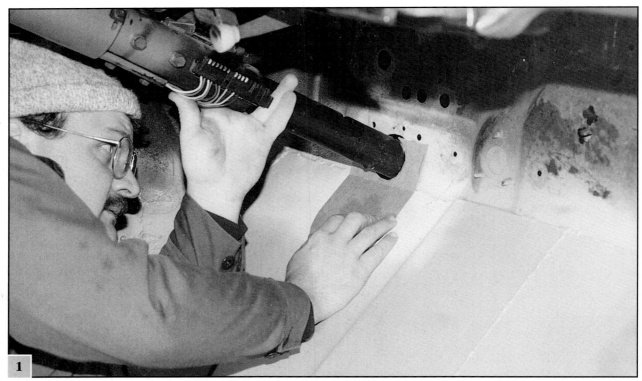

1

First, get the column where it feels right. It helps to have the seat installed, but in a pinch you can take measurements from another car as a guide. Next, cut the stock mounting flanges off the column. We'll be using the stock neutral safety switch, though. After wiring the column in place, we used cardboard templates to make a mounting plate that welds to the column and bolts to the floor.

To steer our 1947 Olds convertible project, we got a 1977 Cadillac tilt/tele column from fellow hot rodder Mike Hawkes. Judging from a trial fit, it looked like it was going to be a good match. We later found that it was dang near perfect. The first step was to clean the stock mounting hardware off the column. We then slightly enlarged the column hole in the floor so the shift arm could fit through, and temporarily hung the column from wires to see where it should go. Once the location was determined, we made templates and fabricated a new mounting plate that would weld to the column and bolt to the floor

(it also covers the hole in the firewall nicely). I would've liked to have used one of the multi-angle column mount collars now available, but it happened that the column went through the floor right where the toeboards meet the firewall; the angle means that the mounting plate has to have a bend in it.

So far, almost everything on this car had been "from the yard," because there wasn't (and still isn't) sufficient demand in the marketplace for anyone to tool up and make 1947 Olds components. Probably a good thing. However, in this stage we were able to use some off-the-shelf parts, namely a column drop from Ed's Twin City Rod & Custom (612-774-6470), and steering U-joints and shafts from Borgeson Universal (860-482-8283).

With the bottom of the column held secure, we put the TCR&C column drop on the column. I like this piece because it bolts to the stock GM column mounting points (stainless buttonheads are supplied), it's strong and good looking, and it's deep enough that it allows you to hide the column wiring and snake it up under the dash, out of sight. It's also *inexpensive,* a very important word in my life as Burger will be happy to tell you. In our case, it sits back behind the dash a little ways, so we simply fabricated a heavy bracket to bridge the gap between the dash and the drop. Later in the car's construction, we also added a stock-style brace from the firewall to the column drop. This stiffens the whole cowl and dash considerably.

With the column in, it was time to hook it up to the steering box. Again, I would've used OEM shafts and joints, but because the Olds firewall is so much farther back than the donor car's firewall, there isn't a stock shaft long enough to do the job. So, after measuring the distance between the end of the column and the steering box shaft, we ordered two Borgeson U-joints, an intermediate shaft, a collapsible intermediate shaft, and a vibration dampener. The collapsible shaft is a nice safety addition, and the vibration dampener does the job of a factory rag joint by absorbing road shocks and vibration before they reach the steering shafts and column. This

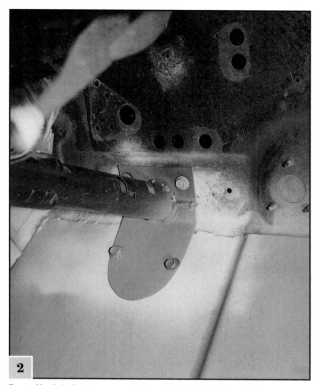

2

Installed it looks something like this. The slightly over-size plate covers an opening in the floor that's necessary to get the stock shift arm through. Obviously this won't be necessary if you use a floor shift.

3

That done, we removed the column and bolted on the column drop. We had to reroute the column wires to the top of the column and remove the metal clip that used to hold them in place.

4 Assembling and installing the Borgeson steering U-joints and shafts was next. All components are splined together and secured with set screws and lock nuts. Note that the dampener is at the bottom, to protect the column and upper U-joint from vibration. A collapsible shaft is a welcome safety addition. One tip: The ends of the shafts can interfere with the operation of the U-joints if they're inserted too far. Check this before the assembly is in the car.

5 We obtained a salvage-yard pedal assembly from a 1980 Olds Cutlass because it matches the planned GM master cylinder and booster, and because the pedal assembly is compact and easy to install.

6

Once we decided where to hang it, it was just a matter of drilling four mounting holes and cutting a larger hole for the brake actuating rod to pass through. The booster should have a rubber gasket on the firewall side; if you save it, it can be used as a template.

improves road feel and extends the life of those components. Once the parts arrived, we bolted them all together as per the instructions and bolted it in place. Safe, good-looking, and the first all-new parts on the Olds.

After mounting the column, it was time for a brake pedal. I personally don't mind a firewall-mounted master cylinder, especially when there's so much room under the hood. I also hate lifting the carpet to check or add fluid on a frame-mounted master cylinder; granted there are remote reservoirs available, but I still like my master cylinders on the firewall. With that in mind, we scrounged a pedal assembly off a 1980 Olds Cutlass. I was pleased to find that the pedal assembly was very neat and compact, and that it

would fit exactly where I wanted it. A tip: If you're in doubt about where to put the column or the pedals, just take a look at where they're located in your late-model driver. In my 1986 Caprice, I simply used my foot to measure the pedal height from the floor, and noted where the pedal was in relation to the column, then duplicated that position in the Olds. Just make sure the pedal won't hit anything in its travel (like the floorboards); then drill four mounting holes and one for the actuating rod, and you're in business. (Just for grins, I also measured the column position relative to the seat and floor. The Olds was within a fraction of an inch there, too.) We'll also add a brace from the pedal assembly to the dash to minimize firewall flex.

IN THE SHOP:

ANCHORING SEATBELTS

If there's one thing that's a mystery to us, it has to be how many really nice hot rods we see that have no seatbelts. We get the story of "They don't look good, they get in the way." Well, guess what folks? They look fine, they might save your life, and they can't get in the way if you wrap them around your midsection! It's borderline embarrassing to have to be trying to convince people they need seatbelts. In the daily driver the first thing you do is buckle up, but in your street rod you think you don't need them—go figure. But, it still seems that there are a lot of rod builders not taking the time to install a set of belts properly. Seatbelts and safety harnesses are available from most rod shops, speed shops, or directly from safety companies like Simpson, Bell, Schroth, and others. There is more to it than just buying matching color belts (and yes, they are available in a color that will look just fine with your new sculptured interior). Let's take a look at some mounting tips that we garnered from experience, observation, and best of all, from the Federal Motor Vehicle Safety Standard and Regulations.

First, whenever possible, go for a shoulder restraint system over the simple lap belt. Granted, the lap belt is much better than nothing, but should you hit something, you might save both your face and your Duvall windshield if you have a shoulder restraint system. If you're not concerned with your face just think what a shame it would be to bend that Duvall, not to mention cleaning up the mess.

OK, three-point systems work just fine for passenger vehicles. Mount the third belt from the B-pillar, and the two lap mounting points from behind the seat. A four-point system is a bit more restrictive, but it also holds you in the car better. It is a bit difficult to turn your body around to back up, but slipping one shoulder out from under the belt will permit you to turn and look over your shoulder. Then, duck back under the belt and you're ready to motor on. The plus side of the four-point belts is the safety and the fact they just look like hot rod belts. The street versions use the normal clip-together belts. This is convenient for your passengers, and also for any rescue-type people who may be trying to get you out of the car should you be involved in a serious wreck. The racer-style connections are not as convenient for getting in and out of the car, but they are VERY safe and definitely will raise an eyebrow when you have someone sit down and then you take the time to "belt them in!"

OK, now you're convinced that you want seatbelts in your street rod. How do you go about installing them? Well, it's a lot of common sense, and in most cases they can be installed in about a half day in the home shop. Let's take a look at what you'll need.

All fasteners should be at least 1/2 inch; we prefer grade-eight bolts and grade-eight washers. Use large flat washers to ensure that whatever the belts are bolted to can withstand the load. It is preferable to mount the belt to the body floorboards using a large washer. Thin floors, rusted floors, or fiberglass floors are not acceptable mounting points. The belt anchor must be able to withstand a test load of 5,000 pounds applied through a body block. Likewise, when mounting the shoulder harness to the B-pillar, it must be anchored into a steel structural member. Screws into sheet metal will not withstand the forces of a crash. A strong anchor point should be fabricated and welded into the pillar. The anchor point can be drilled and tapped to receive a bolt, or a nut and bolt anchor system can be used. This anchor point should be substantial enough to restrain a 5,000-pound force. When in doubt, make it stout!

Now that you have a feel for what is required for proper anchor points, what is the

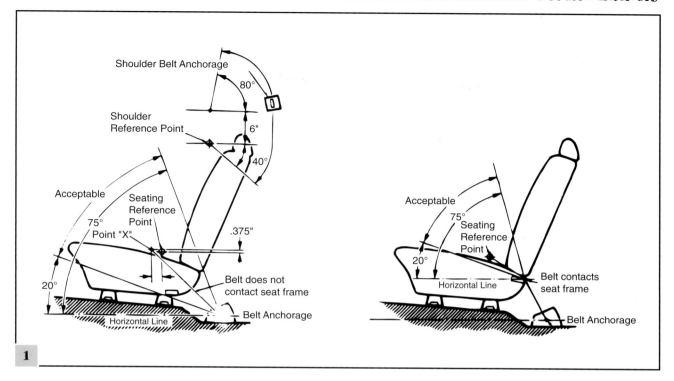

1

correct location for these anchors? Lap belt anchorage points must be a minimum of 6-1/2 inches apart. All anchor points must be rearward of the rearmost belt contact with the seat frame for all seat positions. In general, a line from the anchorage to the seating reference point must form an angle with the horizontal of 20–75 degrees (see fig. 1), unless the seatbelt bears upon the seat frame.

In cases where the seatbelt bears upon the seat frame (see fig. 2) the specified line is determined by the seating reference point and the nearest contact of the belt with the seat frame. (For adjustable seats with no belt-seat-frame contact, the line is drawn from the anchorage to a specified point forward and above the seating reference point with the seat in its rearmost position.)

See figure 1 for the mounting locations of the three-point system. All should be located as per the drawing with the seat in its full rearward and downward position and the seat back in its most upright position.

For sedans, the rear seat occupants can usually be safe with just lap belts. Also remember that mounting the seatbelts properly will only help protect you if the seats themselves are solidly anchored to the floor. If your seats aren't mounted properly, in the case of a serious crash

the seats will break loose from their mounting points, which enables them to go out from under the occupant, thereby rendering the seatbelts nearly useless. Good seat anchors are a must in any safe street rod.

New seatbelts are relatively inexpensive. It is recommended that you use new belts. Junkyard belts can have minor cuts, and may have been wet, left in the sun, and exposed to other things that could destroy the integrity of the belt. Last but not least, always be certain that the belts are mounted clear of any sharp objects, thin sheet metal, or heat. Any of these things could easily cut the belt under load, or the heat of an exhaust system could weaken the belts. Factory-style edge protectors can be gotten from donor cars in a junkyard to protect belts going around objects and out of the pillars. Inertia-type belts allow the most mobility; adapt them to your street rod for more comfort.

Use this information as a guide for installing seatbelts in your car. To really know where and how to install the belts would involve having an engineer design a system for your particular car. However, with good common sense you should be able to devise a system that will work well. As is always the case, if you are not certain of your design or fabrication abilities contact a professional.

Installing a Four-Point Harness

Safety features in street rods is a topic that's not often broached. Sure, the brake systems are good and the chassis construction's safe, but other than basic lap belts (and all too many rods don't even have them!), safety features for the driver and passenger are, at best, minimal.

We've put some 15,000 miles on our 1932 roadster with just lap belts. Frankly, it wasn't the most secure feeling. In late-model cars, "buckling up" is a reflex action, and the shoulder-lap belt combination will keep you in place should you be involved in an accident. We wanted that same kind of protection in the roadster.

With a topless car there is no mounting point at the C-pillar, since there is no C-pillar. That left us with aftermarket belts to choose from, since factory units could not be adapted to the roadster (in many closed cars, factory belts can be fitted, complete with mounting hardware and inertia reels). We opted for a set of four-point belts from Schroth Harness belts.

These belts are constructed with quality webbing and hardware. They also have a feature called ASM (antisubmarining). This feature is designed to minimize whiplash and "submarining" (the effect of sliding out from under the lap belt in a crash) in the case of a head-on crash. Add to that the high-performance good looks of a true belt system, and we were sold on the concept.

To start with, we removed the old single lap belt from the roadster. Then came installing the four-point harness. Since we mounted the Schroth lap belts in the same mounting points, that was simple enough. The belts have plenty of adjustment, and they aren't too long for street rods, a nice feature

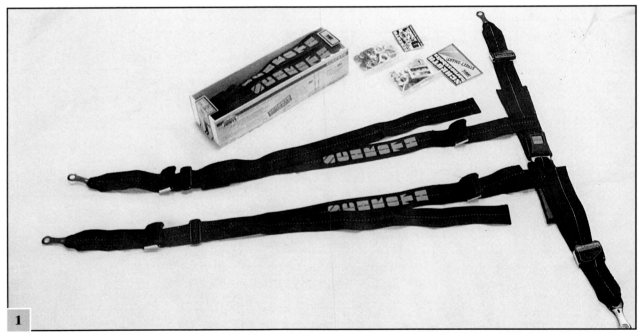

1

The Schroth harness comes complete with all mounting hardware. In the center photo, the old lap belts are removed, and then in the lower photo, the Schroth units are bolted in place. The quality of the new belts is first class.

2

The shoulder belts go over the seat back, then through the floor behind the seat, and attach through the floor with large metal washers, top and bottom.

3

Be sure sharp or abrasive edges cannot come in contact with the belt surface. Use supplied mounting hardware.

4

Pro-street or just a plain hot rod like our roadster, a four-point harness provides high-performance looks and high-performance safety for your hot rod interior. Note the padded lap belts; they provide comfort and safety. Belts are fully adjustable and should be worn snug to provide protection. The clip-on inboard shoulder belt is the ASM "shock absorber," a Schroth exclusive.

in itself. Mounting the shoulder harness is a bit more involved. At this point we must tell you that there is a lot more to belt technology than just bolting them in place. Each installation should be tested with the seat configuration. Since this isn't possible for each installation, the manufacturer and this book are unable to tell you where or how to actually mount the belts in your car. We will, however, give you some general tips.

First, be certain you're mounting the belts to a solid chassis mount. Mounting belts through floors, metal, or (and especially!) fiberglass is not recommended. We mounted the shoulder harness to a chassis cross-member, and the lap belts to a piece of 1/4 x 2-inch angle iron that we had welded into the body's structural skeleton (it's a Wescott body). Both of the mounting points are VERY secure.

We would like to have mounted the shoulder belts farther to the rear, but due to space limitations the belts had to go over the seat back and almost straight down. When feeding belts

through floors and interiors, make sure that nothing sharp can cut or fray the belt.

Installing our shoulder harness involved removing the upholstery from the trunk. Large thick washers (or a 4"x4" square piece of 1/8" flat stock on glass bodies) are used on both sides of the floor to reinforce the attaching points of the shoulder belts. After re-installing the upholstery and a second check to be certain all bolts were tight, the project was complete.

A quick adjustment of the belts and we were ready to ride. The belts are comfortable—you really feel like a part of the car. We think the high-performance safety look is a plus, and the safety factor is "off scale," compared to just lap belts. As we said earlier, perfect mounting of the belts may not be possible, but in case of a crash these belts will keep you in the car, and that often is the difference between life and death in an auto accident. Bear in mind that improper mounting of belts and harnesses can also cause injury. The best recommendation we can provide is to mimic factory mounting whenever possible.

IN THE SHOP:

INSTALLING NEW GAUGES IN OLD DASHES

BY LANE ANDERSON

The time has arrived to decide what to do with the instrument cluster in our 1937 Chevrolet project. Since this car is a driver, not a "billet bullet" and not a "money is no object" exercise, we decided to use what we had.

Our guidelines were low cost, simple design, and ease of maintenance. I have seen more than one of my friends spend an entire weekend disassembling their dashboard to replace a burned-out, "high-tech," bored-in,

indicator light. That is an exercise to avoid and it can be avoided by good design.

We decided to use (steal) two good ideas from two of our friends (what are friends for?); local street rodder Bob Coulbourne contributed the insert gauge design, and Larry Rhodes at Rhodes Custom Auto gave us the tube-mounted indicator bulb idea.

We used the original gauge cluster's back plate or bucket as the basis for our new cluster. Since this is a street rod and not a

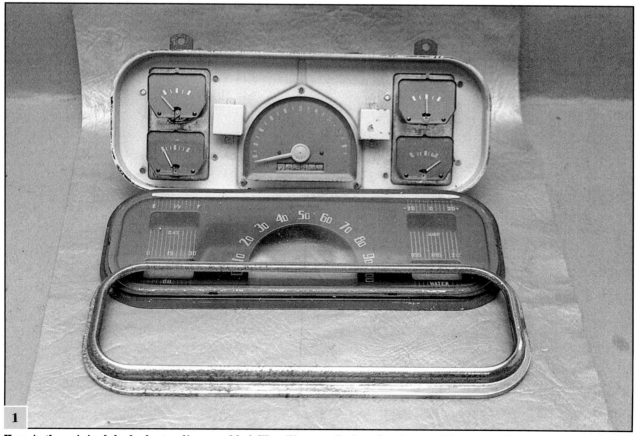

1

Here is the original dash cluster disassembled. We will reuse the bezel and part of the original bucket. We will cut out most of the back, leaving enough of the outer edge to weld the new back plate to. *Lane Anderson*

2

This is the backside of the new back plate, made of 18-gauge mild steel. We cut the gauge holes (speedometer, voltmeter, gas) with a hole saw and drilled holes for the indicator lights (3/8 inch for the oil pressure and temperature, 1/4 inch for high beam and turn signals); then five pieces of 3/4 inch-outside-diameter x 1/16-inch wall tubing (they have a 5/8-inch inside diameter), each 1 inch long, were soldered to the backside. Each tube is placed over an indicator light hole. *Lane Anderson*

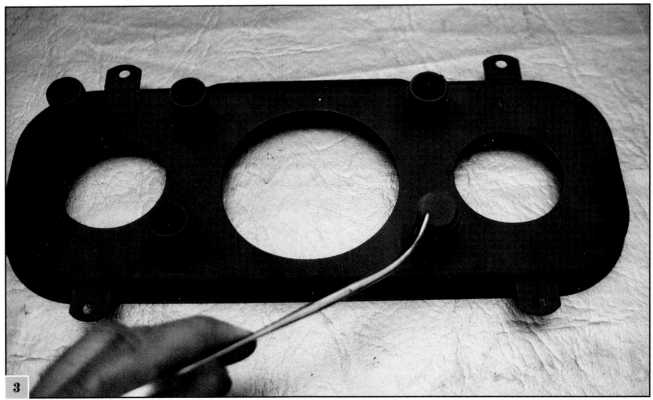

3

The new backplate was tack-welded into the remains of the bucket. Then we cut colored lenses to fit into the five tubes. The lenses are sized to drop into the tubes, and are then secured with a dab of clear silicone caulking. We used four different colored lenses. This time we used colored Plexiglas from the local arts/crafts store. *Lane Anderson*

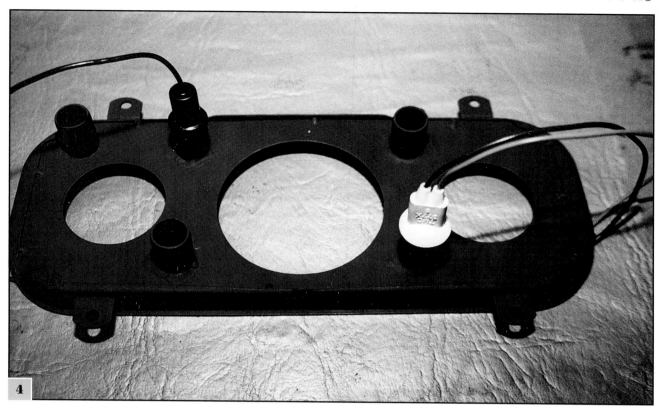

4

The light sockets are made for 5/8-inch holes; NAPA/Balkamp No. LS6225 for the turn signals and high beam indicator, and NAPA/Balkamp No. LS6449 (nongrounded) for temperature and oil pressure. The sockets simply plug into the tubes from behind; they're easy to get to in case a bulb burns out. *Lane Anderson*

5

The bucket was painted satin black and the three Classic gauges were installed as outlined in Classic's directions. The new lens, made of smoked Plexiglas, was glued into the newly painted bezel. The cluster was reassembled in the original manner, with the bezel crimped onto the bucket. The entire cluster is held together and held in place by the four original mounting studs. *Lane Anderson*

6

When the cluster is installed, it looks like it grew there, not like it was bolted on the dash to cover a hole. Best of all, if a bulb burns out, it can be changed in minutes—not days. *Lane Anderson*

restoration, the fact that the chrome on the bezel was shot did not present a problem. We just glass beaded the bezel and painted it the same color as the dash. The Classic gauges, inset behind the smoked lens, and the hidden indicator lights resulted in a smooth, clean-looking dash.

What motivated us to use indicator lights instead of gauges? A good friend of mine (who has proved to be a lot smarter than I thought he was) once told me "spend the money, get a good radiator and fan, and put in an idiot light. I never enjoyed my first car until the heat gauge broke."

IN THE SHOP:

RESTORING HEATERS

BY LANE ANDERSON

F all is the time of the year when you can cruise to your heart's content, without worrying about overheating. Sometimes the opposite may be your problem, when your significant other says "I'm cold, can we turn on the heater?"

If you have a heater in your car, you may well be using one with the old style manual shut-off valve, usually located under the hood. While these valves still work fine, it is so tacky to be seen parked on the side of the road with the hood up, even if you are just turning on the heat!

LEFT
This is our heater front and back. We removed the doors so the chrome didn't blind the camera.

The heater is really rather simple once disassembled. The hardest part was getting the core out of the housing. (The manufacturer must have had a phobia about rattles—it was a tight fit!)

If you did not want to spend the money for a new heater, or just liked the character and simplicity of the original heaters, follow us as we update our vintage heater. This unit was included with a 1937 Chevrolet and was an aftermarket add on. Everything that was done to this heater has also been done to OEM heaters.

The first step was to have the heater core cleaned and pressure tested. Remember that some of the new street rod radiators come with a 22-psi cap. If the core passes this test, and ours did, it's time to start the updates.

A trip through the NAPA catalog found us 12-volt motors, single-speed and two-speeds, with identical dimensions. We chose the single-speed reversible model and adapted it to the unit by simply drilling two holes. The fan hub

3 The old motor on the left, the new 12-volt motor on the right, NAPA No. 6551063. Adapting the new motor required only the drilling of two holes, slightly inboard of the original holes.

4 The heater control valve, NAPA No. BK660-1301. We trimmed the enlarged ends off in preparation for soldering.

5 Our heater with new piping, including the heater control valve, mocked-up for a trial fit. The 5/8-inch-outside-diameter copper tubing and fittings are available at any hardware store.

was drilled to accept the larger diameter of the new shaft.

We could have stopped here and used the heater in its original configuration, but we decided to do two more upgrades. The heater hoses originally came through the firewall and connected at the top and bottom of the heater. This makes it hard to change hoses, harder to tighten the clamps, and just looked goofy with the hoses penetrating the firewall 11 inches apart.

We added a cable-controlled heater valve and rerouted the hose connections to be closer together and to extend forward through the firewall. We used a NAPA No. BK660-1301 heater valve but soldered it into the new piping. The copper tubing is 5/8-inch-outside-diameter "water pipe" just like you find in your basement.

With the addition of a bracket to anchor the end of the control cable, we now have the best of both worlds. Classic styling and total control from inside the car—your significant other will be happy.

6

After the trial fit, we installed the motor and made and installed a sheet metal bracket to anchor the end of the control cable.

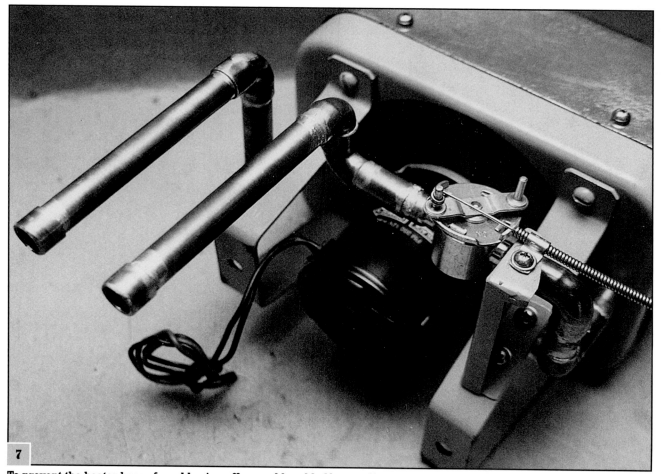

7

To prevent the heater hoses from blowing off, we soldered half a coupling to the end of each tube. Here is the entire updated unit with tubing and control valve installed, and control cable for valve installed and clamped to the new bracket, ready to be installed and enjoyed.

15 Things To Do With Your Hot Rod

BOND WITH THAT BEAUTY 275

TAKE THAT MAIDEN VOYAGE 275

MOTOR OVER TO A CRUISE NIGHT 276

JUST DRIVE 276

TEAM UP FOR A LONG RUN 276

RACE THAT HOT ROD 277

DETAIL, DETAIL, DETAIL 277

ADD THINGS, CHANGE THINGS 277

TAKE PHOTOS 278

SELL IT 278

ENTER AN INDOOR CAR SHOW 279

TAKE A KID FOR A RIDE 279

LET SOMEONE ELSE DRIVE YOUR CAR 279

HEAD TO BONNEVILLE OR THE DRY LAKES 280

SEE YOUR HOT ROD IN A MAGAZINE 280

So you went out and bought that old car. Then you put in a year or more of hard work, making the decisions, finding those rare parts, ordering those trick pieces, and choosing just the right color. The engine is running perfectly, the new wheels and tires are exactly what you've always wanted, and the mile-deep paint is glistening. So what are you going to do with that hot rod now that it is finally finished? Hopefully you thought about that question as your hot rod was being designed and built!

This might seem like an odd question, but sometimes you get so involved in the process of building a hot rod that the notion of what you may or may not do with the car upon completion never enters your mind.

On the other hand, many good hot rods have a real mission that is clear all during the building process, and often that plan is executed very shortly after completion of the car. It could be attending a far-off rod run or going to the local drag strip, but one thing is for sure—after all this work it's time to go out and have some fun with your hot rod!

With those thoughts in mind, we thought maybe we should close this book with a few ideas on just exactly what you might want to do with your hot rod now that it has rolled out of the garage, the license plates are in place, and it's time for driving. Without further ado (and at times with tongue firmly in cheek) we offer you 15 things to do with your hot rod.

1. BOND WITH THAT BEAUTY

That's right, have some special quality time with your hot rod. We prefer evenings, just before turning the lights out and right after a perfect ride (top down, warm summer night, open lake pipes come to mind). Pull the car into the garage. Now get out of the car and pick a vantage point that gives you a great view of, say, the front quarter of the car. Simply sit there and admire your (and others') efforts; remember those special brackets you built, the problems you encountered and overcame. Admire the great lines of the car, the low silhouette of the chopped top, the perfect rows of louvers. Think of things you might like to do in the future, things you'll never change, and everything in between. Quite simply—bond with your hot rod. Think of it as the equivalent of reading your kid a bedtime story. If this sounds weird to you, we're betting you haven't built a hot rod yet.

2. TAKE THAT MAIDEN VOYAGE

Few things will quicken the pulse, moisten the palms, and heighten the senses like that first

Despite the "Lone Wolf" plaques and club jackets, hot rodding is a social activity. Enjoy it with your hot rodding friends; you can swap tools, tell lies, help lift bodies off frames, or just plain hang out.

They're called *hot* rods for a reason! At least once in your hot rod's life, you have to take it to the drag strip to see what it can do. Borrow a helmet and some slicks and have at it. When you start breaking parts, you know you've done it right!

solo run, on the street for the first time. No, we're not talking about those little passes through the neighborhood with open headers and one seat in the car just to prove the car can move under its own power. Those trips are great (although some neighbors may contest that point), but we're talking about heading out in that fresh car for the first time to actually go several miles. The smell of burning paint (hopefully on the engine and headers) mixes with a myriad of new sounds to make this one exciting drive. It will take approximately 500 miles before you really become comfortable with the car and learn all the sounds that are "normal," but that first ride is always special.

3. MOTOR OVER TO A CRUISE NIGHT
There is an organized (a relative term for sure) cruise night within a couple hours of most people in this country. It might be on a Tuesday night or a Saturday evening, but these informal get-togethers are a great place to meet other hot rodders, tell tales of the open road, compare cars and ideas, and just plain hang out. In a couple of hours you can get a real hot rodding "fix" for no money and very little time. You will find one of the great things about street rodding is you can do it anywhere, anytime. You don't need

a racetrack, a fairgrounds, or anything else. Simply an open road and a meeting place is all that is required to have fun with street rods.

4. JUST DRIVE
OK, so you've arrived at that point where you and your street rod are one. Sometimes it's fun to simply slide behind the wheel and go for a ride. Find that favorite road (usually not an interstate) and simply drive into the country. Done right, this trip will block out all the hassles of the day and bring you back to a simpler time when all that really mattered was you and your car. I have found hot rods to be great mood-altering devices and time machines all wrapped into one. Few things can take me back like the rumble of a healthy engine and a dash full of gauges all pointing in the proper directions. Enjoy the drive.

5. TEAM UP FOR A LONG RUN
While a solo drive is probably still my personal favorite, very close behind is the group run to a common destination. Get together with several other hot rodders (I would say five is about the real limit if you want to arrive on time) and head out to a major event. Take that car to the Nationals and enjoy the camaraderie of thousands of other

Don't take hot rodding too seriously. Do you suppose the owner is a dentist?

hot rodders all in town for the sole purpose of enjoying cars.

When choosing your running mates (much like an election) choose them wisely. Be certain everyone is comfortable driving at the same speeds, and has similar fuel ranges. After that it's a matter of selecting a route and heading out. The value of great memories (and laughs if you're doing this whole thing right) accumulated on a 3,000-mile trip is priceless.

6. RACE THAT HOT ROD
That's right—race it. Oh come on, it's not going to hurt the car, and even if it does, if you built the car you can fix the car. It's the beauty of being a hot rod builder! So take the car to the local drag strip (or dry lakes, salt flats, etc.) and go racing. Shoe polish some numbers on the window, uncork those headers, don a helmet, and enjoy the whole experience of drag racing. Do a burnout, pull up to the line, and try to cut a great light. Then leave hard and see what the old car will really do. It may be best to make a couple moderate passes prior to really going full bore, but one thing is for sure—racing a hot rod is fun! If you are racing at a Goodguys Rod & Custom event or similar vintage drag race, you will find yourself in a class against similar hot rods. Warning: If you happen to win your class (or even an elimination or two) you could become seriously addicted to this sport.

7. DETAIL, DETAIL, DETAIL
I find great pleasure in just simply cleaning my hot rods. Not just a simple wash and dry, but a real detail cleaning. Clean and wax the paint, condition the leather, and polish the aluminum. Get the car as clean as possible, polish those Halibrand wheels to perfection, make those leather seats supple and smooth, and, of course, make that paint so shiny you can shave in the mirror image. For reasons I can't explain, this whole exercise is more enjoyable if it is raining outside (or snowing for those with heated garages).

8. ADD THINGS, CHANGE THINGS
The beauty of hot rods is that they are never really finished. There always seems to be something you can add to make the car better, or something to change for a new look or better performance. Been driving that hot rod for a while and looking for a change? How about new wheels, adding flames, or replacing that four-barrel intake with a tri-power unit? It doesn't matter if the changes

277

are big or small, what matters is that the car continues to evolve and keep you involved.

9. TAKE PHOTOS

Much like pictures of kids, you will find many "Kodak moments" with your hot rod. Everything from that photo of your feet sticking out from under the car to the great action shot of the car in motion—lots of photos will help you chronicle the progress of the car. ALWAYS, take photos prior to a major change such as new paint or upholstery; trust us on this one; you will enjoy seeing the car in every configuration. You may even laugh at your "pink period" or the choice of wheels and tires you had 15 years ago. Of course, while the car has changed over the

years, you are still the same hard-body stud-bolt you were 25 years ago. (See No. 4.)

10. SELL IT

Oh calm down. Sure you just finished your car and you can't imagine life without this great hot rod, but guess what Bunky—a time will come when for any number of reasons you will decide the old car must go. Maybe your kids are grown and you're selling that fat-fendered sedan and building a Hi-boy roadster. Maybe your kids have just arrived and you're selling that roadster to buy a fat-fendered sedan, or possibly you are looking for the comfort and style of a large late-1930s luxury rod. Tastes change, garage space is limited, new challenges are needed, and the old

Hot rods aren't just fair-weather friends, and don't let a little rain stop ya. Especially if you drive a roadster. Learn to enjoy that rain suit!

11. ENTER AN INDOOR CAR SHOW

To the neophyte hot rodder, there may seem to be little difference between the indoor show and the outdoor show, but trust me when I tell you there can be a world of difference!

For the most part, outdoor rod runs tend to be fun outings where only cars that want to be judged are subjected to that portion of the event. Many times awards are presented on a totally subjective format such as Editors' Pick, Club Choice, or what have you.

In almost all inside shows, there is REAL judging. Judging sheets, a team of judges, scores, and the all-important (to some people) first place, second place, and third place award winners in each class. We have a lot of problems with inside car shows. First, cars are often awarded points for how many modifications have been done to the car, with little or no regard for the quality of work within each modification. Example: One Model A coupe has a chopped top with knots on the doorpost where each cut was made, and the doors no longer line up properly. Across the show floor sits a stock-top Model A coupe with a flawless door fit, something that takes many hours to accomplish. The chopped coupe gets points for having a chopped top, while the stock-height coupe receives none. This can often lead to a very well-built and highly detailed car losing to a car with less craftsmanship.

Actually, truth be known, the whole thing of "winning" seems to cause problems. For that reason we recommend you participate in all indoor shows with a "Display only, not for judging" sign in the window. The exception to this rule would be any cool, small car show put on by a local hot rod club that has been in existence for more than 20 years.

12. TAKE A KID FOR A RIDE

If it's your kid all the better, but get a youngster in your hot rod and go for a ride. Let them experience firsthand the rough ride, the healthy exhaust note, and all the cool gauges. You get to experience the wide-eyed grin, the cool questions, and the fun of watching a young person realize that hot rods are cool. When you get back to the shop, show them how the car works; show them how to make things and fix things. You just might end up with a really great garage buddy for years to come.

13. LET SOMEONE ELSE DRIVE YOUR CAR

Sounds weird, but swap off cars and get a glimpse of your pride and joy going down the road. It's amazing how many things you'll notice when you follow behind, pull alongside, and

car is sold. It's a tough thing to do, but if you built the car, it will forever be "your" car. The pain of selling your hot rod is muted by the cash influx for that project in the garage that is awaiting paint, chrome plating, and upholstery. Oddly enough, you may see your old hot rod all the time, or it may simply disappear, never to be seen again. I have sold several cars I have built over the years. One, a 1934 Pontiac I built, I see often. The car has been changed, but it is still a beautiful car and a part of me still thinks of it as "my car." Others, like a 1939 Ford pickup I built, I never saw again even though the new owner lived within a hundred miles of my house. Whatever the case may be, there are memories forever from each and every hot rod. (See No. 9.)

Above all, drive your hot rod—to the store, to work, to the coast, to the other coast. That's what they're for!

view in the rearview mirror your very own hot rod. I guarantee you will find a couple things to change, modify, or adjust after this experience. Plus you will be amazed at how good the old car looks at speed.

14. HEAD TO BONNEVILLE OR THE DRY LAKES

Just in case you get to thinking you've seen it all, or worse yet you know it all, head out to Bonneville or the dry lakes events. There you will be among some real old-timers, hot rodders who have 50 years experience making old cars go fast. You'll meet guys who have the perseverance to work on a car all year to race it for one week.

You'll come away with a sense of history, a sense of family, and a pride in being a part of this great hot rodding hobby/sport.

15. SEE YOUR HOT ROD IN A MAGAZINE

It's a funny thing, this hot rod hobby. One of the best things that can ever happen to a hot rod/hot rodder is to see that special hot rod in a magazine. A small shot with a caption at a street rod event is very cool. But the big one, the

mother lode, the major deal, is to have a full-color feature done on your car. Few things will make a car as immortal, as recognized, and as validated as a full feature. Should you be lucky enough to have your car selected for such an honor, do the editor, yourself, and everyone involved with the car a huge favor and be honest when you fill out the tech sheet. For the uninitiated, a tech sheet is given to every owner who has his or her car featured. On this sheet the owner provides information on the car such as what year, make, model, suspension, engine, and interior are used on the car. The sheet also asks WHO did the work. Now here's a tip, if you've never held a spray gun, don't write "owner" on the line that reads, "Paint by:" Also, if you purchased the car, it might be nice if you mentioned the small fact that the original owner actually built the entire car, but you did change the interior and the wheels. If every owner would do this, it would make it easier for both the editor and the owner to attend future rod runs. Beyond this minor point, enjoy the 15 minutes of fame provided by a magazine feature article; there is truly something special about seeing your car in a magazine.

Appendix A

The Ten Commandments of Hot Rodding

1. Cast not aspersions on the unpainted, nor upon the four-doors, nor upon the two-tone blue '46 Hudson sedans. *Detroit smiles on all its creations.*

2. Thou shalt not covet thy neighbor's Deuce. *OK, maybe just a little bit, because he probably enjoys it.*

3. Honor the gray beards. They are the keepers of the flame, and have much to teach. *Ask them to explain tuning and maintaining six Stromberg 97s, and you'll be running EFI for the rest of your life.*

4. Let not your hot rod suffer beneath a coat of pink paint, for that color is reserved for cosmetics sales. *Remember in the early 1990s when every rod run started to look like a* Miami Vice *set? Yeeesh. Thank god for Boyd Red and Sikkens Black.*

5. Thine alloy wheels shall have five, count them, five spokes—not six, not four, not three. And two spokes are right out. *One exception here, too—and that's for American 12-spoke spindle mounts and those nifty-keeno new ET 10-spokers. Great hot rod look.*

6. Thou shalt not decorate thine hot rod. Stuffed animals, crybaby dolls, fringed cushions, and crocheted "Don't Touch" signs will lower thine sperm count.

7. Murals are an abomination unto thine rod. Stick to scallops and flames. *The whole van thing died in the 1970s—why didn't it take murals with it?*

8. Thou shalt not trailer thine hot rod, unless it operateth not. *The exception to this is if your hot rod has gone over the edge and become a race car, and you're actually towing it to a race for the purpose of racing.*

9. Chop not for the sake of chopping. *Some cars actually look good stock height.*

10. Thou shalt have fun.

Appendix B

Source Guide

97 Heaven
4542 Roslyn Rd.
Downers Grove, IL 60515
630-968-8187
Rebuilds Stromberg 97 and other vintage carbs. Sells parts and tools.

A-1 Racing Parts
770 Rte. 28
Middlesex, NJ 08846
732-968-2323
Repro Mustang II suspension components.

Accel Performance
8700 Brookpark Rd.
Brooklyn, OH 44129
216-398-8300
Performance ignition parts, distributors, and aftermarket EFI parts and kits.

Aeroquip
1695 Indian Wood Circle
Maumee, OH 43537-0700
419-891-5100
High-performance plumbing and fittings.

Air Ride Technologies
2762 Cathy Lane
Jasper, IN 47546
812-482-2932
Air bag suspension kits, parts, and accessories.

Air-Tique
209 Kimberly Drive
Cleburne, TX 76031
817-641-6933
AC and heat systems for hot rods, customs, and specialty vehicles.

Alan Grove Components
27070 Metcalf Road
Louisburg, KS 66053
913-837-4368
Custom alternator/AC brackets for many hot rod engines.

Aldan Shock Absorbers
646 E. 219th St.
Carson, CA 90745
310-834-7478
Performance shocks, springs, and coil-overs.

All Ford Parts
1600 Dell Ave.
Campbell, CA 95008
408-378-1934
Original and repro parts for 1928–48 Fords.

A&M Soffseal
104 May Drive
Harrison, OH 45030
513-367-0028
Weather stripping and rubber parts.

American Autowire Systems
150 Heller Place
#17 Westside
Bellmawr, NJ 08031
800-482-9743
Wiring kits, panels, harnesses, and electrical components.

American Racing
19067 Reyes Ave.
Rancho Dominguez, CA 90221
888-279-4335
Custom aluminum wheels, including the classic Torq-Thrust five-spoke.

American Stamping
8719 Caroma
Olive Branch, MS 38654
601-895-5300
Stamped reproduction 1932 Ford frame rails.

ARP
531 Spectrum Circle
Oxnard, CA 93030
800-826-3045
High-performance hardware for racing and street use.

Art Morrison Enterprises
5301 8th St. E
Fife, WA 98424
253-922-7188
Performance chassis, suspensions, and components for street or racing.

Belmont's Rod & Custom
138 Bussey St.
Dedham, MA 02026
781-326-9599
Hot rod parts, new and used. Extensive selection of vintage speed equipment, both new and NOS.

Billet Specialties
340 Shore Drive
Burr Ridge, IL 60521
800-245-5382
Billet aluminum wheels and accessories.

Bill's Hot Rod Co.
1064 E. Edna Place
Covina, CA 91724
626-332-1915
Custom AC and alternator brackets.

Bitchin' Products
9392 Bond Ave.
El Cajon, CA 92021
619-443-7703
Replacement steel floor pans, firewalls, and other hot rod parts.

Blower Drive Service
12140 W. Washington Blvd.
Whittier, CA 90606
562-693-4302
Blowers, blower drives, and custom EFI setups.

Bob Drake Reproductions
1819 NW Washington Blvd.
Grants Pass, OR 97526
800-221-3673
Ford reproduction parts.

Bob's Classic Auto Glass
21170 Hwy. 36
Blachly, OR 97412
800-624-2130
Flat glass for all cars from 1920 to 1960; tinted or clear.

Borgeson Universal Co.
187 Commercial Blvd.
Torrington, CT 06790
860-482-8283
Steering shafts, U-joints, couplers, vibration dampers.

Brassworks
289 Prado Rd.
San Luis Obispo, CA 93401
805-544-8841
*Hot rod radiators and
performance water pumps.*

Bright Works
106 Loretta Ln.
St. Paul, MN 55115
651-429-4439
*Polishing and buffing supplies and
equipment.*

Brookville Roadster
718 Albert Rd.
Brookville, OH 45309
937-833-4605
*Reproduction steel Ford bodies; 1929
roadster and roadster pickup, 1931
roadster and roadster pickup,
and 1932 roadster.*

Bruce Horkey
Rte. 4, Box 188
Windom, MN 56101
507-831-5625
*Repro pickup bed floors in wood,
truck boxes and parts.*

Carrera Racing Shocks
5412 New Peachtree Road
Atlanta, GA 30341
770-451-8811
Shocks, coil-overs, springs.

Chassis Engineering
119 N. 2nd St.
West Branch, IA 52358
319-643-2645
*Hot rod suspensions, frames, and
components. Engine-swap kits.*

Chris Alston's Chassisworks
8661 Younger Creek Drive
Sacramento, CA 95828
916-388-0288
*Chassis kits, suspensions, brackets,
\roll cages, wheel tubs, and
other hot rod and racing parts.*

Classic Instruments
P. O. Box 1216
Crooked River Ranch, OR 97760
541-548-1940
*Full line of hot rod gauges in
a variety of styles.*

Clay Smith Engineering
5870 Dale St.
Buena Park, CA 90621
714-523-0530
*High-performance cams and
valvetrain components.*

Coach and Chassis Works
1445-A Babcock Blvd.
Pittsburgh, PA 15209
412-821-1900
*Fiberglass 1934 Plymouth/Dodge bodies
and parts, 1948 Chevy pickup parts, and
other fiberglass components.*

Coker Tire
1317 Chestnut St.
Chattanooga, TN 37402
800-251-6336
*Repro tires for vintage cars, including
whitewalls, racing tires, and new wide-
whitewall radial tires.*

Competition Cams
3406 Democrat Rd.
Memphis, TN 38118
800-990-0853
*High-performance cams and
valvetrain components.*

Cooling Components
3968 I-40
Proctor, AR 72743
Hot rod radiators, fans, and shrouds.

Cornhusker Rod & Custom
R. R. 1, Box 47
Alexandria, NE 68303
402-749-1932
*Hot rod chassis, flathead waterpump
kits, flathead tranny adaptors, and other
flathead accessories.*

Covell Creative Metalworking
106 Airport Blvd., Ste. 201
Freedom, CA 95019
800-747-4631
*Metalworking tools and videos. Also
offers metalworking workshops across
the country.*

Currie Enterprises
1480 N. Tustin Ave.
Anaheim, CA 92807
714-528-6957
*Custom 9-inch Ford rear ends, gears,
and components.*

C. W. Moss
402 W. Chapman Ave.
Orange, CA 92866
714-639-3083
Repro parts & accessories, street rod parts.

Dennis Carpenter Reproductions
P. O. Box 26398
Charlotte, NC 28221
704-786-8139
Reproduction parts and rubber for Fords.

Denny's Drive Shaft Service
1189 Military Rd.
Kenmore, NY 14217
716-875-6640
*Custom-built drive shafts, yokes,
U-joints for street and race.*

Deuce Factory
424 W. Rowland Ave.
Santa Ana, CA 92707
714-546-5596
*Manufacturer of 1928–34 Ford
suspension and chassis parts.*

D. F. Metalworks
17872 Metzler Lane
Huntington Beach, CA 92647
714-841-6200
*Grilles, hood latches, body components
for street rods. Also custom fabrication.*

Earl's Performance Products
825 E. Sepulveda
Carson, CA 90745
213-830-1620
Performance plumbing, lines, and fittings.

Early Wheel Co.
P. O. Box 1438
Santa Ynez, CA 93460
805-688-1187
*Steelies, painted or chrome,
custom offsets.*

The Eastwood Co.
580 Lancaster Ave.
Malvern, PA 19355
610-640-1450
*Free catalog with restoration tools,
supplies, videos, and books.*

Eaton Detroit Springs
1555 Michigan Ave.
Detroit, MI 48216
313-963-3839
Custom springs for cars and trucks.

Edelbrock
2700 California St.
Torrance, CA 90503
310-781-2222
*Performance engine parts,
including heads, intakes, carbs,
and dress-up items.*

Egge Machine
11707 Slauson Ave.
Santa Fe Springs, CA 90670
800-866-3443
*Pistons and other engine rebuild parts
and kits for vintage and obsolete
engines.*

Energy Suspension
1131 Via Callejon
San Clemente, CA 92673
714-361-3935
*Polyurethane suspension bushings,
engine and tranny mounts.*

Engineered Components, Inc. (ECI)
P. O. Box 841
Vernon, CT 06066
860-872-7046
*Hot rod brake kits, disc conversions,
master cylinder mounts, and other brake
components.*

**Engineering &
Manufacturing Services**
P. O. Box 24362
Cleveland, OH 44124
216-541-4585
*Stamped sheet metal patch panels, rear
pans, floor pans, firewalls, rocker panels.*

Fatman Fabrications, Inc.
8621-C Fairview Rd., Hwy. 218
Charlotte, NC 28227
704-545-0369
Independent front suspension kits and components and complete chassis.

Flatlander's Hot Rods
1005 W. 45th St.
Norfolk, VA 23508
757-440-1932
Traditional hot rod bodies, frames, and parts. Finned Buick drum conversions for early Ford brakes.

Ford SVO Motorsport
44050 N. Groesbeck Highway
Clinton Township, MI 48036
810-468-1356
Crate motors and high-performance engine and chassis parts for Fords.

Gardner-Westcott
10110 6-Mile Road
Northville, MI 48167
248-305-5100
Chrome and stainless fasteners and fastener kits.

Gennie Shifter
930 S. Broadmoor Ave.
West Covina, CA 91790
626-337-2536
Shifters, handbrakes, cables, and other engine control accessories.

Gibbon Fiberglass
132 Industrial Way
Darlington, SC 29532
843-395-6200
Fiberglass bodies and parts for Ford cars and pickups.

Glide Engineering
10662 Pullman Ct.
Rancho Cucamonga, CA 91730
909-944-9556
Hot rod seat frames.

Godman Hi-Performance
5255 Elmore Rd.
Memphis, TN 38134
901-761-5949
High-performance plumbing and tools for brake and fuel lines.

Griffin Racing Radiators
100 Hurricane Creek Road
Piedmont, SC 29673
864-845-5000
Custom radiators in aluminum or copper/brass.

Halibrand
P. O. Box 100
Wellington, KS 67152
800-824-7947
Quick-change rear ends and parts, custom wheels, NOS flathead engines.

Haneline Products
P. O. Box 430
Morongo Valley, CA 92256
760-363-6597
Gauges and engine-turned dash panels.

Harwood Industries
13240 Hwy. 110 S.
Tyler, TX 75705
903-561-6338
Fiberglass bodies, parts and accessories.

Headers by Ed
P. O. Box 7494
Minneapolis, MN 55407
612-729-2802
Headers, header kits, and flanges for more than 100 engines.

Heidt's Hot Rod Shop
1345 N. Old Rand Rd.
Wauconda, IL 60084
847-487-0150
IFS and IRS kits and components.

High-Performance Coatings
550 W. 3615 S.
Salt Lake City, UT 84115
800-456-4721
Thermal and friction coatings for exhaust and engine components.

Holley Performance Products
1801 Russellville Rd.
Bowling Green, KY 42101
270-782-2900
High-performance carbs, intakes, ignition, and other components.

Hot Rod Air
9330 Corporate Drive, Ste. 303
Selma, TX 78154
210-651-0040
Air conditioning parts and systems for vintage vehicles.

Hot Rod and Custom Supply
1304 SE 10th St.
Cape Coral, FL 33990
941-574-7744
Traditional hot rod products and speed equipment.

Hot Rod Carburetion
203 E. Elizabeth
Holden, MO 64040
816-732-5566
Multiple-carb induction systems and air cleaners.

Howell Engine Developments
6201 Industrial Way
Marine City, MI 48039
810-765-5100
Wiring harnesses and parts for electronic fuel injection systems.

IDA Automotive
Rte. 9 and Texas Rd.
Morganville, NJ 07751
732-591-1245
Fiberglass Willys bodies, custom EFI systems.

I&I Reproductions
15513 Vermont Ave.
Paramount, CA 90723
562-531-8117
Reproduction parts for Chevrolets.

Iskenderian Racing Cams
16020 S. Broadway
Gardena, CA 90247
213-770-0930
High-performance cams and valvetrain parts.

Jacobs Electronics
500 N. Baird St.
Midland, TX 79701
915-685-3345
High-performance ignition components.

James J. Durant Enterprises
P. O. Box 7278
Newport Beach, CA 92658
Steel mono leaf springs for hot rods.

**Joe Smith Antique Ford
and Street Rod Parts**
2140 Canton Rd. NE, Suite C
Marietta, GA 30066
800-235-4013
Repro parts for early Fords and street rods.

Koolmat
26258 Cranage Rd.
Olmsted Falls, OH 44138
440-427-1888
Insulation for firewalls, floorboards, and other heat shield products.

Lobeck's V8 Shop
560 Golden Oak Parkway
Cleveland, OH 44146
440-439-8143
Hot rod parts, complete chassis, turn-key cars.

Lokar, Inc.
10924 Murdock Drive
Knoxville, TN 37922
865-966-2269
Shifters, cable sets, throttle linkages, pedals, emergency brakes, and other hot rod products.

Magnum Axle Co.
P. O. Box 2342
Oakhurst, CA 93644
559-877-4630
Hot rod axles, suspensions, frames, brake kits.

Mallory Industries
Spring Lane
Farmington, CT 06032
860-409-7806
Ignition systems and components.

Mark Williams Enterprises
765 S. Pierce Ave.
Louisville, CO 80027
303-665-6901
High-performance rear ends, custom-length axles, third-members, and brakes.

Martz Chassis
P. O. Box 538
Bedford, PA 15522
814-623-9501
Front and rear suspensions, chassis, and fabrication.

Master Power Brakes
110 Crosslake Park Rd.
Mooresville, NC 28117
704-664-8866
High-performance brake kits, disc brake conversions, master cylinder mounts, and brake system components. Also rebuilds vintage master cylinders.

Modern Flathead
9103 E. Garvey Ave.
Rosemead, CA 91770
626-572-0938
Stock and performance parts for Ford flathead V-8s and four-cylinders.

Mooneyes USA
10820 S. Norwalk Blvd.
Santa Fe Springs, CA 90670
562-944-6311
Moon discs, Moon tanks, manifolds, valve covers, and much more. Full line of nostalgic rod and custom components.

Mopar Performance
248-853-7290
800-348-4696
Performance equipment for Mopar engines and vehicles.

Mr. 40s
7343 El Camino Real, #156
Atascadero, CA 93422
805-462-2214
Hot rod parts, specializing in 1940 Fords.

MSD Ignition
1490 Henry Brennan Drive
El Paso, TX 79936
915-857-5200
High-performance ignition components, including distributors, coils, plug wires, and more.

Mullins Steering Gears and Hot Rod Parts
2876 Sweetwater Ave., Suite 2
Lake Havasu City, AZ 86406
520-505-3032
Steering boxes (Vega, Saginaw, and others), steering shafts, steering columns, and other hot rod components.

New Port Engineering
2760 Newport Rd.
Washington , MO 63090
636-239-1698
Bolt-in replacement electric wiper drives for vintage cars.

O'Brien Truckers
5 Perry Hill
North Grafton, MA 01536
508-839-3033
Cast-aluminum engine accessories, air cleaners, and car club plaques from vintage or new molds.

Offenhauser Sales Corp.
5230 Alhambra Ave.
Los Angeles, CA 90032
213-225-1307
Speed equipment, intakes, valve covers, and other engine accessories.

Old Chicago Street Rods
16169 SE 106th Ave.
Clackamas, OR 97015
503-655-1941
Fiberglass bodies and parts for Chevrolet cars and trucks.

Outlaw Performance
P. O. Box 550, Rte. 380
Avonmore, PA 15618
724-697-4876
Fiberglass bodies, Pro/Street chassis, and hot rod parts.

Painless Wiring
9505 Santa Paula Dr.
Fort Worth, TX 76116
800-423-9696
Wiring panels, wiring harnesses, and electrical components for hot rods.

Pertronix
440 E. Arrow Hwy.
San Dimas, CA 81773
909-599-5955
Breakerless electronic ignition kits for points-type distributors.

Pete & Jake's Hot Rod Parts
401 Legend Lane
Peculiar, MO 64078
800-334-7240
Hot rod suspensions, chassis, and components. Full line of hot rod parts.

Posies
219 N. Duke St.
Hummelstown, PA 17036
717-566-3340
Leaf springs for hot rods and customs, full line of hot rod parts.

Pro Shocks
1715 Lakes Pkwy.
Lawrenceville, GA 30043
770-995-6300
Hot rod shocks, coil-overs, and springs.

PS Engineering
2675 Skypark Dr., #102
Torrance, CA 90505
310-534-4477
Traditional cast alloy wheels.

Pure Choice Motorsports
2155 W. Acoma Blvd.
Lake Havasu City, AZ 86403
520-505-8355
Complete line of brake and fuel line plumbing and components. Offers plumbing kits customized to fit your car in steel or stainless steel.

Radir Wheels
P. O. Box 166
Montville, NJ 07045
973-334-3470
Vintage-style cast-aluminum wheels.

Repeat Seats
1225 Namekagon Loop
Hudson, Wisconsin 54016
715-386-6202
Quality used bucket seats.

RB's Obsolete Automotive
7711 Lake Ballinger Way
Edmonds, WA 98026
425-670-6739
Bolt-on suspension kits for Chevys. Full line of hot rod parts, specializing in Chevy cars and trucks.

Rod Bods
1703 Greg St.
Sparks, NV 89431
775-358-4261
Reproduction steel 1932 Ford roadster bodies.

Ron Francis' Wire Works
167 Keystone Road
Chester, PA 19013
800-292-1940
Wiring kits, component panels, and electrical components for hot rods.

Rootlieb Inc.
P. O. Box 1829
Turlock, CA 95381
209-632-2203
Reproduction steel hoods, fenders, running boards, splash aprons for Fords and other makes.

Roy Brizio Street Rods
263 Wattis Way S.
San Francisco, CA 94089
650-952-7637
Hot rod chassis, components, and fabrication.

SAC Hot Rod Products
633 W. Katella Ave.
Orange, CA 92867
714-997-3433
Ford frame rails, chassis, suspensions, and components.

Sanderson Headers
517 Railroad Ave.
South San Francisco, CA 94080
650-583-6617
Headers for a wide range of hot rod engines, in both traditional and over-the-frame styles.

Sharp Enterprises
1005 Cole St.
Laclede, MO 64651
660-963-2330
Chrome and stainless steel fasteners and hardware.

So-Cal Speed Shop
1357 E. Grand Ave.
Pomona, CA 91766
909-469-6171
Traditional hot rod parts, also fabrication and turn-key cars.

Speedway Motors
P. O. Box 81906
Lincoln, NE 81906
402-474-4411
Huge selection of high-performance, hot rod, and racing parts and accessories.

Stainless Specialties
P. O. Box 781035
Sebastian, FL 32978
561-589-4190
Stainless mufflers, exhaust tubing, U-bends, sidepipes, clamps, and accessories.

Steele Rubber Products
6181 Highway 150 E.
Denver, NC 28037
704-483-9343
Reproduction rubber parts and weather stripping for American cars and trucks back to 1920.

Steve's Auto Restorations, Inc.
440 SE 174th Ave.
Portland, OR 97236
503-665-2222
Reproduction steel 1933–34 Ford roadster and cabriolet bodies and parts. Also custom body and chassis fabrication.

Super Bell Axle Co.
401 Legend Lane
Peculiar, MO 64078
816-758-4504
Tubular and I-beam dropped axles, spindles, brake kits, and other traditional front-end components.

TANKS, Inc.
P. O. Box 400
Clearwater, MN 55320
320-558-6882
Hot rod gas tanks in steel, stainless steel, and polyethylene for a variety of cars from 1928 to 1962.

TEA's Design
20385 15th St. NW
Rochester, MN 55901
507-289-0494
Upholstered hot rod seats and matching fabric.

Tilton Engineering
25 Easy St.
Buellton, CA 93427
Gear reduction starters, master cylinders, pedal assemblies, clutches, hydraulic clutch throw-out bearings, and more.

Total Cost Involved
1416 W. Brooks St.
Ontario, CA 91762
909-984-1773
Full line of hot rod chassis, suspensions, and components.

United Speedometer
2431 University Ave.
Riverside, CA 92507
909-684-0292
New gauges as well as vintage gauge restoration/repair.

US Auto & Title
P. O. Box 17325
Rochester, NY 14617
716-342-5769
Vehicle titling service.

US Radiator
6921 S. Avalon Ave.
Los Angeles, CA 90003
323-778-5390
Hot rod radiators.

Vintage Air
10305 IH 35 N.
San Antonio, TX 78233
800-725-3203
Performance air conditioning and heater systems for vintage cars.

Vintage Development and Design
512 5th St.
Nevada, IA 50201
515-382-6674
Cast-aluminum engine accessories for small-block Chevys, vintage Chevys, and GMC six-cylinder specialists.

Walker Radiator Works
694 Marshall Ave.
Memphis, TN 38103
901-527-4605
Hot rod radiators, fans, and cooling system accessories.

Wescott's Auto Restyling
19701 SE Hwy. 212
Boring, OR 97009
503-658-3183
Wide selection of mostly Ford fiberglass bodies and parts.

Wheel Vintiques
5468 E. Lamona Ave.
Fresno, CA 93727
559-251-6957
Steel smoothie and rally wheels, hubcaps; chromed, plain, or powder-coated.

Wilwood Engineering
4700 Calle Bolero
Camarillo, CA 93012
805-388-1188
High-performance brake systems and accessories.

Winter Performance Products
2819 Carlisle Road
York, PA 17404
717-764-9844
Quick-change rear ends and high-performance rear end components.

Wood N' Carr
3231 E. 19th St.
Signal Hill, CA 90804
562-498-8730
Restoration and parts service for woodies.

Zoop's Products
931 E. Lincoln St.
Banning, CA 92220
909-922-2396
Serpentine belt, pulley, and bracket systems, and other hot rod parts.

Appendix C

Club List

Australian Street Rod Federation
P. O. Box 556
Southport D.C. Queensland 4215
http://home.vicnet.net.au/~asrf/welcome.htm
One year, AU$72.00. Very active in government and safety concerns. Sanctions events, hosts a Technical Advisory Committee.

Canadian Street Rod Association
P.O. Box 308, Station "U"
Toronto, Ontario M8Z 5P7
phone: 800-334-4408
fax: 905-682-9729
E-mail: csra@csra.on.ca
http://www.csra.on.ca/
One year, CN$36.00. Includes subscription to Canadian Street Rodder *magazine.*

Delaware Street Rods, Inc.
P. O. Box 334
Rockland, Delaware 19732
http://www.delawarestreetrods.com

East Coast Timing Association
44 Ravenwood Drive
Fletcher, NC 28732
phone/fax: 828-684-3009
E-mail: LandSpeedRacer@email.msn.com
Conducts land speed trials at Maxton Air Force Base in Maxton, NC.

Early Ford V-8 Club of America
P.O. Box 2122
San Leandro, CA 94577-2122
fax: 925-447-2920
One year, $30, includes six issues of V-8 Times *magazine. Restoration oriented.*

Goodguys Rod & Custom Assn.
P.O. Box 424
Alamo, CA 94507
510-838-9876
http://www.goodguysgoodtimes.com
One year, $25, includes 12 issues of Goodguys Goodtimes Gazette. *Sponsors numerous hot rod, musclecar, and VW events throughout the country.*

Inliners International
14408 SE 169th
Renton, WA 98058
425-228-2028
http://www.Inliners.org/
One year, $24. Monthly newsletter with ads, features, tech info, etc. Devoted to users and fans of high-performance inline engines.

Kustom Kemps of America
Route 1, Box 1714, Bill Hailey Drive
Cassville, MO 65625-9743
417-847-2940
fax: 417-847-3647
http://www.kkoa.com
Sponsors custom car events, publishes Trendsetter *magazine.*

Kustoms of America
Lebanon Pike
Nashville, TN 37214
615-885-1279
fax: 615-883-5329
http://www.kustomsofamerica.com/
One year, $25. Includes monthly StyleLine *magazine. Sponsors custom car events.*

Michigan Hot Rod Association
phone: 810-771-7110
http://www.mhraonline.org
Association of Michigan clubs, sponsors the Detroit Autorama.

Minnesota Street Rod Association
2510 94th Way
Brooklyn Park, MN 55444-1185
http://www.msra.com/
One year, $25. Monthly newsletter. Sponsors "Back to the '50s Weekend," holds association events throughout the state, and has a legislative watchdog committee.

Mississippi Street Rod Associatoin
P. O. Box 799
Terry, MS 39170-0799
http://www2.netdoor.com/~samhowel/

National Street Rod Association
4030 Park Avenue
Memphis, TN 38111
901-452-4030
http://www.nsra-usa.com/
One year, $28. Includes monthly subscription to StreetScene *magazine. Sponsors annual Street Rod Nationals and 10 regional events.*

Secrets of Speed Society
P.O. Box 957436
Hoffman Estates, IL 60195-7436
312-558-9338
http://www.classicar.com/clubs/soss/ssshome.htm
One year, $30 (bulk mail) or $35 (first class mail), includes quarterly magazine. Devoted to Model T, A, and B Ford hop up and performance.

Southern California Timing Association
2517 Sycamore Drive #353
Simi Valley, CA 93065
805-526-1805
fax: 805-584-8518
http://www.scta-bni.org
Sanctions land speed racing at El Mirage and Bonneville. One-year associate membership, $50, includes 12 issues of SCTA Racing News, T-shirt, and rule book.

Specialty Equipment Market Association (SEMA)
P.O. Box 4910,
Diamond Bar, CA 91765-0910
909-396-0289, ext. 172
http://www.sema.org/
One year, $150 for clubs, associations, and individual dues. Other rates apply for manufacturers and business in the automotive aftermarket industry. Publishes SEMA News, a monthly magazine. Association does lobbying on the state and national level on behalf of the aftermarket industry and hobbyists.

United Street Rods of Idaho
11260 Valley Heights Ct.
Boise, ID 83709
208-362-6233
http://usri.org
One year, $5. Monthly newsletter. Association of Idaho Clubs, primarily a legislative lobbying group.

Utah Salt Flats Racing Association
P. O. Box 27365
Salt Lake City, UT 84127-0365
801-467-8628.
http://www.saltflats.com
Sanctions regular land speed trials at the Bonneville Salt Flats. One year, $35. Includes four-day gate and pit pass to World of Speed event at Bonneville Salt Flats, monthly newsletter.

Wheels of Time Street Rod Assn.
P. O. Box 111
Breinigsville, PA 18031
http://www.wheelsoftime.org/main.htm

Index

Accessories, engine-driven, 235
Air cleaners, 243–245
Birdsall, Dick, 148, 149
Bodies,
    fiberglass, 51
    steel, 51
Body modifications,
    channeling, 52
    chopping tops, 44–46, 52, 93–95
    deciding what you want, 51
    decking, 53
    frenching, 48–50, 52
    louvers, 54
    nerf bars, 53
    nosing, 53
    pie sectioning, 52
    rolled pans, 53
    sectioning, 43, 52
    shaving, 52
    suicide doors, 52, 53
    tunneling, 50, 54
Brake boosters, 204, 205
Brake fluid, 208
Brake lines, 207, 208, 213
Brakes, anti-lock, 206, 207
Brakes, front, 199–203
    disc, 200–203
    drum, 199, 200
Brakes, installing, Mustang II front, 209–211
Brakes, rear, 203, 204
    disc, 203, 204
    drum, 203
Carburetors, 233, 234
Carpeting, 257
Chevrolet Sedan, 1932, 146, 147
Chevrolet Sedan, 1948, 154, 155
Chevrolet V-8 engine, birth of, 21
Chop Jobs, aborted, 34
Chopping tops, Ford F-100, 85–92
Cleaning, entire car, 37, 38
Collision damage, assessing, 40
Dashboard and gauges, 252–254
Dents,
    assessing, 40
    fixing, 62–67
    repairing, 48–50
Door latches, installing, 82–84
Drivetrain, installing, 238, 239
Dzus button, installing, 96–101
Echols, Gary, 146, 147
Electronic fuel injection, 232, 233
Emergency brakes, 206
Engines,
    Chevrolet big-block, 224, 225
    Chevrolet small-block, 223, 224
    Chrysler hemis, 229
    Ford flatheads, 225–227
    Ford small-block, 227
    which to choose, 223,

Exhaust, 235–237
Firewalls, fixing, 47
Floors, fixing, 41, 42, 47
Ford coupe, 1940, 152, 153
Ford Roadster, 1932, 156, 157
Ford Roadster, 1936, 150, 151
Four-point harness, installing, 264–266
Frame modifications, 118–124
    boxing, 118, 119
    "C"ing, 121
    cross-members, 119, 120
    Pro/Street, 121
    subframes, 123, 124
    X-Members, 120, 121
    "Z"ing, 121
Frame repair, 118
Frame swaps, 117, 118
Frames,
    aftermarket, 112
    evaluating an aftermarket, 116, 117
    evaluating an original, 112, 116
    Ford, 109, 110
    GM, 110, 111
    Mopar, 111, 112
    other stocks, 112
Front axle, locating, 164, 165
Gauges, installing, 267–270
Gribble, Kevin, 156, 157
Gribble, Randy, 156, 157
Hammer forming, 102–107
Heaters, restoring, 271–273
Ignition,
    crank-trigger, 235
    electronic, 235
    points-type, 234, 235
Interior
    material, selecting, 255–257
    pattern, selecting, 257
King, Wes, 150, 151
Lentz, Rea, 16
Master cylinder, 204
Model A sedan, 1929, 158–160
Model T roadster, 1923, 158–160
Motor mounts, custom, 133–136
National Hot Rod Association (NHRA), 18
National Street Rod Association (NSRA), 26
Norman, Mark, 152, 153
Parks, Wally, 18
Patch panel, 48
    hammer-welding, 68–74
Pedal, location and mounting, 251, 252
Peterson, Robert, 18
Pikes Peak Hill Climb, 16
Plastic filler, 33–34
Plastic-media blasting, 55–58
Plumbing, 207, 208, 212–221
Power steering, swapping, 186–189
Rear axles, 174, 175, 179
    Ford 8-inch, 174

Ford 9-inch, 174
    quick-change, 174, 175
Rear springs, fat Fords, installing, 190–193
Rickey, Roger, 154, 155
Rod & Custom magazine, 26
Rust, 33
    assessing, 38, 39
    removing, 55–61
Safety, 254, 255
Sandblasting, 55
Seatbelts, 254
    anchoring, 262, 263
Seats, 247–249
Shifter linkage, designing, 240–242
Shifters, 237
Shock absorbers, 167, 168
Shocks, coil-over, 179
Smith, Leroy, 158–160
Smith, Mike, 158–160
Southern California Timing Association, 16
Springs,
    coil, 177, 178
    leaf, 176, 177
Steering column,
    hanging, 258–261
    mounting and selection, 249–252
Steering, 170, 172
Street Rod Nationals, 26
Stripping,
    dip, 57–60
    manual, 60, 61
Subframe front suspension, installing, 137–144, 161
Subframes, 172, 173
Suspension, front, 163–174
    lowering, 168–170
    upgrade kits, 173
Suspension, front, independent, 172
    installing, 182–185
Suspension, rear, 174–181
    early Ford, 175, 176
    independent, 179–181
    solid axle, 174, 175
Swap meets, 31
Transmissions,
    automatics, 237
    manual, 237, 238
Valves,
    combination, 206
    hold off/metering, 206
    proportioning, 206
    residual pressure, 205, 206
Vermin, 35
Wheels, choosing, 194–197
Willys Sedan Delivery, 1934, 148, 149
Wood,
    repairing and replacing, 47, 75–81
    rotten, 33, 39, 40
X-members, custom tubular, 125–132